Putting Management Theories to Work

Marion S. Kellogg

Manager, Individual Development Methods
General Electric Company

Revised by

Irving Burstiner, Ph.D.

Associate Professor, CUNY
Baruch College of Business
and Public Administration

A SPECTRUM BOOK   PRENTICE-HALL, INC., Englewood Cliffs, N.J. 07632

Library of Congress Cataloging in Publication Data

KELLOGG, MARION S
   Putting management theories to work.

   (A Spectrum Book)
   Includes bibliographical references and index.
   1. Personnel management. 2. Industrial
management. I. Burstiner, Irving. II. Title.
HF5549.K345 1979   658.3   79-17083
ISBN 0-13-744490-7

Originally published © 1968 by Gulf Publishing Company, Houston, Texas
© 1979 by Prentice-Hall, Inc., Englewood Cliffs, New Jersey 07632

Editorial/production supervision and interior design
    by Donald Chanfrau
Cover design by Peter Ross
Manufacturing buyers: Cathie Lenard and Barbara Frick

A SPECTRUM BOOK

10 9 8 7 6 5 4 3 2 1

Printed in the United States of America

PRENTICE-HALL INTERNATIONAL, INC., *London*
PRENTICE-HALL OF AUSTRALIA PTY. LIMITED, *Sydney*
PRENTICE-HALL OF CANADA, LTD., *Toronto*
PRENTICE-HALL OF INDIA PRIVATE LIMITED, *New Delhi*
PRENTICE-HALL OF JAPAN, INC., *Tokyo*
PRENTICE-HALL OF SOUTHEAST ASIA PTE. LTD., *Singapore*
WHITEHALL BOOKS LIMITED, *Wellington, New Zealand*

Putting
Management
Theories
to Work

Marion S. Kellogg was elected vice president-Corporate Consulting Services for the General Electric Company in 1974. She has been with General Electric since 1944 and has held a series of operating assignments in the employee relations function. Her fields of expertise include management by objectives, employee/manager relations, selection, placement, development, and manpower planning for professional and management employees. She's the author of numerous management articles and has authored five books, including "What to Do About Performance Appraisal" and "Talking With Employees: A Guide for Managers."

A former business executive, Irving Burstiner is currently Associate Professor of Marketing at the Baruch College of Business & Public Administration (City University of New York). He has published in professional journals, co-authored a general management text, and authored "The Small Business Handbook." He owns the Creative Management Institute, a management and sales consulting firm.

Contents

Preface to the Revised Edition, xi

Preface to the First Edition, xiii

I

RELATIONSHIPS WITHIN
THE ORGANIZATION

1 The Dilemma of the Modern Manager 1

The Rise of Nonprofit Organizations ◆ Increased Numbers of Professional Workers ◆ Current Trends Are Likely To Continue ◆ Study the Behavioral Scientists ◆ The Theory Isn't Always Practical ◆ We Cannot Overlook Traditions

2 The Partnership Analogy 15

Consent by Competent Parties ◆ A Common Purpose ◆ Partners Retain Their Individuality ◆ Investment, Contribution, Rights, and Rewards ◆ Free Flow of Information ◆ There Is More Risk ◆ Basic Elements of a Partnership ◆ The Translation ◆ Is This Partnership Relationship Workable?

3   So You're a New Manager   25

See Your Manager ♦ Clarify Key Responsibilities ♦ Get To Know Employee Capabilities ♦ Formulate Sound Relationships With Professionals ♦ The Stage-Setting Meeting ♦ Plan Your Own Time

4   Fact-Finding Phase I: Individual Work   34

Advance Groundwork ♦ Documentation ♦ Boning Up on Interviewing Skills ♦ Individual Adaptation ♦ Encourage Employee Preparation ♦ The Meeting ♦ After the Meeting

5   Fact-Finding Phase II: Work Programs   45

Your Preparation ♦ Structure of Meeting ♦ Your Role ♦ The Participants and Their Roles ♦ Learn About Group Interaction ♦ The Work Program Meeting ♦ Additional Fact-Finding

6   First Major Decisions—Work Programs and Resources   56

Key Decisions ♦ The Department's Function ♦ Work Priorities ♦ What To Do About Each Project ♦ Sum Up the Decisions ♦ Match Resources With Priorities ♦ Does the Total Program Meet Your Standards? ♦ Planning the Meeting With Your Manager ♦ Involve Key Professionals ♦ Making Your Recommendations

7   Organization and Staffing   65

The Organizing Process ♦ A Few Basic Principles ♦ Position Design ♦ Is All the Work Delegated? ♦ Relationships Between Positions ♦ Systems and Procedures ♦ Staffing ♦ "Un-Staffing" ♦ Does Your Manager Agree? ♦ Think and Move Quickly

8   Organization Changeover   76

Acceptance Needed ♦ Critical Factors in Reorganizing ♦ Establish a Personnel Planner ♦ Fill Positions Reporting to You ♦ What if an Individual Refuses? ♦ How To Handle Displacements ♦ Early Communication ♦ Repeat at Lower Levels ♦ Time Span ♦ Your Personal Attitude ♦ Organization Review

9   The Groundwork for Motivation   86

Broaden Traditional Job Description Content ♦ Encourage Cross-Examination of Jobs ♦ Supplement Job Descriptions With Work Plans ♦ Objectives of Individual Negotiation ♦ Keep the Employee "In Charge" ♦ Plan for Employee Growth ♦ How To Ensure Individual Commitment ♦ Your Behavior Contributes to Commitment

10 Sustaining Motivation Toward Organization Goals   98

Information Systems—Feedback ◆ Is Your Example Being Followed? ◆ Renew Commitment to Work Goals and Plan for Individual Growth ◆ Make Adequate Preparation ◆ Let the Employee Brief You on Progress ◆ Keep the Focus on the Future ◆ Managerial Option ◆ Ground Rules for Growth Discussion ◆ How To Factor Development Goals into Current Work ◆ Planning Developmental Action on a Group Basis ◆ Reward Through Internal Satisfaction ◆ External Reward Is Also Necessary ◆ Rewards Must Be Congruent With Accomplishment

11 Fighting Obsolescence   112

Fight Obsolescence in Yourself ◆ Selecting New Employees ◆ Upgrade Knowledge and Keep an Open Mind ◆ G-2 Intelligence ◆ Don't Keep Employees in the Same Job Too Long ◆ Watch Out for Individual Over-Involvement ◆ Make Sure Your Assumptions Are Valid ◆ An Improvement Goal in Every Work Plan ◆ How You Do It Counts ◆ Don't Let the Improvement Goals Become Repetitive ◆ Your Personal Visibility ◆ Recycle the Work of the Organization ◆ Express Positive Attitudes About Change

II
RELATIONSHIPS
WITH INDIVIDUALS

12 How to Help the Beginner   127

A First Job Is Critical ◆ The Case of Anthony Michel

13 Over the Hill? What To Do About It   140

The Story of Harry Anderson ◆ Summary and Implications

14 Challenging the Promotable Employee   153

Aids to Evaluating Employee Potential ◆ The Case of the Promotable Account Representative ◆ Summary

15 The Excellent But Nonpromotable Specialist   167

The Specialist Is Needed ◆ The Case of the Vibration Specialist ◆ Summary

16 **When a Manager Reports to You**   **180**

The Case of the District Manager ◆ Summary

17 **What About You?**   **193**

Know Yourself ◆ Think About Your Job—And the Next One ◆ Manage Your Time Intelligently ◆ Put Something New into Your Work ◆ Self-Feedback Will Improve Learning ◆ Get Help from Your Manager ◆ Set an Improvement Goal for Yourself ◆ Keep Your Manager Informed ◆ Incorporate Your Career Interests into This Job ◆ How to Get Ready for the Future ◆ Summary ◆ Recommended Plan

Preface
to the
Revised Edition

Despite modern advances in management/organization theory and behavioral psychology—and the availability of sophisticated managerial tools—management today still remains much more an art than a science. Indeed, it may well remain an art forever.

Among other factors, the difficult task of planning, organizing, guiding, coordinating, and controlling the activities of an organization's employees has been further complicated in recent decades by new technology, significant changes in the economy, accelerated growth in government employment and the burgeoning of not-for-profit organizations, the attenuation of family, home, and religious influences upon the individual, and the emergence of newer lifestyles. To the neophyte, the managing role presents a formidable maze of often-frustrating, trial-by-error tactics and maneuvers.

Marion Kellogg's book bridges the gap between management theory and actual practice. It is an intelligent and intelligible work that will be as timely and helpful to the harried manager (or manager-to-be) in the 1980s and beyond, as it is today. It is, in effect, a blueprint for managing cooperative endeavors within all types of organizations.

Irving Burstiner

Preface
to the
First Edition

This book is written for managers who desire to improve their skills. Its purpose is to show how to manage complex work performed by individuals whose personal knowledge and talents may individually surpass those of the man to whom they report. It is, of course, only a foundation upon which each will build, experiment, and adapt, and from which each will ultimately develop his personal style.

Based on the enormous changes which have already occurred in working life and on current and predictable trends, certain assumptions were made in planning the book. First, most managers will reach their organization goals through the work of professional specialists. Certainly other kinds of workers will continue to be employed, but the most dramatic change in managing concepts will occur in the relationship between the professional manager and the professional specialist. Part I of this book focuses on the nature of this relationship and its practical implications for accomplishing work.

Second, while the manager and those who report to him are a working team, there are inevitable problems of individual growth and motivation. These must be worked out on a one-at-a-time basis, even though sound principles of group dynamics may contribute to problem solution. Part II takes five universal and critical problems faced by almost every manager. Through simulated dialogue and editorial commentary, sound approaches to solution are outlined.

Third, a manager may in the future find himself in a variety of organizations as well as in the more familiar profit-making business institution. The work is not markedly different, but interests, priorities, and motives may present less well-explored challenges. For this reason, the functions and settings used for illustrative purposes are deliberately varied.

To unfold the managing process as logically as possible, the book is arranged so that a manager is taken from the point of his selection through his key decisions on work, organization, and staffing, to his eventual concentration on sustaining and improving motivation to accomplish organization objectives economically. There is no implication that the reader should be a new manager. He may be new; he may merely aspire to manage. Or, and this is more likely, he may be one of the countless number who learned their skills the hard way. His purposes may be to compare what his experience has taught him with current recommendations and to add new methods to those he already uses successfully.

Regardless of experience, the message of the book should be clear: Between management theory and practice there is an inevitable gap. This fact should not result in condemning nor ignoring the theory. It should, instead, encourage a manager to move toward the ideal, to experiment as he does so and, finally, to make an individual adaptation which represents for him a workable balance.

Marion S. Kellogg

I

RELATIONSHIPS
WITHIN
THE
ORGANIZATION

1

The Dilemma
of the Modern
Manager

Today's manager faces a dilemma: the advice of management theorists and social scientists just does not seem to coincide with the day-to-day life in corporations. To perform successfully, the manager must blend the actions of several fellow employees with the advice of social scientists. The manager must juggle and balance theories with reality until he or she is able to cope with his or her own particular situation in a reasonable way.

Because the social sciences have lagged the physical sciences, we in the management field have been content to rely on lore handed down from one manager to another when looking for ways to improve our skills. Because measurement tools have been either non-existent or impotent, there has been little formal valuation of this handed-down information. But important changes are occurring which both demand and permit a full exploration and revision of managing philosophy and practices.

THE RISE
OF NONPROFIT ORGANIZATIONS

One change is the growing number of nonprofit institutions. In earlier decades, a manager was usually employed by a private enterprise with a strong profit motive. Today, however, he or she is just as likely to work in another sector of the economy. He or she may direct a hospital or charitable organization, be a college administrator, head a technical bureau or agency supported by government funds, or be part of the military structure.

As Ginzberg and his associates pointed out in *The Pluralistic Economy:*

In the decade 1950–1960, nine out of every ten net new jobs . . . reflected . . . the activities of the not-for-profit sector . . . In 1929, 4,465,000 individuals (calculated on a full-time equivalent basis) were directly employed by government and nonprofit institutions; they contributed 9.7 per cent of the employed labor force . . . by 1960 both the number and percent had risen significantly. In that year . . . more than one in five of all those employed, were directly employed in the not-for-profit sector.[1]

This analysis further indicated that the increase in government positions accounted for most of the rise, and that professional and technical workers predominated in these positions. However, they pointed to startling increases in other areas as well. Teachers accounted for more than half of the total of government employees, and college-trained individuals in the health profession increased from just under 200,000 in 1900 to more than 1.1 million in 1960.

Bringing these statistics into present-day focus, the number of government employees reached the 15 million mark by 1976. That same year, elementary and secondary school teachers totaled some 5.2 million.[2]

IMPACT ON MANAGING

This trend in employment from predominantly profit-making institutions toward nonprofit ones places additional demands on managing skills. Profit-seeking is a strong motive for outdoing competitors by controlling costs, improving quality, and incorporating innovative features into products and services. The absence of this motive creates a vacuum. Unless leadership in nonprofit institutions can spur professional workers to set and meet standards of high performance, there will be deterioration of output despite the increasing investment of human resources.

The mission of a nonprofit organization must be clear. Needed results should be specified and communicated. Employees should be dedicated to achieving their common purpose. These situations do not happen by chance. They require effective managing and a special relationship between manager, employee, and the organization as a whole.

INCREASED NUMBERS
OF PROFESSIONAL WORKERS

A second major change is the nature of positions available and the training of those employed in these positions. "Employment of professional, technical and kindred workers more than doubled between 1947 and 1964,

[1]Eli Ginzberg, Dale L. Hiestand, and Beatrice G. Reubens, *The Pluralistic Economy* (New York: McGraw-Hill, 1965).

[2]Bureau of the Census, U.S. Department of Commerce, *Statistical Abstract of the United States, 1977* (Washington: Department of Commerce, 1978).

rising from 3.8 million to over 8.5 million."[3] The number is still increasing; actual 1976 statistics reflect a total of 13.3 million professional and technical people in our work force.[4] Some of this rise stems from advancing industrial technology, the increased automation of factory processes, and the appearance of whole new technologies. The continued defense effort of our country has dictated technical investigation at an unprecedented rate. The education level of the typical American has increased and there are larger numbers of educated individuals available for employment.

The shift to more demanding, complex jobs in all sectors of the economy, matched by better-educated and informed employees to fill them, has placed added strains on traditional managing methods. Employees capable of suggesting ways to improve their work and the output of the organization are likely to resent not being able to do so. Employees trained to work toward high standards, but finding managers accepting less or unable to distinguish high from mediocre quality, are likely to feel frustrated and experience a conflict of values.

Managers in authority over and responsible for work they not only cannot do but cannot evaluate properly, may experience anxiety and feel unable to cope with the situation. Some managers race to keep up with all the new knowledge in the specialized areas with which they deal. But they know that this must be a losing race. In the end, managers must revamp their skills to deal constructively with people who are individually superior in their special fields.

PROFESSIONALS REQUIRE DIFFERENT MANAGEMENT METHODS

This necessary renovation of management skills sets the stage for a new relationship between the manager and the professionals who report to him. On this point, Drucker wrote:

> Every knowledge worker makes economic decisions—whether he be a research engineer deciding to continue or drop a project, an accountant deciding what cost definitions are appropriate to the business, a sales manager deciding where to put his strongest salesmen, or a market researcher defining the market in which a product competes. To make the right decision the knowledge worker must know what performance and results are needed. In turn, the knowledge workers must be 'excited', to use Mr. Kappel's word. He cannot be supervised. He must direct, manage, and motivate himself. And that he will not do unless he can see how his knowledge and work contribute to the whole business.[5]

---

[3]"The Outlook for Technological Change and Employment," Appendix, Vol. 1, *Technology and the American Economy*. Studies prepared for the National Commission on Technology, Automation and Economic Progress, February, 1966.

[4]*Statistical Abstract*, 1977.

[5]Peter F. Drucker, *Managing for Results* (New York: Harper & Row, Pub., Inc., 1964).

Military leaders recognize the needed change in managing concepts. Over a decade ago, Major Tatum wrote: "First, the manager should remember that he is a manager of specialists. His primary responsibility is to create the environment in which his specialists can successfully apply their skills." Later in the same article: "The description of his job as a 'manager of specialists' is different from traditional formulations. Therefore, many of the tried and true leadership 'principles' may no longer be applicable, particularly those based on the assumption that the manager knows best (because of experience factors) and does not need the advice of lower-ranking specialists."[6]

PROFESSIONAL WORK IS DIFFERENT

Professionals are likely to be different from other employees, just as their work is different from other work. Their managers cannot use the old ideas of skill, care, and effort as yardsticks for judging success. Professionals are given a problem to solve or a result to accomplish. Or they may decide what the problem is that needs solving or what the needed result is. The measure of their success is whether the problem is solved satisfactorily, or whether they worked on the "right" problem, or whether they have contributed to or accomplished an organizational objective. If the solution is ingenious, if it displays great thoroughness and organization, if it was worked on night and day, the professionals may be complimented for these things. But the fundamental issue is whether specified goals have been met.

This objective standard of success motivates professionals to exert major influence on the goals of the organization and on their work goals. As a minimum, they must be committed to achieving these goals. This forces a change in both managing concept and the nature of the manager-professional relationship.

CURRENT TRENDS
ARE LIKELY TO CONTINUE

Both trends—more jobs in nonprofit institutions and more professional employees—are likely to continue. Here is what the National Commission on Technology, Automation, and Economic Progress reported:

> Industry projections . . . indicate that the rate of job growth will continue to be higher in the service-producing industries than in the goods-producing industries. . . . The largest increase in manpower requirements in the

---

[6]Major Lawrence B. Tatum, "Manager-Specialist Relationships: A Theory," *Air University Review*, Vol. 18 (November–December, 1966).

service-producing sector is expected to be in Government, nearly all in state and local government. Employment requirements in medical and other health services establishments (excluding government services) are expected to increase by more than one-half between 1964 and 1975. It is anticipated that manpower needs will increase in practically every professional and technical field—including teaching, counseling, the natural sciences, engineering, programming, the health professions, the social sciences and social and welfare work . . . By 1975, manpower requirements for professional technical and kindred workers are expected to rise by more than one-half to 13.2 million. As in the past, requirements for salaried managers and officials are likely to continue to increase substantially during the next decade because of the increasing dependence on trained management specialists—buyers, department store heads, and purchasing agents—by business organizations and Government agencies. In addition, occupations such as hospital administration are developing, which will probably absorb some management and planning functions currently performed by non-management personnel.[7]

These predictions underline the changing nature of jobs and employees. The manager who wishes to adapt his or her managing skills to meet current and future needs must assume a continuing trend toward a greater professionalism of work and the work force. He or she must develop relationships with employees which encourage and reward their contributions to the formulation of organization goals, allow greater freedom of choice in doing work, and emphasize self-measurement and personal growth.

STUDY THE BEHAVIORAL SCIENTISTS

How does one learn to do this? A logical place to begin is with management literature. Unfortunately, the classical literature supports the old order of things. While many of the fundamentals hold true, it is difficult for a hurried manager to see through to the hard core of usable theory and information.

The journals are even more confusing because they are written by a variety of authors in a variety of situations. Some authors are theorists, some practitioners; some function at levels where they are surrounded by the old school; some function at levels where the managers are old school and employees are "new breed." At their best, journals represent the confusion of this transition period. Any manager reading with an open mind will be startled to find clear-cut evidence *for* participative management followed the next month by so-called clear-cut evidence *against* it.

Nor is much help probably available from the manager's manager. It is very likely that he or she developed his or her own skills with little help during a different era. That individual probably has not analyzed the manag-

[7]*Technology and the American Economy.*

ing process well enough to sort out useful information and make it available to subordinates.

Social scientists are hailed for providing sound inputs for the learning manager. When we examine their writings, it is clear that the best minds have observed the changing situation and anticipated the trends. In fact, social scientists have much to contribute to an improved understanding of the management process and interpersonal relationships. Let's take a quick look at a few of the outstanding theorists of the last decade.

ARGYRIS ON ORGANIZATION

In 1957, Chris Argyris looked at industrial organization and perceived the unfortunate impact of the formal, typical pyramid-type structure on the motivation of the individual. He wrote:

> Assuming that the healthy individuals are not to be changed, one way to reduce the 'negative' (from management's point of view) informal behavior is to change the formal organizational structure so that the employee experiences more activity than passivity; greater relative independence than dependence; uses more, rather than less, of his important, rather than skin-surface abilities; has a longer rather than a shorter time perspective; and finally, is in an equal if not higher position than his peers.[8]

HERZBERG ON ATTITUDES TOWARD WORK

At about this same time, Frederick Herzberg and his associates investigated the attitudes of professional workers toward their jobs—attitudes which affect both internal satisfaction and productivity. In his earlier surveys, he was primarily concerned with engineers and accountants, some of whom had supervisory functions, but all of whom were personally doing some individual work in their respective functions. The question, "What do people want from their jobs?" got the following responses:

> When our respondents reported feeling happy with their jobs, they most frequently described factors related to their tasks, to events that indicated to them that they were successful in the performance of their work, and to the possibility of professional growth. Conversely, when feelings of unhappiness were reported, they were not associated with the job itself but with conditions that *surround* the doing of the job. . . . The factors that lead to positive job attitudes do so because they satisfy the individual's need for self-actualization in his work. . . . First, jobs must be restructured to increase to the maximum the ability of workers to achieve goals meaningfully related to the doing of the job . . . The individual should have some measure of control over the way in which the job is done in order to realize a sense of achievement and of personal growth.

[8]Chris Argyris, *Personality and Organization* (New York: Harper & Bros., 1957).

Herzberg pointed out that this approach was not possible at that time for most blue collar workers. But, as automation eliminates more and more routine jobs, managers can design new positions and restructure existing ones with maximum motivation in mind. He concluded, however, that achievement alone is insufficient for motivation, that it "must lead to a feeling of personal growth in the individual accompanied by a sense of increasing responsibility," and that the manager must find ways to reward accomplishment in a discriminating fashion. With respect to employee participation in decisions affecting his work, he wrote:

> Within certain limits, it is likely that more latitude . . . can be given to individuals to develop their own ways of achieving the ends that are presented to them by a centralized authority. This is a reasonable solution to the problem of motivation, more reasonable than the usual formulation of participation.[9]

MCGREGOR ON ALIGNMENT
OF PERSONAL AND ORGANIZATIONAL GOALS

Almost concurrently, Douglas McGregor was addressing himself to many of the same issues in his much-quoted and misquoted book. He wrote this practical evaluation of individual involvement and influence on the organization:

> Perfect integration of organization requirements and individual goals and needs is, of course, not a realistic objective. In adopting this principle, we seek that degree of integration in which the individual can achieve his goals *best* by directing his efforts towards the success of the organization. 'Best' means that this alternative will be more attractive than the many others available to him . . . It means that he will continuously be encouraged to develop and utilize voluntarily his capacities, his knowledge, his skill, his ingenuity in ways which contribute to the success of the enterprise.

In this same book, McGregor presented two opposing hypotheses on which managers build their philosophy and personal style of managing. In Theory X, he postulated that employees dislike work, avoid it if possible, and try to get away with minimum performance. Acceptance of Theory X leads a manager to stress close supervision, heavy direction and control, and monetary incentives for better performance. In Theory Y, he supposed that employees may find satisfaction in their work, are willing to accept responsibility, will strive to achieve organization objectives, and will find their personal growth rewarding.

McGregor advocated Theory Y as the more desirable of the two hypotheses, admitting that it is not practical in all cases at the present time. Theory

---

[9]Frederick Herzberg, Bernard Mausner, and Barbara Bloch Snyderman, *The Motivation to Work* (New York: John Wiley, 1959).

Y leads a manager to grant employees greater freedom of choice in their work, to provide better information about organization objectives, and to work toward improved relationships with employees. That he saw the practical limitation in its immediate adoption by managers for all employees was clear when he wrote: ". . . a number of applications of Theory Y in managing managers and professional people are possible today."[10]

LIKERT: CONDITIONS FOR THE NEW MANAGING CONCEPTS

In 1961, Rensis Likert consolidated many of his conclusions in the book *New Patterns of Management*. His recommendations on observations of organization structure and the management principles and practices of successful managers in business and government, reinforced those of Argyris, Herzberg, and McGregor. He suggested that managers strive for general rather than close supervision, greater employee freedom to set work pace, the alignment of personal and organization goals, and interest in the employee's well-being.

Likert pointed out at least two practical conditions which shed light on the complexity of the new skills which will be required of managers. The first is the ability to be aware of the employee in a very special way: "Supervision is, therefore, always a relative process. To be effective and to communicate as intended, a leader must always adapt his behavior to take into account the expectations, values and interpersonal skills of those with whom he is interacting." This understanding of individual differences and the varying reactions to managing practices is demanding of the person who wishes to work toward the expected conditions of the future. This is a considerably more difficult way of managing, requiring much greater sensitivity on the part of managers.

Likert suggested a second condition:

> An organization operating under the newer theory is not free from conflict. Conflict and differences of opinion always exist in a healthy, virile organization, for it is usually from such differences that new and better objectives and methods emerge . . . The central problem, consequently, becomes not how to reduce or eliminate conflict, but how to deal constructively with it.[11]

BLAKE ON MANAGERIAL STYLE

Blake evolved a description of the managing style most likely to generate sound interpersonal relationships between manager and employee:

[10]Douglas McGregor, *The Human Side of Enterprise* (New York: McGraw-Hill, 1960).
[11]Rensis Likert, *New Patterns of Management* (New York: McGraw-Hill, 1961).

Political democracy itself leads people to want and to exert a voice in those matters that affect them. Cultural concepts of excellence leave people uneasy with conditions that fail to measure up to what they know is attainable. Modern concepts in the areas of health and advanced education place a high value on doing things in the 'best' way. Another value is away from status, based on 9,1 power with deference as the basis for relationship, and toward the 9,9 use of hierarchy stemming from accomplishment and merit. This tends to lead to relations which are open, communicative, and problem solving, rather than closed, suspicious and problem generating.[12]

It is possible, of course, to find real differences among these social scientists. There is nevertheless a remarkable body of consistent data and interpretation.

THE THEORY ISN'T ALWAYS PRACTICAL

Suppose that a manager is armed with the theorists' vision of the new managerial role. He or she understands their reasons and they seem sound. He or she determines to try them out. What happens?

The manager begins, perhaps, with the idea of providing more opportunity for employees to influence their goals and allowing more freedom to choose how goals will be met, commitment dates set, and standards established. An employee named Art Canning is called in. Something like the following scene may very well occur.

"Art," says the manager, "what do you think you ought to be doing during the next six months?"

Art, who is the shop engineer for a refrigerator-freezer assembly area and has held this job for the past seven or eight years, looks a little startled and replies: "You know darn well what I ought to be doing—keeping that line moving."

"Yes, yes, I know that, but what will that consist of?"

"Fixing anything that goes wrong."

The manager feels exasperated but remains patient exactly as expected. "Well, what will go wrong?"

"Listen, if I knew that it wouldn't happen—we'd fix it ahead of time." Art isn't quite as patient as his manager. The manager beams: "That's just what I had in mind—couldn't we prevent some of these failures?"

Art looks at his boss with pity. "Yeah, if I were out there right now I probably could."

---

[12]Robert R. Blake and Jane S. Mouton, *The Managerial Grid* (Houston: Gulf Publishing, 1964). (Note: The 9,1 position represents a manager with little concern for the people in the group; the 9,9 position represents the team-centered manager who accomplishes the task with the assistance of committed people.)

Art knows his job. He has done it well for years. He is not used to thinking in terms of goals. He is used to responding to the immediacy of the problems that beset him. He does not even get the drift of what his manager wants of him. The manager has not communicated his intention very well, nor has he displayed much understanding of the nature of Art's work. If the manager concludes from his discussion that Art is not a suitable subject for experimentation with new managing methods, he could be doing Art an injustice. He should realize that between theory and application a lot of development work needs to be done. The theories must be adjusted to *this* individual in *this* situation doing *this* kind of work.

CHANGE REQUIRES MIND PREPARATION

A manager who attempts to get an employee to commit himself or herself to a date for completing a particular assignment may well run into a similar situation.

> Suppose that the treasurer of a bank asks a programmer: "Mary, when will we be able to have the first report on the ABC situation?"
> "Probably a couple of months or so. I can't be sure."
> "Could you pin it down a little more specifically? I really need to know when I can expect it."
> "I don't think so. First we need all the data from all the department heads and they're very slow in getting it to me. I just know they're going to be late. Then we've had to re-do the program for the new computer and it isn't working right yet. It's got to be debugged, and I don't know how long that will take. Then the printout equipment . . ."

Mary goes on, building a case for a later and later date. The more the manager presses, the more defensive Mary becomes. The manager says to himself, "This isn't the way it's supposed to work at all. Setting one's own date is supposed to generate commitment to meet it. All I'm getting is static."

The manager forgets that any sudden change in his behavior is likely to cause apprehension among those who report to him. If Mary is used to being asked to complete a report by a certain date and then working very hard to meet it, asking her to set her own date may well cause her concern and make her wonder if the manager has somehow been dissatisfied. Change requires preparation, understanding, and acceptance, if it is to be successful. Even then, its introduction has to be carefully timed, and a thoughtful and sound decision made as to whether it is better done gradually or abruptly.

It is also common for the manager to decide to apply some of these newer ideas to his management. If greater autonomy and upward influence are the order of the day, he has a few things to discuss with the boss. So one day after the two have finished reviewing a new product application, he takes the plunge:

> "Henry," he says, "I've had a feeling for a long time that we are being much too conservative in our product development programs. Our line is very narrow, and the additions we make to it are so similar to the ones we already have that they don't really broaden our market very much. It seems to me that we should diversify and deliberately work toward more radical changes in current product lines. This would make us quite a different company in ten years than we are today. We would have so much greater possibility for company growth, and there would be more attractive job opportunities for all of us."
>
> Henry grunts. "Who'd pay for all that? The owners of this company know what they want and what they're willing to invest, and they make decisions about things like that. The rest of us just do our jobs."
>
> "But couldn't I at least put together a proposal for them to consider and try to show . . ."
>
> Henry interrupts. "I suggest you just go back and make the product application we've been discussing work properly so that at least one new customer is happy."

The lower-level manager goes away pretty disillusioned about his influence on the company or even on his own work. He may feel, as a result, that the theorists are way off base, do not know what they are talking about, or that their ideas only apply to academic institutions.

WE CANNOT OVERLOOK TRADITIONS

Most institutions—whether public or private, profit-making or non-profit-making—have been around for quite a while. They have traditions and inbred ways of doing things. The people who have grown up in them find it hard to change and break old habit patterns. It is even hard for them to think of different approaches and different ways of working life.

Change will come gradually in some quarters. The important thing is that it *is* beginning. Mechanization and computerization are stimulating it from one direction. New professional employees with different values from those already employed are stirring things from the bottom up. If we can draw on past experience, once change begins, it picks up momentum.

But, we should not give the impression that *a* change will occur and then be finished. As our knowledge increases, even greater advancement will be possible in managing philosophy and practices. Meanwhile, a manager needs first to become acquainted with the current and anticipated state of his profession.

> It is beginning to be possible for the industrial manager to be a professional in this respect. He can draw upon a reasonable and growing body of knowledge in

the social sciences as an aid to achieving his managerial objectives. He need not rely exclusively on personal experience and observation.[13]

Next, he needs to learn how to *apply* this body of knowledge. Dunnington put it very well when he wrote:

> One might conclude that managers, as a matter of course, would extensively use the resources of the behavioral sciences. We find, however, that there is considerable variability in the degree and manner of utilization . . . Although there are similarities among organizations and individuals, there are also important differences. It is the similarities which permit the behavioral scientist to generalize. It is the differences which make the application of findings and theories difficult.[14]

We can safely conclude that managing concepts are changing, and with good reasons. Current theorists and behavioral scientists can offer a general advice for the manager who wants to keep pace, but it is the manager alone who must reconcile theory and practice. The following chapters are designed to help the manager make this reconciliation by acting in ways which will achieve organizational goals as well as encourage personal growth. We need a workable model of the manager-professional relationship to aid us in exploring possible courses of action; the legal partnership is such a model.

---

[13]McGregor, *The Human Side of Enterprise.*

[14]Richard A. Dunnington, "The Application of the Behavioral Sciences to Management," in *The Personnel Job in the Changing World,* Management Report No. 80 (New York: American Management Association, 1964).

2

The
Partnership
Analogy

The term partnership has been so overworked and sentimentalized when applied to the employee-manager relationship that a little brainwashing is needed before examining the worthwhile implications such a relationship might have.

Partnership, for example, does not mean that a manager says frequently: "My employees are my partners!" . . . and then acts very much like their boss.

There are many other situations wrongly labeled partnerships: the sort of benevolent parent-child relationship; the manager who is a partner when in trouble but is "in charge" when things are going well. The manager who abandons his or her responsibilities and lets employees do what they think best is certainly not a partner. Neither is the manager who claims that he or she and the employees are partners and then uses the art of indirection to cajole them into saying and doing what is "right."

The dictionary defines a partnership as "The legal relation existing between two or more competent persons who have contracted to join in business and share the profits." Looking at the legal meaning, it is possible to set up a useful analogy within both profit and nonprofit organizations. *It is not a perfect one, of course,* but it helps highlight important points about the kind of relationship which should be encouraged among professionals to make explicit the value of their individual contributions and their absolute dependence on each other to achieve their goals.

Defined in a very broad fashion, a professional is a worker who deals with a complex body of knowledge which he or she is determined to enlarge.

The worker has considerable freedom of choice about the way work is done. His or her standards of performance or work values are largely self-determined and dictated by the objective requirements of the problem or investigation being pursued.

This definition implies that the professional's field requires concentrated study over a fairly long period of time. The professional then, will usually (though not invariably) be a college graduate. The methods used in a particular field are many and require complex, innovative decision-making to decide how to obtain needed information. The facts of the total situation determine when a satisfactory result has been reached. For this purpose, feedback from others may be helpful—but the professional makes the final evaluation of its technical adequacy because he or she originally defined and stated the problem.

It is possible to argue endlessly about who is included in such a description of "professional," but this serves no useful purpose. From the point of view of achieving excellent work results, the more who fit the definition, the better. From the point of view of establishing effective, satisfying relationships, the more who fit the better. (It should be noted, however, that the Fair Labor Standards Act defines professional work, and employers are bound to adhere to the definition for purposes of computing pay.)

One category of employee should be singled out for special mention—the manager. This individual deals in a complex field of knowledge; has considerable freedom of choice about how to do his or her work; performance success is dictated by the objective requirements of organization goals. This fits the description of professional.

Viewed this way, the relationship between a manager and the professional employees who report to him or her is a relationship *among professionals*. They are engaged, of course, in different fields of work but are equally bound by objective standards and equally involved in complex, innovative decision-making. This makes the concept of their legal partnership an even more attractive analogy. Let's look at some aspects of this relationship.

CONSENT BY COMPETENT PARTIES

Legally, there is no partnership without the consent of the individuals involved, and they must be capable of understanding what they are agreeing to. The consent is usually formalized by a contract outlining the terms of the agreement.

In industry and in nonprofit organizations a detailed contract is rarely drawn up. The usual arrangement is a written salary offer which probably outlines little more than the name of the employee's position and the initial compensation to be received for it. While working in the organization, the employee may find his or her job changed in quite dramatic ways with little warning. Notification of compensation changes may be in writing, or it may only be by word of mouth.

This rather casual handling of important matters appears to stem from and reinforce a basic disregard for the professional's identification with his or her work. It discourages such identification. And in so doing, it tends to lessen the desire to achieve and prevents much of the self-satisfaction and self-realization which might otherwise be inherent in doing the work.

If we were to move closer to a partnership arrangement, the *investment* of each party—manager and individual workers—would be carefully identified prior to employment. This means that the contribution of each would be explored and agreed to; the issues of liability and potential reward or compensation would be clarified. The parties involved would openly investigate each other's qualifications or assets. The manager would pre-plan the work of the open position so that its specific contribution to organization goals would be clear. The prospective employee would make a candid evaluation of the worthwhileness and feasibility of the organization goals and his or her probable contribution to them. If the employee decided to enter into the agreement he or she would have determined to accept whatever risks might be involved.

This could not be only an initial effort made at the time of employment. As the organization is restructured or organization goals shifted or positions redesigned or filled with new incumbents, agreement of the individuals involved would be important.

A COMMON PURPOSE

Under the law, partners pool their individual interests for a common purpose not in opposition to their personal goals. This partnership provides a way for each to pursue his or her own ends under more favorable conditions than could be provided for alone.

If professional employees and management are on different sides, it can hardly be viewed as motivating a high level of cooperative effort. For the professional who identifies with the work he or she produces, the partnership ideal has far greater advantages.

For example, today's engineer or scientist needs facilities, equipment, and money. Often he or she needs knowledge from disciplines. A social worker needs the help of doctors, available hospital facilities, law enforcement agencies, and so on. Even an administrator in a private foundation needs information-gathering channels and legal and financial inputs, to mention only a few requirements. So that pooling personal talents with those of other professionals working within an organization structure which facilitates work and provides needed resources makes a great deal of sense. Professionals, however, whether managers or individual workers, need to align their personal objectives with the organization objectives. They can only commit themselves fully if they feel the two are in harmony.

PARTNERS RETAIN THEIR INDIVIDUALITY

The law protects the individuality of partners. The agreement holds only as long as the parties to it remain in the firm. If one or more withdraws, the partnership is dissolved.

In recent years, there has been a tendency to play down individuality, to seek the good team workers and one who will not rock the boat, especially in industrial and business organizations. Many popular writers have viewed with alarm the stress on conformity or "fit," telling the boss what he or she wants to hear, and the like. Accounts have undoubtedly exaggerated the point for many firms. Nonetheless, they have done little to make these organizations attractive to creative, professional workers who pride themselves on their independence. Professionals feel that much of the importance of their work comes from their individually different approaches to problems and their unique perspectives.

The partnership is a sound solution to the problem of individuality within an organization. There is a pooling of interests by the members and there is a common purpose to be achieved. But there is also explicit recognition of the dependence of the organization on its members as individuals and of the purpose of each in joining the organization. Professional work under this concept, then, cannot be an impersonal, automatic assembly-line process.

Just as the identity of the outstanding artist or writer is obvious from the style of his work, so the professional—manager or individual worker—desires and, if his work is good enough, deserves similar recognition. There are some important implications to this. The professional needs to develop his or her quality and abilities to the point where they find clear expression and outlet in his or her work. Yet this must be done in such a way that the total goals of the organization are enhanced. In turn, the climate of the organization must encourage this development and include ways to recognize and reward it. Expected *results* must be defined—not just activities to be completed. Professionals should know what resources are available to them so that maximum energies can be devoted to making innovative *and* legitimate work choices.

INVESTMENT, CONTRIBUTION, RIGHTS, AND REWARDS

A partnership agreement outlines fairly precisely the initial and continuing investment of each partner and how the profits will be divided. These are not necessarily equal in amount or content for all partners. One may make a larger initial investment than others. For one, the investment may be money; for another, skill.

A well-established senior lawyer, for example, who takes a "junior partner" does so usually with the understanding that the senior partner brings more contacts and know-how to the business. The already established law practice has a certain monetary value, so the senior partner's share of the profit is correspondingly higher. The younger partner expects to work harder and do more of the routine work. This is an investment on his or her part in return for the benefits of the older person's experience. The level of reward is rightfully lower than the senior person's, at least for the time being.

If, however, a senior corporation lawyer wishes to expand and diversify his or her practice to include tax work, a partner with the same expertise and maturity may be sought. In this case, the terms of the agreement are equal or more nearly equal.

In the industrial analogy, if a manager hires a young Ph.D. solid-state physicist with only summer job experience, the manager must contribute a great deal of technical know-how, business judgment, knowledge of organization, and work methods. Since the manager's contribution is expected to be larger than that of the young physicist, the pay is also considerably higher. The physicist accepts these terms, so that he or she can learn from the manager or from others in the organization. The manager's risk is higher, too, with this physicist than with another more experienced individual. So the manager's reward should appropriately be greater.

If, on the other hand, the manager sees a market to be tapped if he or she only had certain technological know-how in the organization, and hires the best pro to be found in this field, the contribution is more nearly equal. The rewards should be more equal also. In both cases, however, each party looks at his or her own probable contribution and the contribution of the other and agrees to the reward terms based on the relation between the two.

What changes would the partnership concept imply between professionals in profit or nonprofit organizations? The legal liability of the individual for the total result cannot, of course, be literally translated. More emphasis can, however, be placed on individual responsibility. This would necessitate more emphasis on sound selection for all parties concerned. The professional would evaluate others with whom he or she would be associated in the hopes that they, including the manager, could contribute substantially to the outcome of his or her personal work. The manager who has the hiring responsibility would check out the professional competence of the prospective employee and make certain that the employee could add important strengths to the total group.

Next, since the investment and contribution of each would be carefully spelled out in advance, each would be aware of what was expected by the other. This would permit self-evaluation as well as evaluation of the adequacy of others' performances. The individual worker would have a real stake in the adequacy of the manager's performance, for example, as well as that of the other associates. Frank discussions of ways and means of improving might well be quite common.

Compensation and reward would certainly be handled differently. As it is now, managers have, in most cases, the bulk of the power in their hands. The personnel office or higher levels of management may establish guidelines for them varying from permissive to absolutely inviolable.

In any event, the professional—manager or individual worker—once hired, has little to say about his or her own compensation. He or she really has only two choices: stay under existing conditions or leave if unfairly treated and protests go unheard. There is some feeling that the professional should not discuss salary, that money is beneath his or her dignity. But if the relationship were that of partners in a common venture, the reward basis would be agreed to in advance. Ground rules could not be changed without the consent of those involved. The basic considerations would most probably be the initial investment of the individual—how much talent and experience, how many useful contacts and similar needed attributes one brings to the organization—and the defined contribution or results expected of him or her. This implies much greater specificity ahead of time and much better measurement of individual results than exist in most organizations today.

FREE FLOW OF INFORMATION

In a partnership, each party is entitled to complete information about the firm's business and has access to its books. Two issues are involved here. One is privilege; the other is responsibility. The professional should be able to know the business facts about the organization of which he or she is a member. Most organizations today realize that this free flow of information permits more intelligent work choices and better alignment of work with needs.

On the other hand, there is more than the "right to know" involved. The professional who takes his or her personal liability seriously has a responsibility to find out. One cannot excuse oneself on grounds that he or she worked toward an incorrect goal through ignorance. That person must define goals only after the most careful exploration of what is needed. An individual cannot claim that he or she overspent the budget because of ignorance as to what the funding limitation was. It is incumbent upon the partner to find out. The manager and the individual professional worker share responsibility for the exchange of relevant information.

THERE IS MORE RISK

In most areas, professionals—managers and individuals alike—gain by establishing something like a partnership arrangement. The individuality of each is protected. Their roles are more clearly defined. Their shares of the rewards are delineated.

There are other implications which may not be so attractive. Partners share the *risks* of the organization as well as its rewards. There is much less protection. Each is at the mercy of his or her associates' work. If one fails to do his or her share, the rewards of the others may suffer.

Under these conditions, each partner evaluates the gain of continuing the partnership. Each must question if the arrangement still contributes to personal goals and if the terms still seem fair. The higher risk brings other implications; if partnership thinking were translated into business and non-profit agency settings, professionals would be compelled to involve themselves in the goals of the organization, its methods, its management competence, and the total quality of its output. The pressure on them for excellent performance could be higher. Most would experience an increased sense of urgency and drive for accomplishment.

BASIC ELEMENTS OF A PARTNERSHIP

Summarizing, then, the fundamentals of a partnership and some of the key implications are:

1. Partners have a common purpose.
2. The common purpose serves their individual interests.
3. Each person must be committed to certain accomplishments.
4. Each must be committed to staying abreast of information affecting his or her sphere of contribution.
5. Each evaluates on a continuing basis the importance of the partnership arrangement to personal goals.
6. Each evaluates on a continuing basis the contributions of the partners.

7. The partners share in both the risks and rewards involved in their activity and have access to full information about the firm.
8. The basis for risk, rights, and reward is a negotiated agreement based on the initial investment and the expected contributions of each partner.
9. Major changes in the work require the consent of the partners.
10. The partnership may be cancelled according to the terms of the previously negotiated agreement.

THE TRANSLATION

Can these be translated into the industrial and nonprofit organization settings?

1. *Common purpose.* The output for which the professionals—manager and individual workers—are responsible.
2. *Serving individual interests.* If the output is accomplished, it should bring some result each person is seeking for him or herself—greater knowledge, career advancement, recognition of competence by other professionals, personal satisfaction, and so on.
3. *Commitment to accomplishment.* Each dedicates his or her working time to what has been agreed upon. For the manager, it may be providing funds or figuring out work flow between sections or departments. It may be supplying technical know-how or making plans involving risk decisions. For the individual professional worker, it may mean evolving the process or the information or the new design needed for a successful product.
4. *Commitment to currency of knowledge.* If each is to make a specialized contribution to joint output, it goes without saying that each must be up to date in his or her specialty and, preferably, ahead of competitors.
5. **and 6.** *Self-evaluation of benefits from association with each other.* The relationship is subject to evaluation by all professionals involved. The manager appraises the individual worker's progress toward the anticipated professional contribution. The individual professional similarly evaluates the effectiveness of the manager's efforts to facilitate work. The continued conscious evaluation of the benefits of the partnership and the decision to continue it or not are useful spurs to self-motivation.

7. *Shared risk and reward.* The conscious decision to continue working together because of total benefits each is receiving from the association makes the monetary reward more acceptable. And the continuing availability of full information about how well the organization is meeting its objectives permits and encourages improvements in performance to help increase the probable reward.

8. *Prenegotiated basis for sharing.* Each party—manager and individual professional worker alike—agrees to meet certain objectives on the basis of a clearly defined reward or compensation system.

9. *Major changes require consent.* Substantial changes in objectives, in expected contribution, in compensation, and in other important working conditions need the specific agreement of all members of the organization involved.

10. *Cancellation.* The conditions under which professionals may cancel the agreement are also defined. If the evaluation of the contribution of other members is negative, or the benefits of the partnership become less than satisfying, or the basis for assigning reward or lack of it seems unfair, any party may decide to discontinue—providing he or she follows predetermined rules. Termination practices are, therefore, clarified.

IS THIS PARTNERSHIP RELATIONSHIP WORKABLE?

Current management thinking is very close to it. Theorists of the last twenty to thirty years have stressed the importance and "rightness" of the trend toward self-control and self-measurement. They have emphasized the need for alignment of personal values and goals with those of the organization and have recommended open and full information exchange. They have decried the role of the manager as "judge" and urged that of "helper."

But in the hierarchical organizations in which most employees function, it is difficult to find a way to go from traditional relationships toward recommended ideals. A model or pattern is needed. Those who wish to improve their managing success or other kinds of professional work could match their attitudes and actions against such a model. The legal partnership relationship has much to recommend it for this purpose.

An exact translation is, of course, impossible. Even if we signed a contract and spelled out its exact terms as legal partners do—and maybe we *should* move in this direction with professionals—we could not legally establish partnership inside a corporation or a government agency, as examples.

In addition, we are burdened with tradition, industrial history, organization philosophies, established management practices, and all sorts of benefit plans, pay practices, and expectations on the parts of the individuals involved. Often these are quite inconsistent with those of a partnership.

To move in the direction of the partnership ideal, moreover, involves a change in the manager's concept of self, role, power, and contribution. The manager would need to see the individual professional worker as an ally and associate. For the professional, it would imply greater risks than he or she may currently enjoy. It would eventually mean a long delayed overhaul of personnel practices. Since the parties involved are employees of a company or agency, they have a relationship to the organization as well as to each other. Since professionals are unlikely to work alone, they have additional relationships to other employees.

All these factors complicate application of the partnership model. But they do not make it impossible. They make an exchange of relevant information and an improved understanding of the role of each employee even more important. They establish certain limits on the freedom of each professional to negotiate an acceptable agreement with the other. They reduce some of the risk for all parties and make possible an organization continuity which might otherwise not exist.

In other words a "perfect" partnership may be an impossibility. But the very factors which limit it offer some compensations and permit the application of partnership principles—with promise of very real rewards for doing so—to a far greater extent than currently in use.

Organizations have a choice. They can encourage a relationship among employed professionals which is more like that existing between management and nonexempt employees. But this situation is likely to generate work and personal attitudes which will degrade professional work and discourage innovation. Or, they can move in a direction closer to the partnership concept, thus dignifying the status of the professional workers, encouraging their active involvement in the affairs of the total organization, and increasing their commitment to achieve needed results. The latter choice seems definitely worth the effort.

3

So You're
a New Manager

On Friday you were just one of the gang—a professional employee with four years' experience in the firm. You had trained for your job for at least four years. You probably took night courses, too, some at a local university and some offered by your employer. You really wanted to understand and contribute to the basic field in which you were making your career.

Then a month ago, rumors started that your boss was moving to a new job in another department. One day you were called to the front office and told that you were being considered as a replacement. You were pleased and flattered to be considered. You did your best to make a good impression. Later though, a lot of questions went through your mind. "What if they pick ME? What would the people I work with think? Can I handle the job?"

You knew that if it were offered to you, you would take it. But you did not go all out for it mentally. You reserved a little question in case someone else was selected. Then you were called back to the front office and told that the job was yours if you wanted it. There were some other words about having every confidence in your ability to do well and so on. But you did not hear much of that.

Now it is Monday, and a little stage fright has set in. You have not trained for managing. Where do you begin?

There are undoubtedly a number of employees and associates who have already asked for time to see you or who will do so very shortly. Probably the mail includes a number of "urgent" requests for your help in expediting this or finding out what is wrong with that. While such requests cannot be ignored, you have a first major choice to make. You can let the demands of others guide your managerial life, or you can resolve not to spend your working time just fighting fires, surviving emergency situations, stop-gapping, and pinch-hitting. A really successful manager will get ahead of and stay ahead of as many of these problems as possible and deal with those that remain in an orderly, rational fashion. So, resolve to be a pro at your new work. Set aside a certain amount of time each day for the constructive, longer-range kind of thinking and action that is needed. In the beginning, this ought to be at least 50 to 60 percent of your time.

SEE YOUR MANAGER

Begin by seeing your manager. If your manager does not ask to see you, ask to see him or her. No matter how thoroughly your predecessor reviewed work matters with you, it is desirable, even necessary, to get information from the person to whom you are now accountable for results. Assumptions that work underway should be continued, that the current dollar and man-power budget is the right one, even that the charter or mission of the department will remain as is, are simply not valid. Often, one staffing change triggers a series of thoughts about other moves that might increase overall effectiveness. Often, too, since communication is limited by personal wishes and past experience, any understanding gained through your predecessor may be incorrect or place emphasis on the wrong matters.

So, it is essential that you review a number of items with your manager. Make it clear that this is a preliminary discussion subject to change as you develop firsthand knowledge of the situation.

CLARIFY KEY RESPONSIBILITIES

First, clarify the role of the department which you will be managing. What is its purpose or charter or mission? What does your manager count on it to do in the organization? This information gives you the broad frame of reference on which to base your current and future work programs.

Second, list the major results that the organization is expected to achieve and by what date and according to what priority. How does your manager see these results contributing to the total operation he or she runs? This information will tell you the specific relationships which you should establish and maintain on a healthy give-and-take basis. It will also permit you to take whatever steps may be necessary to insure that interrelated work is scheduled accordingly.

The third item to document is any limitation placed on your authority. Is there a limit to the amount or rate of money you spend? Is there a head count which effectively limits the size of the organization? If there are pooled facilities or work groups serving several parts of the organization, what priorities have been set for your work?

Fourth, discuss any feeling or impression—favorable or unfavorable—that your manager may have developed about employees, organization structure, work habits, and the general effectiveness of the organization which you are now managing. As you work in your new position, you can watch for evidence to verify or refute his or her thoughts on these subjects.

Fifth, are there any specific assignments that your manager wishes to give you personally? These may be matters for his or her use, for use by associate managers, or for customers.

Finally, do you have any recommendations or questions to discuss with your manager? It is perhaps too soon to raise major questions involving substantial change, unless you have been deeply involved in a problem or study of some sort and have convictions about it which your new status and the new information and perspective available to you will not change.

FIGURE 3-1   Clarify These Matters With Your Manager

---

1. Your department's role in the overall operation

2. Major results to be obtained—with dates and priorities

3. Limitations on your authority

4. His or her view of the organization's effectiveness

5. Your specific, personal assignments

6. Your recommendations and questions for discussion

Inevitably, some items discussed will be quite specific and clear. Others will tend to be less well defined. Log these as areas for thought, investigation, and better formulation on your part. Follow your thought with further discussion and agreement with your manager. Both of you will be more satisfied and have a better chance of accomplishing objectives if expected results and ground rules are defined.

GET TO KNOW EMPLOYEE CAPABILITIES

Now that you have a clear idea of what is expected of you, probably the next action should be a review of every available piece of information about the individuals who will be working with you. If you have never managed before, you will tend to see yourself carrying the ball, perhaps helped by an able assistant or two. Wipe this image from your mind.

Unless your title is only for prestige, you should organize to get results rather than try to produce them by yourself. Your role is obtaining and assigning adequate resources to solve problems, making sure that priorities are correct and information adequate. You should facilitate the department's work by anticipating favorable happenings so that they may be exploited. It is your job to foresee difficulties in time to avoid them, hopefully influencing future events rather than merely responding to them. You insure quality output on schedule—but not by masterminding work. Instead, you find capable individuals to undertake the effort and then challenge them, expecting top professional output and reviewing results objectively in the light of internal or customer needs. You should contribute what you can to minimize barriers. Share your past relevant experiences as appropriate. This is a full-time job. It precludes continuing work on pet projects of your own. This would deprive professional employees of the managing contribution they deserve to have from you.

This means that you must depend on the employees who staff your organization to accomplish needed work. So you had better know everything that there is to know about their abilities. If you worked closely with them before, you have an advantage because you already know a great deal about what they are working on and how they go about their work. Perhaps you even know how heavy their work loads are. But you also have a very real disadvantage. Your relationship with them has changed; you are now called upon to make judgments about their work and contribution against the background of *business* or *organization* or *customer* needs. This is a different context from your earlier, more specialized view. Then, too, since you knew them as friends or associates you will have biases and prejudices about them—both favorable and unfavorable—which will make it harder for you to make sound, objective decisions about their work.

An examination of the personnel file of each member of the department is a good place to begin. Get the facts about each individual's education and experience. See what has been recorded about his or her performance assets and liabilities and, if available, career interests and probable growth potential.

If yours is the usual situation, it is quite probable that the recorded information is woefully inadequate. Set up a procedure for documenting information about each employee; get your secretary started preparing folders for your day-to-day use. Make a list of what you personally observed in the past about each person's performance strengths and weaknesses, adding whatever information is in the files. Try to translate these into the requirements for their positions as now structured and the kind of contribution they are likely to make to the department. List any questions that you have about their current assignments.

These notes are your first data for your personnel records. You will want to supplement them, of course, through later individual and group discussions.

FORMULATE SOUND RELATIONSHIPS
WITH PROFESSIONALS

A productive relationship which encourages excellence of output is not apt to develop by chance. First of all, unless you were brought in from another department or from outside the firm, you do not start from a zero position. This situation calls for a little reflection and analysis on your part. What has your past relationship been with each member of your organization? Even if everyone acts the same as before and pretends nothing has changed, this is obviously not the case. You are now in a position to affect their work assignments, their salaries, and their careers. They are in position to contribute greatly or moderately to results for which you are responsible—to affect *your* success or failure in significant ways. Recognizing this interdependence, you need to work with them to set the relationship ground rules between you. The first things that you do and say will have an important impact because you will be under close scrutiny during your early "appearances."

Since most of the people who report to you are professional employees trained to set their own standards, you have the opportunity to move in the direction of a partnership relationship to capitalize on these qualities. If you worked with them, they think of you as an associate, and this will favor the partnership concept. On the other hand, if they had a superior-subordinate kind of relationship with your predecessor, based on a hierarchy of power, you have some things to overcome.

So you need a plan of action for your first meetings with employees. The plan does not have to be elaborate. First, you will want a group meeting to set the stage for your working relationship and to outline some of the early actions that you want to take. Later, you will want an individual meeting with each person to review his work and his feelings about it. You will also need a series of work program or project reviews to provide specific data about the current status of work and future alternative actions.

In each of these meetings, you need to make explicit what your work is, what the professionals' work is, and how you will work together for excellent results. You also will have to demonstrate by your actions—both in these meetings and later—that you mean what you say.

THE STAGE-SETTING MEETING

Opening Remarks.   Begin by telling employees that you have been thinking about how you and they can best work together to obtain needed, excellent results. Tell them of your conviction that the key to much of your joint success is a sound working relationship. Their investments in the future of the department are their full talents applied to their professional work. Yours is providing needed resources to match work priorities and anticipating future demands on the organization in order to respond properly and influence the future favorably whenever possible. Both of you have responsibilities for keeping each other informed and increasing your competence to do your part of the job better.

Let employees know that you intend to keep them informed of what you are doing to make it easier for them to do their work, and that you count on them to let you know quickly about their significant successes or failures. You hope that they will evaluate your contribution to their work as you will theirs to the organization, so that both can decide how beneficial the association is and what might be done on both sides to make it more helpful.

Establish Common Purposes.   Put in writing the major commitments of the organization (the ones you worked out with your manager). Whether you use a blackboard or an easel or hand out typed sheets, make sure that all see what has been tentatively agreed to. Add the dates by which each should be completed. If there are long-term projects, give the milestone dates by which major phases of the projects will be accomplished. Indicate whatever priorities have been set for these. Be sure to acknowledge that you do not know enough about the details to determine how easy or how hard it will be to accomplish these projects, or whether the effort assigned to each is adequate, or whether the money being spent matches the schedule. Indicate your need for their professional judgment throughout. Specify that you would like to hold a full-scale, detailed review to examine just where all major programs stand, how likely they are to meet customer and internal company expectations, and what might be done to improve their outcome. In all probability, this series needs to be organized along program or product lines. Assign the responsibility for organizing these review sessions to an appropriate program director or coordinator, or a project or product manager if such exists, or to an appropriate key specialist. Set a date or dates when this will be done. Give them enough time—a week is perhaps a good average—to review their own work, their evaluation of it, and make alternate suggestions for improving quality, reducing cost, completing it sooner.

Exchange Information.   Invite frank discussion of things employees like and do not like about the department, the work, the organization structure, the paper work processes. Ask for any constructive ideas for improving the situation. This part of the meeting is critical. Their comments may be brutally frank or criticisms may seem petty or unfounded. But, if you show annoyance, irritation, or unwillingness to devote thought to the issue, you imply that your opening remarks were shallow words. You dampen the desire to live up to the ideal of full information exchange between you. So particularly in your early meetings, you need to feel and show honest acceptance of whatever you are told. Better definition of what you need to tell each other can come later. Make notes of things that seem important to them, whether they seem important to you or not, and, of course, note items requiring action on your part. These points may well supply some of the content for your own management goals.

Make Action Plans.. Tell those in the meeting that you would like to meet with each of them individually. If possible, work out the schedule on the spot. Make it clear that there are several reasons for these meetings. First, you want to be sure that information about education, experience, and other matters relating to their qualifications is known to you and documented in your personnel files.

Second, you want to review their salary situation. This review is not, of course, to grant or refuse increases so soon, but to be sure that you know how their jobs are evaluated for salary purposes, what action has been taken for each and when, and also to hear expressed any feelings each may have about his or her salary situation.

Third, you want to review each person's total work load to be sure that you know what each feels he or she is accountable for producing for the organization. Is it making use of their special talents? Do they feel it is taking them in the direction of personal career interests? You want to know whether the work is satisfying, whether he or she is learning from it and feels challenged by it, and if this individual would like to suggest changes in what he or she is doing. Naturally, you must make it clear that all of you share responsibility for obtaining results expected by the overall organization. But within this framework, individual interests can and will be served.

Ask that each person be prepared during the meeting to point out any problems or barriers he or she is encountering in getting work done, what that person believes the probabilities are that due dates can be met, and what the two of you can do to improve the odds that they will. Explain that you would also like to walk through each work area to meet all employees at their work stations and to make certain that you are thoroughly familiar with the working conditions, facilities, and equipment assigned to each. If possible, work out a schedule for doing this before closing the meeting.

Close the Meeting. Close by repeating the highlights of what you expect of them and what they should expect of you. Confirm the action plans you made during the meeting. Make it a habit to open and close meetings promptly so that all of you can schedule your time. This is a small courtesy, usually much appreciated by professional people whose personal output stops when they are in meetings. But do not continue a meeting until the announced closing time unless its objective has not been accomplished or something of real importance has come up which deserves the attention of the entire group. And do not let a meeting peter out. Keep the action crisp and bring it to a definite closing when the business has been completed.

Figure 3-2 summarizes the steps for your stage-setting meeting.

FIGURE 3-2   Agenda for the Stage-Setting Meeting

---

1. Opening remarks—define your relationship.

2. Establish common purposes—results expected of the department.

3. Exchange information. What is on their minds? What do you see ahead?

4. Make action plans:
   a. individual meetings,
   b. work area tours,
   c. work program or project reviews.

5. Close meeting—summary.

PLAN YOUR OWN TIME

Work out a preliminary action plan for yourself. You now have personal assignments obtained from your manager and a few additional items agreed on at your stage-setting meeting with employees. You have a schedule of personal visits to each work area in your organization and individual meetings with each professional worker. You have a series of work reviews to learn the status of major work commitments.

What other events are likely to occur and need time allocation? Does your manager hold regular meetings of any kind? Is there a fairly heavy volume of correspondence which comes in on a daily basis and needs attention? Are you serving on any committees or task forces in place of your predecessor? Do you need to review the finances of the department with the treasurer or accountant? Are important customers scheduled to visit you? Do you need to consolidate relationships with associate managers in other parts of the organization? Do you have to find someone to take over or get started in your former job?

Block out in a general way when you might do these things. Sit back for a moment and look at what you have laid out. Will you finish your review of the people, the work, the facilities, and so on, in time to make the basic decisions you are facing fairly quickly? These decisions are:

- ◆ Are talented people in place to do the work that needs to be done?
- ◆ Is the work planned and organized with sufficient ingenuity to meet or beat department goals?

- Is the output of the department excellent in both quality and quantity?
- Are employees being rewarded adequately for their contributions—both in terms of their personal satisfaction and growth and in terms of compensation?

If the answer is no in any one of these respects, what should be done about it?

Develop a sense of urgency in the organization that will challenge, stimulate, and increase dedication. Start with yourself. Perhaps you can speed up your reviews and meetings. Do not become so hurried that you cannot give adequate attention to what you are hearing and seeing and you fail to make adequate written notes for later reference. But at least speed up to the point where you and those who report to you are visibly pushing forward, visibly putting a little extra into each day, visibly making it clear that much needs to be done, and it is of such importance that it cannot wait for tomorrow or next week.

4

Fact-Finding
Phase I:
Individual Work

As a professional engaged in managing work and responsible for results produced largely by professional employees, you need to make at least two critical decisions. First, do the individuals who report to you have the talent to do the work assigned to them? Second, is this work essential to the organization? If the answers to both are yes, the first corollary question to be tackled is: are conditions such that each person is able to carry out his or her assignment effectively? That is, does he or she have the manpower, facilities, tools, work methods, paper work flow, facilitating organization, and so on, to permit excellence of performance?

The second corollary question is: Does the individual want to produce the needed result with distinction? Has he or she an interest in the field or technology involved? Does it represent a learning experience for him or her? Does it take the individual in the direction of career interests? Does it promise recognition or other rewards?

Answering these questions and making the fundamental decisions require that you sit down with each employee for a fact-finding session. In one sense, this interview may be extraordinarily difficult. You want individuals to speak freely about themselves and their work, yet both of you are keenly aware that the information discussed will be used to help you decide on the employee's qualifications and what his or her work future should be in the organization you manage. Only with carefully laid groundwork and with preparation by both parties is the meeting likely to be successful.

The fact that the personnel involved are professional employees, hopefully possessing considerable independence and curiosity, will help. And your words and actions to date about a partnership concept—whether you have used the term or not—will help too. For the meeting is not at all one-sided. The professional employee also has decisions to make. He should be encouraged to view this meeting as an extraordinary opportunity to show you the investment of skill and talent he is making to meet the objectives of the department and to give you his appraisal of the benefits he is receiving in return or what he feels he should receive. The meeting can legitimately, then, be structured as an information exchange.

ADVANCE GROUNDWORK

Assuming that you have already discussed your desire to confer with each person to review his or her work and how he or she feels about it, some additional groundwork is now in order. A personal note to each individual, confirming time and place and restating the purpose and agenda in more detail, is desirable. It might read something like this (in your own words, of course):

> Dear Susan:
>
> At our meeting next Tuesday morning at 10 o'clock, I thought we might use the small conference room on the second floor so that we would both be away from phones and have uninterrupted time together.
>
> As you know, it is my purpose to learn as much as I can about what you and your associates are working on and get your professional estimate of the likelihood of success. Later, when we look at work programs, there will probably be a second opportunity to review this same information in a slightly different light. It would be helpful at this first meeting, therefore, if you could emphasize your personal association with the work. By this I mean, be prepared to present a list of your major responsibilities, saying briefly where each stands with respect to completion time and also with respect to funding, inputs from others, quality (current and prospective), anticipated obstacles to successful completion, and similar points. In addition, be prepared to discuss your personal feelings about this work. Do you think this is desirable, important work for the department to undertake and for you to be associated with? Is it using your talents and abilities? Is it leading you in a desired career direction? What recommendations do you have for the work and for your association with it?
>
> I think I also mentioned that we should review basic information about your education and experience to be sure that personnel records reflect the current status of your qualifications. We will also discuss your salary situation so that we both know where that stands and how you feel about it.
>
> You may well have related matters to add to our agenda. If any require prior investigation on my part, I hope you will mention them ahead of time so that it can be done.
>
> I hope you will seize this opportunity to get out on the table all the matters, favorable and unfavorable, which affect your ability and willingness to do excellent work. We can look at them thoughtfully and either reinforce or minimize them as the case may be. Incidentally, we should probably allow two hours to cover this ground and plan to add to it or subtract from it as seems desirable at the time.
>
> I am very much looking forward to our discussion.
>
> *Bob*

You may want to attach an agenda such as the one following so that each person sees what will be expected of him or her in the course of the meeting.

You will need to prepare for these meetings in three ways. First, decide precisely what you will cover in the meeting, what information you will want to record in at least note form, and how you will record it so that the high points will be readily available to you later for your decision making. The second kind of preparation will be to refresh your knowledge of interviewing so that you conduct this delicate conference with skill. Third, bring to mind everything you know about the person you are seeing to be sure you adjust the interview to his unique situation.

FIGURE 4-1   Suggested Agenda

The agenda will vary according to how well you know the individual you are interviewing, your past relationship with him, and your knowledge of his current work and past performance. A basic pattern, however, might be the following:

1. Opening remarks (you):
   a. purpose of meeting
   b. comment on past and current relationship

2. Review of major work goals by employee:
   a. purpose of position
   b. current work status
   c. effort devoted to each
   d. evaluation of contribution of others
   e. major current and anticipated obstacles and problems
   f. managerial help needed
   g. likelihood of success

3. Employee's reaction to current work:
   a. evaluation of worth to business
   b. evaluation of work to career
   c. recommended changes

4. Quick review of employee's personal and job history data:
   a. verify and update current records
   b. review salary situation

5. Relationship of employee's work to department goals:
   a. review "fit" with department goals
   b. input and output points—related work
   c. managerial contribution
   d. priority set by manager's manager

DOCUMENTATION

The way you record work-related information elicited during this meeting will depend on the nature of the work being discussed. If you are responsible for large, complex technical projects, professionally planned and documented on a PERT or similar system, it may only be necessary to put new information into the system or adjust milestone charts to reflect this new information. Otherwise, 5 × 8 cards labeled to identify the work program, project, investigation, or service may prove useful.

Record on these cards the major phases of the work, who is responsible for each phase, their beginning and expected completion dates, and major problems or obstacles to completion. File the cards by work program. As each individual is interviewed, his or her comments may be entered on the appropriate card. When work programs are reviewed, individual comments will be readily available. These work program cards may also be grouped later according to the key results or goals to which you and your manager agreed. You may then evaluate how well the work in progress contributes to the results which you are currently committed to accomplish.

With respect to the personnel information, it will be helpful if you make your notes as factual as possible. When you record judgments, guesses, or opinions, label them as such. These notes may be handwritten in the personnel files already started.

You may also find it useful to start a separate log of managerial actions that you ought to take or consider taking, or questions you want to investigate. A plain piece of paper, one side devoted to "people" actions and the other to "work" actions, is probably all that is needed.

BONING UP ON INTERVIEWING SKILLS

Hopefully, some time in the past you have taken a good skill improvement course in interviewing. If not, there are a number of good books on the subject largely devoted to interviewing for a particular purpose such as employment or appraisal discussion. If you can abstract from the specific subject matter and focus only on the technique of the interview as such, it may be useful to read one or more of these.[1]

There are, however, a few basic conditions which make it easier to conduct a good interview, and you should at least be sure these are met.

[1]For example, see: Glenn A. Bassett, *Practical Interviewing* (New York: American Management Association, 1965); Richard A. Fear, *The Evaluation Interview* (2d ed.; New York: McGraw-Hill, 1972); Felix M. Lopez, *Personnel Interviewing* (Rev. ed.; New York: McGraw-Hill, 1975).

Keep the Interview as Uninterrupted as Possible.   Have reasonable privacy so that all involved feel free to say what they wish. It is essential that there be a minimum of (preferably no) telephone or visitor interruptions to cause distraction or inability to follow a coherent train of thought.

Follow a Pattern of Questioning.   Decide in advance the areas you want to explore. Draw up the outline for doing this and, if possible, the actual wording of questions you will use. Both these practices increase the reliability of the information you obtain and help ensure that you do cover all areas. Questions at random and on the spur of the moment often prove to elicit incomplete data.

Do as Little Talking as Possible.   Except when you wish to explain or contribute to the discussion in some predetermined way, ask your question and be quiet. Your purpose is to obtain information. The best way to do this is by listening to the interviewee. Managers know this but sometimes fail to apply it. Their tendency is to talk too much.

Ask Big Enough Questions Requiring More Than a Yes or No Answer.   A simple yes or no actually tells you very little. You want to know as much as possible about this individual—personal interests, ambitions, standards, and talents. This sort of information is not likely to come out of the courtroom yes or no answer.

   Ask questions like: "Tell me how you feel about this assignment: Is it good for us to be working on? Does it use your talents? What are you learning from it? Tell me anything else I ought to know about this piece of work, both from a company point of view and from yours." And then be quiet so that the employee can organize his or her thoughts and answer coherently. Do not be afraid of a few moments of silence. If the individual needs prompting at some point say: "And don't forget about . . ." Or if he or she is vague on some point of interest, you might say: I'm very interested in that. Could you tell me a little more about it?" . . . or, "Give me an example or two."

Look and Sound Interested and Receptive.   When the interviewee is talking, show attention, be responsive, nod, or in any way indicate that you are following closely. If you fail to communicate your interest, the person may feel he or she is taking too much time and leave out information that you would like to have.

Redirect Conversation if Overelaborate or Off the Track.   If the person does wander off on tangents or get too involved in unwanted detail, interrupt firmly but with a smile and pull his or her attention back to the point. For example, you might say in a pleasant tone of voice: "You certainly have thought about that a great deal. But I'm afraid we must get back to the subject of drafting support. What is your feeling about that?" Or, "Headquarters investigations always do involve some extra paper work. We have to recognize the good effects they have as well. What *other* events have affected results recently?"

These few suggestions are not enough to make you a good interviewer, but perhaps they will serve to remind you of things learned earlier or at least encourage you to read and think about the importance of the interviewing skill.

INDIVIDUAL ADAPTATION

Reflect on Your Past Relationship, if Any.   Before you see each person, you will want to give specific thought to him or her as an individual. What has your relationship been in the past? How will it affect your new relationship? Has the employee given you information about him or herself, their work, interests, and so on, which might now be of personal concern? If so, do not plan to pretend you have forgotten or want to ignore it. Instead, plan to reassure the individual that you do remember and would like to work with him or her in the most helpful way possible to take joint remedial action if that appears to be in order. Any pretense that the past is blotted from the record or the slate wiped clean is not only false, but doomed to create insecurity and suspicion, neither one of which is likely to make it easier for you to work together.

Review Available Personnel Information.   Review whatever you know or were able to find out about the person from others. What appear to be his or her areas of contribution? What are his or her limitations? How experienced is the individual in his or her professional field? Is the salary about right for the contribution? You may need help from a personnel or administrative component on these matters and should get it if you do.

Consider the Individual's Work and the Department's Goals.   Next, review the common purpose you share—the agreed-upon commitment to the business or agency. Discuss what he or she contributes to it and what priority it has in the list of commitments you have made. Recognize that unless each professional involved commits him- or herself to what you have agreed to achieve, your agreement is worth very little. Recognize, too, that you cannot legislate or order that commitment: it must be aroused. So work out how you will discuss the employee's role in the department's scheme of things with him or her, considering what you know or have been able to find out.

Suspend Judgment.   Finally, resolve to suspend judgment about what is being done or should be done until you have heard the entire story and how he or she feels about his work and future.

ENCOURAGE EMPLOYEE PREPARATION

Your letter will have outlined the reason for holding the meeting with this person and indicated the material to be covered. It is worth making a telephone contact two or three days ahead of time to make sure that he or she will be prepared. A quick statement, something like, "Just wanted to be sure you'll be ready for our session on Thursday. Is there anything special you wanted me to look into in advance?" is probably all that is needed to let the employee know that you are placing considerable importance on this meeting.

THE MEETING

Your meeting with each person should, of course, be private. Try to arrange it so that both of you are sitting at a table or in comfortable chairs as in a social meeting. Avoid placing the other person in a straight chair at the side of your desk while you rock back and forth in a swivel chair, thus automatically indicating a difference in status.

Review Purpose.   Begin by making a short speech. Tell the employee, at risk of repetition, that in accepting your job you agreed to accomplish certain things for the business or organization. Explain that you realize the agreement is worthless unless this person agrees that these things can, and will, be done. Point out frankly that you feel you are in a rather unaccustomed position. You are responsible for meeting certain commitments and your work is to facilitate their accomplishment. This is a new kind of work for you and you are determined to do a professional job of it. You, therefore, have two interests—one, that your associates who are doing the work to meet commitments are competent to do it, and two, that the work itself matches and challenges their abilities. For your part, you will do your best to see that the effort devoted to a project matches its priority, that the organization structure *assists* the flow of work in the department, that suitable resources are available on an economic basis and match assigned priorities, and similar managing work. To put it another way, you are dependent on every employee's output and that of his or her associates. So you are naturally concerned that full talent should be channeled toward accomplishing the department goals. In doing this, you want this person to feel that his or her own best interests are being served—getting internal satisfaction, contributing to professional reputation, forwarding career objectives, and so on. You hope that this person will have something to say about his or her feelings on this subject a little later in the meeting.

Past and Current Relationship. Refer to your former relationship with the worker if one existed. If it was a pleasant, give-and-take relationship, say that you hope it will continue, that you enjoyed the exchange and sharing of ideas or interests, and that you need and want this to continue even more than before.

If it was not a pleasant one, if there was hostility or lack of understanding between you, tell the person that you recognize what existed in the past, and that you hope both of you can figure out why it was so and improve it. Meanwhile, perhaps he or she will be willing to channel criticism of you into useful feedback information. You want to be able to count on the individual to bring to your attention things which he or she feels are unfortunate or wrong or harmful to the organization.

If the relationship was so close that you exchanged confidences, say that you hope he or she understands that you value your close relationship highly. Let the individual know that you count on it as a help to the department and hope that he or she will continue to be open and frank concerning comments and suggestions. Moreover, your awareness of this person's feelings and attitudes puts you in an excellent position to be of help. This help would not, of course, be at the expense of any other member of the organization, but in a way which you hope you will eventually be able to achieve with the others.

Review the Individual's Major Responsibilities. At this point, turn the meeting over to the employee. No matter how well you feel you already know what he or she is doing—in fact, especially if this is the case—listen with solid attention and open mind. Make notes of what is said.

It is probably best to have the employee begin by describing his or her position. List all the major pieces of work for which he or she is currently responsible, whether or not they have actually been started. Then review the percentage of time currently spent on each. Find out if he or she feels the time devoted is appropriate to the importance or priority placed on each.

Then have the worker briefly state just what has been done and what is left to do. Avoid too much detail, because some of the same material may be covered again when you review key work programs. If he or she has the information, find out how much money remains for completion compared with what needs to be done and the time left to do it. Have the individual evaluate how well those who are contributing information or drawings or other inputs to the work are doing, considering volume, time, and quality.

In particular, ask how satisfied those who are receiving data or information or drawings from him or her feel about his or her work. Again consider volume, time, and quality.

Ask the employee to review the major obstacles encountered, whether they are likely to recur, and what additional ones he or she will probably face before the work is completed. Finally, get this person's estimate of how successfully each piece of work will achieve its purpose in terms of quality, finish date, and customer or client expectations.

Employee's Reaction.   Next, ask the worker to talk about how he or she feels about each responsibility. Is it a valuable piece of work? What will it contribute to the business as a whole and to the department specifically? Knowing what this individual knows now, should it have been undertaken in the first place? Is it worth continuing? What would be the penalty for stopping now? What would he or she recommend in its place, or how could its future course be altered to make it more valuable?

Does it use the worker's talents? Is it forcing him or her to enlarge professional know-how? Does it coincide with career goals? Is the worker using it to enhance his or her reputation? When the value of a piece of work is questioned, ask the worker what would better serve organizational and employee interests? If a piece of work is beyond his or her capability, is it because of a technical or administrative deficiency? Can this individual suggest what help or information or changes might remedy the situation? In general, what are his or her career interests?[2] What are the major strengths on which he or she can build a career? Is the worker limited by geographical preferences, desire to specialize in an area not particularly needed by the business, or unwillingness to work extended schedules?

If possible, get the individual to sum up personal, overall reaction to his or her present position. Every job has some elements which are not ideal. Taking this into account, just how does he or she feel about the work and what reasonable recommendations does this person have to make about it?

Review of Personal History Data.   Quickly review with the employee the information about his or her education and experience which are in the personnel file, allowing the person to add any additional facts which ought to be included. Review the salary value for this position as currently established, where his or her salary is with respect to any maximum that exists for this work, how long it has been since the worker has had a merit increase, and his or her understanding of how salaries are administered in the department. How does the employee feel about his or her salary treat-

[2]See Chapters 11 and 12 in Marion S. Kellogg, *What To Do About Performance Appraisal* (New York: American Management Association, 1965).

ment generally and about the current pay level specifically? Try to correct any misunderstandings the individual has about the process, but if he or she feels underpaid, avoid argument. Merely make a note of the reaction and promise two things—first, to review his or her position once it has been more clearly defined to be sure it is evaluated properly according to the plan used in the organization, and, second, to make the work "contract" clearer between you in the future so that both of you can better evaluate when he has earned an increase.

Relationship of Individual Work to Department Goal. Then take the meeting ball back. Briefly review your list of commitments to your manager, and show the employee how each of his or her responsibilities satisfies completely or contributes to or fails to contribute to one or more of them. Where the individual is one of several contributing, try to identify who the others are, and make notes to be verified later. Then review what you see as your needed contribution to his or her work and to the broader department goal it serves. Get any additional thoughts the person may have. Don't overlook such things as funding, changing priority on use of pooled facilities, specialized consultation either with you or supplied by someone else, supporting help from technicians or other services groups, publicity for good results, coordination of related work, leadership with respect to modification of ideas or planning emphasis, and similar items.

Then show the employee where the goal to which his or her work contributes fits in the priority system and why organization-wise this priority was set. If it is high on the scale and he or she believes that it is rightfully so, there is no problem. If he or she thinks that it is too high, ask the employee to review the work again in the light of the overall reasons for placing it there and be prepared to present his or her case at the later work program review. If it is low on the scale, and the employee agrees, ask him or her to consider if it should be continued at all, and if not, what might be substituted. If he or she feels that the priority is wrong, again ask for reasons. These can be reviewed at the time of the work program review.

If the employee's work is isolated from that of the associates, set a date for submission of oral or written ideas and recommendations concerning his or her work package and your contribution to it. If the employee's work meshes with others, he or she will have the opportunity of presenting these thoughts to all involved at the work program reviews.

Closing. Close the meeting by reaffirming your interdependency. Point out that you want to move towards the condition in which each of you sees clearly what you must both do individually to meet your joint commitment to the firm's business, and each of you has confidence that both important contributions will be made. Check with the employee to be sure he or she has gotten as much as possible of the information he or she wanted from the meeting. If not, take additional time to explore areas of interest or to point out when you will have the information if it is not now available.

AFTER THE MEETING

If you can, avoid scheduling anything immediately following your individual meetings with employees. Give yourself time to organize your notes for easy, later reference. Give yourself time, too, to reflect on what you have heard. List items which may require action. For example, employee capability does not match work assigned—too great, too little, wrong field, and so on. Or, breakdown in flow of work between two parts of the organization. Or communication failure upward or downward or crosswise. Or, incorrect effort assigned—too much, too little, wrong rate. Be quite specific in your notes so there is no chance of later confusion. You will need to refer to those items which appear to require action when you have reached the point of decision.

When each employee has been given a turn to review his or her work, you will find yourself in possession of an enormous number of facts, impressions, and half-ideas. You still need an integrated picture of where work stands with respect to your commitments, where the critical hold-up items lie, what the probability is that the organization can meet its commitments, and how the probability can be improved. You are still in the fact-finding stage. Avoid drawing conclusions at this point. Keep your mind open.

5

Fact-Finding
Phase II:
Work Programs

The next logical phase of your fact-finding (although it may overlap individual discussions) is looking at the objectives, status, key problems, and proposed future course of each major work program for which your department is responsible. Your meetings with professional employees should have given you fairly detailed understanding of major parts of each program. The project or program review meetings, therefore, need to be structured to emphasize the flow of work *between* individuals and components, the common understanding of the objectives or specifications for each program, its relationship to and importance in the business plans of the firm or overall organization, and customer expectations and likelihood of their realization. These points focus the attention of each employee on his or her own work, to be sure, but do so within the perspective of the overall business picture or organization objectives. For proper emphasis, review programs in order of their priority.

YOUR PREPARATION

The professional staff needs to understand clearly what they are trying to do as an organization, where work stands now, and what is ahead. You need basic information about the status of work and its likelihood of success to make sound decisions about the adequacy of the organization, staffing, assignment of resources, and so on. Each specialist in the department has some of this information; probably no one has an integrated picture unless there is a project or product engineer, a program director, or a coordinator responsible for just such an overview.

The managerial task facing you, then, is to expose all of the relevant, important information so that all the professionals have a sound basis for making their respective decisions. This needs to be done whether the information involved is favorable or unfavorable. You must get the unfavorable information so that all of you can identify and begin to take necessary steps to improve the situation.

Inevitably, some gaps in work accomplishment, some failures in performance are likely to come to light. No one *likes* to admit them. It takes a very special kind of managerial skill to get complete work information out on the table. Prepare yourself thoroughly in order to be effective at this. You need to develop a pattern for the meeting which will allow you to stimulate, not inhibit, discussion and create a role for participants which will emphasize their importance and their concern for the department's success. You also need to think through how you will keep track of information as it unfolds during the meeting and the kind of action plans you need to make before the meeting is closed.

STRUCTURE OF MEETING

The meeting should have several parts. First, review the total picture related to the work program under discussion—the need for it, customer and competitive situation, financing, and relative priority. Second, there should be a presentation, to which many participants may contribute, about the basic work. Discuss objectives, accomplishment to date and with what resources, work remaining to be done, and available resources for doing it. Next, try to evaluate the likelihood of the program's success: the chief problems to be licked, the time situation, the money situation, and so on. Next, identify critical factors and important barriers or difficulties inherent in various courses of action which might be taken. Finally, a set of action plans should be evolved consisting of the steps which you and others must take to shed light on the unknowns, to help ensure that critical factors will be favorable, and in general, to minimize possibility of failure. These steps are shown in Figure 5-1.

YOUR ROLE

Your role in the meeting is to make the exchange of full information an actuality. This means setting a personal example. You must show by your words and actions that you value the thoughts of the participants and depend on them, encouraging their full participation, rewarding disclosure of unpopular ideas or information or recommendations. It is your job to help participants break out of their established patterns of thinking by giving

FIGURE 5-1   Work Program Meeting Agenda

---

1. Stage-setting remarks for the full exchange of information

2. Presentation of the overall picture from the organization's point of view

3. Program status review

4. Evaluation of the likelihood of success. Key questions for discussion:
   a. What important technical, business, or administrative "unknowns" exist?
   b. What are the major problems and barriers anticipated?
   c. What factors are critical to success?
   d. On what other organizations are we depending and for what?
   e. What alternate courses of action should be considered?

5. Action plans

---

them information that they may not have had before, using terminology different from what they are accustomed to, speaking from a different perspective than they possess, asking questions which get below the surface or more customary modes of thought. It means employing devices which will help them break out of their personal work stereotypes and involving them in the drive toward the required end results. It means encouraging differences of opinion in the hope that by identifying why differences exist, new facts or clouded facts may come to light.

THE PARTICIPANTS AND THEIR ROLES

The participants' roles should be structured to contribute to their individual purposes as well as to group purpose and management purpose. First of all, do not hesitate to break through organization lines when deciding who should attend. Probably every professional employee who plays an important role in accomplishing the program's objectives should be present, whether or not he or she reports directly to you. This will improve the meeting in three ways. First, there will be a minimum of second-hand information. Second, each participant will get a first-hand feel for the whole program, which will allow that person to make decisions on the basis of what is best for the success of the total program or project. And third, individual accomplishment will be recognized in a small way, and the possibility of personal defense exists if failures are brought to light.

When extending invitations to the meeting, make sure that each person understands the objective of the meeting and the rough outline the discussion will follow so that he or she can prepare adequately. Put the key questions to be discussed in writing and emphasize that you are interested in everyone's opinions, ideas, and suggestions.

To help achieve an integrated picture, appoint a leader to organize the presentation on the status of the work program and what is ahead for it. If a project or product engineer or program director has overall responsibility for the program, that individual should be given this responsibility. Otherwise, a respected senior specialist might be a wise choice. Make sure he or she understands that you would like those responsible for major phases of activity to speak for their own work.

LEARN ABOUT GROUP INTERACTION

The work program meeting does not involve the same principles of human behavior as your individual meetings with employees. A participant's relationship with other participants has an impact on what he or she says and does and how the other people respond. In addition, his or her interaction with any one person is observed by others and may also stimulate response from others. There is, therefore, more likelihood that new ideas may develop. Emotions will probably be stronger and either stimulate or inhibit, depending on whether participants are focusing on the common interest of the group or some noncontributing personal interest. A group of highly competent professionals, devoting their full attention to solving problems and to integrating information as a basis for sound decision-making, has enormous potential. But it can only be realized if you provide the proper conditions.

Make Sure That All Understand What They Are Trying to Accomplish for the Department and Themselves. This seems obvious. Yet managers frequently have an objective so clear in their minds that they *assume* it is shared by others. In reality, each person comes to the meeting with his or her own objective—to sell a particular idea, to get more manpower assigned to his or her effort, to "show up" well in front of associates, and so on.

Since these private goals may well interfere with effective problem-solving, they must be minimized. You can do this by publicizing well in advance what needs to be accomplished and its importance to the department and to those who will participate in the meeting. In addition, outline what you expect each participant to contribute prior to and during the meeting so that no one is caught off guard. If possible, involve participants in the objective by having them prepare various materials in advance. This makes the meeting more effective and arouses interest. At the time of the meeting, reiterate its purpose, the role of the participants, and your own role. Present the compelling reasons why this objective has great importance to the assembled group, and relate the overall objective to individual objectives as much as possible.

Focus Attention on the Problem or the Issues, Not on Individual Performance. Avoid discussion of personalities or measurement of individual accomplishment. Where does the work stand? Why is it lagging at certain points? What can be done to put it back on schedule? What are the roadblocks ahead, and how can they be overcome? Have the real reasons for failure or likelihood of failure been uncovered?

Help Participants Express Themselves. If one or more are not taking part or if the discussion is dominated by a few, ask for the advice, opinions, or experiences of the silent ones.

Avoid Playing the Expert. If questions are asked in a conscious or unconscious attempt to find out how you are thinking on a certain point so that the attendees may follow suit, toss the question back to the group or to someone in the group who is close to the information and might logically be more knowledgeable on the subject. On the other hand, do not dodge answering questions or giving information which you logically should know.

Set a Climate for Full Discussion. Reward those who contribute ideas and information by an appreciative thank you. Show pleasure if there is argument or contradictory information, and devote your efforts to getting the reasons for the difference of opinion out on the table. If possible, deliberately spark the airing of differences. These discussions are most likely to bring out information not previously available to everyone. They usually develop considerable involvement in the issues rather than in more subjective views and wishes.

Do Not Be Afraid of Silences. If a question is asked and the response is not immediate, or if a heated discussion ends abruptly and silence follows, do not rush in to ask another question or immediately rephrase one already asked. Give the participants time to collect their thoughts. Wait out the silence for a few moments. If then nothing is said or the group is distracted by a tangential remark, ask the question another way or take it apart a little and ask about some aspects of it. Often, silence permits the spontaneous offering of a valuable piece of information.

Set the Limits of Authority of the Group. For example, the group at the work program meeting is to present and exchange information, spark new ideas, and consider alternate courses of action for the future. But the group probably will not make the decision even though a consensus is reached. Other programs must be considered, and final decisions reserved until all the evidence is in. Be sure the group understands this. On the other hand, make it clear that decisions you make will be managerial ones—priority, resources, and so on. The decisions of how to accomplish individual goals will still rest with the individual, to be made within the framework of the business or administrative decisions and established organization.

THE WORK PROGRAM MEETING

Set the Stage.   Before turning the meeting over to the individual responsible for the review of the specific work program, make it clear that you expect and need every participant's active help in presenting, verifying, and evaluating factually where things stand, how well they are going, the likelihood of success, and what might be done to improve it.

Appoint a Recorder.   Ask that one of the participants make notes of identified bottlenecks, needed information, unsolved problems, disagreements about the status of work items, and decisions on actions to be taken. It is often helpful to put these on a blackboard or large chart pad so that all may see what is being recorded as the meeting progresses. This simple device underlines these as group-identified problems and stimulates the volunteering of additional items or more exact modifications of ones already recorded.

Present the Big Picture.   Next, briefly describe the organization's overall plans as they relate to this particular work program, the market strategy insofar as it has been developed, and the current customer and competitive picture. Participants can then keep these data in mind to evaluate better the presentations and discussions.

Review the Program Status.   Then, hand the meeting over to the individual who organized the presentation. Make it clear that it is the person's responsibility to present, with the assistance of selected others, an objective picture of the work program. These presentations should try to clarify, to add information, to make estimates based on personal experiences, and basically to analyze all information with a view towards recommending what needs to be done for *this* program in the future.

Listen and Take Notes of Important Points and Encourage Participants to Do So as Well.   Even though a recorder has been appointed to take notes for later distribution, keep the work program cards you made up for your individual interviews in front of you, verifying what is already there, annotating as necessary, and adding new information and new items for investigation. The other meeting participants may also want to make notes. If the project is already programmed by PERT or some similar method, any new data which comes to light should be fed into the system.

Stimulate the Exchange of Information. This is your major function. Ask questions throughout the meeting which focus attention on what the program is designed to accomplish. For example:

- Will this feature really fill a customer or client need?
- How does this design or this piece of creative writing or this phase of the work program contribute to the specified goal?
- If you had only half as much money or twice as much money, what would you do differently?
- About how much will it cost us and will its effect on value to the customer or client make this expenditure desirable?

You can help participants make sounder estimates of completion dates by asking such questions as:

- What is the earliest date by which this can be finished and what (explicitly) would have to happen in order to meet it?
- What is the earliest date by which this can be finished and what (explicitly) would have to happen in order to meet it?
- What is the latest date by which this will be finished and what things (explicitly) would cause the presumed delays?

When events are named as advancing or hindering progress and are within the spheres of activity of other participants, verify with them the likelihood of their happening. Contribute any personal experiences you have had in similar situations which might provide useful data and encourage the other participants to do so also.

When dates or other factual information critical to the status of work or its prognosis are given, what person has *first-hand* knowledge of this? Has he or she, for example, seen the product component functioning in test? Has he or she personally verified that all major expense items were in the most recent report? Has consumer data been seen? The objective here is to be certain that critical work really stands as it is presented, and that assumptions are not being made on the basis of rumor or casual conversation. This is especially important when departments outside of your own are involved.

The tone of voice and expression you use in asking such questions can either stimulate or impair discussion. If you give the impression that you are "grilling" the employee and do not believe what he or she is telling you, ground will be lost and information curtailed. If you sense that the group is or might be unfavorable to your question, try putting a checklist of questions on the blackboard. They can serve as thought provokers for each participant to look at and answer as appropriate. If, in addition, you reward admissions of having made unwarranted assumptions or statements of unfavorable information with a warm: "Thank you for being so candid. It's important for us to know the bad as well as the good things," thoughtful, quiet-voiced probing will not affect the climate adversely. It may also help the climate, if you make it clear that *all* participants may, and in fact should, question each other. Because no one is able to see him- or herself and his or her work completely objectively, the questioning can help each put events into better perspective.

Naturally, on this point, your intention must show through. If it is your honest desire to pull together basic facts for the problem-solving attention of all the participants and you use the simple devices mentioned, you should not have too great a problem. However, if the group experienced censure from your predecessor, they may have built up a resistance to frank discussion of work problems. If, on the other hand, your real motive is to get facts so that you can "hang" one of the employees or pass the buck or berate the employee publicly, all the devices in the world are not likely to conceal this for very long.

Discuss the Likelihood of Success.   Once the prepared presentations have been made, an evaluative discussion is in order. You might open this by simply saying: "All of us have a stake in the success of this program. Would each of you give us your frank opinion on whether we are going to be able to realize our goals if we go along as we are at present? Take ten minutes and make a few notes on paper, and then let's hear from each of you."

Or, if you feel that individuals would be reluctant to speak frankly, you might divide them into two groups. Group I has the task of coming up with all the reasons why the overall goal will be met, with perhaps relatively simple or minor changes in plan or effort. Group II must come up with all the reasons why it will probably not be met unless certain important or major changes are made. Give the groups the opportunity to go off to other rooms to work, and plan to reconvene after an hour or so (the time will depend on the complexity of the program). After the initial round of presentations, time to prepare rebuttal may be in order.

Hopefully, from this kind of presentation-discussion there will be sufficient factual data available to identify key problems besetting major work programs and to permit weighing various important changes, alternate courses of future action, that might make the difference between success and failure. If the number of persons working on the program is large enough, a third group might even be formed with the task of doing this. In any event, certain things should certainly become clear—key problems and barriers to success; "unknowns," that is, technical, administrative, or other specialized information needed but not immediately available within the group; and critical factors, factors upon which success depends and which, therefore, should receive special attention. In addition, the advantages and disadvantages of alternate ways of proceeding should be apparent. Each of these areas needs follow-through.

Make Action Plans. Before closing the meeting, certain plans should be made quite specific. With respect to the "unknowns," you will want to ask various specialists to do a little analysis or investigative work or to consult with others who may have more directly applicable knowledge. This may also be true with respect to suggested ways of proceeding with work programs when a little more investigation is needed. Other unknowns may be associated with the performance or needs of your associates in other departments. These you may need to add to your personal work program for explorations.

In addition, make notes of critical items and "points of no return" in work projects. You will wish to explore these personally after the meeting. This may be a delicate matter. Presumably, an individual has the responsibility for certain work and has given you its status. If you tell that person you wish to verify its status, he or she may feel that you do not trust his or her report. Yet, if the item is truly a critical one, you cannot afford to take any risk with it. Telling the truth quite simply and involving the individual in the further effort is the best course of action in such a case.

As an example, when the group has finished its review, you might sit back and say something like this: "As I view this program, it appears that the functioning of component A and the availability of material B are the critical items for success at this stage. Do you agree?" (If the group does, then go on; if not, resolve the disagreement.) "Joe, in view of this I think you and I should make a personal on-site review of where A stands, and Jane and I of where B stands. If we find anything that either relieves the pressure that we feel about these items or increases our concern, we'll report back to all of you." Such a course of action seldom provokes antagonism.

Another action you need to take is to consult with your associates in other departments who are supplying your organization or who may be acting as your "customer," that is, waiting to receive information, materials, or products from you. You covered these things during the program review, but usually contacts between employees are with their counterparts in other organizations. You need to build strong relationships with your own counterparts and make sure that they agree with you on anticipated timing, priorities, funding, specifications, and all the rest.

Close the Meeting.   Finally, the participants need some signal as to whether to go forward full speed with the work program, to hold up effort at least temporarily, or whether to change course in some way proposed during this session. You should make this clear in your closing remarks. Also point out that until all programs have been reviewed, firm commitments cannot be made as final adjustments may be needed if there should be conflicts over needed resources.

Stress again the interest that you all share in the success of the program under discussion, your pleasure at the frankness of comments given, and the fullness of information, both favorable and unfavorable. Review the actions that you now must take and the decisions to be made in the light of the total work of the department, the available resources, and the business plans of the firm.

ADDITIONAL FACT-FINDING

Each of the work programs involving more than one professional should be reviewed in this way until you have a complete picture of all the work currently underway in your department.

Before reaching final decisions, at least one further discussion or review is needed. Looking over the agreements reached with your manager about what is expected of the organization and of you personally, are there any areas not covered in the current work of the department? More than this, is there other work which the organization might undertake which would be more important in the long run than some things now underway? Or, is there other work which if started now might place you in a significantly advantageous competitive position? Or, is there alternate work which might better serve clients or customers? A final meeting to discuss these points is desirable. Give participants adequate warning of the intent of the meeting and try together to arrive at a priority listing of all the desirable work projects. Try, too, to decide if the top items on this list should replace the lowest priority projects already underway. Would there be economic penalties for stopping some work and starting new work at this point? Would needed manpower, money, and physical resources be available? What other problems would such a shift create?

Having made this tentative new work priority listing, you are now armed with the information you need for decision-making. Your associates have done their job. Now it is your turn to make the contribution.

6

First Major Decisions— Work Programs and Resources

Managers often have the mistaken notion that having accepted a new position, their only responsibility is to dig in and perform. In fact, however, you owe your manager at least two important things at a very early date. The first is an accurate, verified report of exactly where current commitments stand and the likelihood of their being met on time and as specified. The second is a well-thought-out set of recommendations of what immediate, if any, and certainly longer-term changes in commitments, resources, organization, and staffing are required to permit the department to fulfill its assigned role with distinction.

Needless to say, these first recommendations will not be the last. Every manager's understanding of what the department is trying to do, could do, and what is limiting accomplishment, grows with time and changes as conditions change. It is especially important to recognize that you cannot make all of the required evaluations by yourself. While your personal inputs to these decisions may improve with time, you will always need information from professionals and from your manager and your associates, who have broader knowledge or different perspectives.

Neither can you expect all the inputs to come from employees, associates, and others. *You* must evolve a realistic but challenging picture of what the department's potential for contribution is. This is an important, demanding, creative effort on your part comparable in every respect with the technical inventions of the engineer or the creative analyses and behavioral predictions of the psychologist.

As preparation, your reviews with individual professionals have given you a good picture of where each one stands with respect to his or her assigned responsibilities and some feeling for his or her commitment to achieve them. Your work program reviews have given you an even better understanding of where major projects stand and what may be hampering their progress.

Your further careful, personal exploration of factors critical to the success of specific programs, of the contributions of other organizations to the department's work, and of the expectations and complaints of customers or clients have given you insights into the way the department looks to others. All these data permit you to make a sound evaluation of the current probability of success of each work program or project.

KEY DECISIONS

Basically, you have three decisions to make about the department:

1. Are you doing the "right" work supported by suitable physical resources?
2. Do you have a sound organization which facilitates work?
3. Are talented people in suitable jobs?

The decisions are, of course, interrelated so that while each may be made independently, each, in turn, needs to be adjusted based on the other two. Steps in making these decisions are outlined in Figure 6-1 on page 62 and discussed in this chapter.

THE DEPARTMENT'S FUNCTION

In tackling the decision about the right work, it is wise to go back to the function which the department is expected to fill in the organization. You discussed this point with your manager in one of your early meetings. Having looked in some detail at what is going on in the department, does your understanding remain the same, or do his or her thoughts and comments now seem to have a different meaning? Do you now envision a somewhat different role as sounder and having more potential? If either of the latter two situations applies, it would be a good idea to initiate brief discussion with your manager on the subject. This requires that you take your thoughts out of the vague, general stage, and write them down quite specifically. *Briefly* describe just how you now envision the department's function and what this would mean in terms of output produced. Better still, specify any alternate roles in the same way and use the comparison as a basis for reaching agreement.

WORK PRIORITIES

Based on the function you agree to achieve, the next step is to review the list of work programs underway in the department. With what you now know about their progress and specifications, do you agree with the originally assigned priorities? Add to this list any new work you and your associates feel is desirable to undertake soon. As previously mentioned, it may well be that some of these newer projects should displace some of the lower priority items already underway. Support the ranking by data on the estimated potential dollar market over a specified period of time (or if this is inapplicable in your situation, a clear statement of the added results to be achieved), the investment to date in dollars and in manpower, and the anticipated new investment.

The priority listing must be tentative at this point until you take the next step—a critical look at the likelihood of success and the conditions which must be provided to increase the chances of success. This involves the careful scrutiny of data collected about each project, preferably in order of importance to the business.

WHAT TO DO ABOUT EACH PROJECT

Each project needs to be considered thoughtfully in the light of five basic questions:

1. Will this project meet the business or organization target expected if it is completed, and will it be on time?
2. What actions must be taken to complete it in the way it should be done?
3. What is the cost of required actions in terms of manpower, money, physical resources? What is the effect on other work? On other departments which may need to contribute? Can these be sold?
4. Are the consequences of failure to accomplish this program such that the work should be continued? Or, is the likelihood of success so low or the cost of completion so high that these factors outweigh the advantages of continuing?
5. If a program or project should be dropped for any reason, what, if any, work should be substituted and at what cost? Can it be sold?

Let's give each of these questions closer scrutiny.

1. *Will this project meet the business or organization target expected if it is completed, and will it be on time?* Get out your work program cards and review your notes. The opinions and estimates of indi-

vidual workers are critical here. Are they unanimous, one way or the other, or is opinion divided? How surmountable do the obstacles ahead appear to be? Have you personally or has anyone in the organization faced similar obstacles before and managed to overcome them? If some of the outcome appears very worthwhile and possible but other parts do not, further market or client inputs may be in order. How much flexibility exists in the target? How satisfied would customers or clients be with a modification of the result? How critical is the timing? In the end, you will make a decision on this point, and it will almost certainly involve risk-taking. The pros will give you their best estimate of the chances of success. You need to decide if these are high enough, if the capabilities of the individuals who will do the work are strong enough, and if your managing skills are good enough to contribute to the result. If you decide affirmatively, you take the risk.

2. *What actions must be taken to complete the program in the way it is needed?* Presumably, this point was discussed at great length at both the individual and work program review meetings. Your own explorations after these meetings gave you additional information. Among the things to consider are:

- adding manpower
- changing the ratio of professional and nonprofessional talent assigned to the project
- appointing a program planner to lay out work efficiently and follow up on performance
- assigning specialized talent to critical areas
- establishing parallel programs for certain high-risk parts of the project
- making additional physical resources available
- changing the direction of the program
- structuring the organization to support the work more effectively
- employing consulting help
- subcontracting certain parts of the program
- establishing progress review procedures with appropriate senior specialists in attendance
- setting up "devil's advocate" teams to identify obstacles and bottlenecks before they are met
- taking more time to complete work

For safety's sake it is best to have in mind at least two ways of going forward, each improving the likelihood of success. Again on this point, you will want to involve key professionals in your choices.

3. *What is the cost of required actions in terms of manpower, money, physical resources? What is the effect on other projects? On other*

departments which may need to contribute? Can these be sold?
Obviously any decision on a course of future action should be
weighed in terms of its cost. And this added cost must be balanced
against the cost of delayed completion or failure to meet specifications fully. Possibilities for funding should be discussed with a suitable financial associate. Additional manpower needs will be discussed with the personnel organization. Effects on other work programs should be taken into account if it is necessary to shift manpower or financial support away from lower priority programs. Discussions with associates in other departments may be necessary or
helpful to determine their ability to change their contribution or
effort on your project in some way.

When the cost of needed actions has been estimated at least
roughly, the question of ability to sell upper levels of management
merits consideration. Usually the selling comes after you have
looked at all programs, all needed changes, all costs, and all alternatives so that you can present to your manager the total plan for the
next period of time. If a certain plan of action is unlikely to sell, an
alternate had better be found before going further.

4. *Are the consequences of failure to accomplish this program such
   that the work should be continued? Or is the likelihood of success so
   low or the cost of completion so high that these factors outweigh the
   advantages of continuing?* One possible course of action is certainly
   to stop work, particularly if the program or project faces large investments and the odds of success appear poor or the market doubt-
   ful. It is particularly important for an engineering manager to face
   this possibility squarely. Even the best technical people become so
   involved in a piece of work that they are unable to see the desirability of cutting it off at a certain point. As a result they may work
   on something long after it is reasonable to expect it to pay off. All
   managers, however, need to look realistically at what the penalty
   would be for stopping certain work totally and perhaps substituting
   something more promising in its place. It may well be that this
   penalty is lower than the cost of continuing.

5. *If a program or project should be dropped for any reason, what, if
   any, work should be substituted and at what cost? Can it be sold?*
   Since choosing a substitute for a dropped work program would be
   the first piece of work originating under your management, its
   choice has special importance to you. If the earlier listing of old and
   new work with priorities was made with care, what should be substituted may already be pretty clearly in mind, or at least the choice
   may be narrowed down to two or three promising alternative projects. You will want, however, to pay special attention to the following factors to be sure you are off to a good start with a good decision:

- its probable contribution to customer or client needs
- its interest to your associates in other departments
- the likelihood that its accomplishment would lead to new, promising areas of work
- its timing with respect to investment needs
- the competitive advantage that it would supply
- required special experience and talent in place or readily available
- strong commitment to its success among the professional staff

If this kind of decision is made, again you must consider how it can be sold to the manager to whom you report. And this "sale" may take just as careful planning to be successful as any piece of work you have ever done.

SUM UP THE DECISIONS

When each of the programs has been looked at against the five questions, and decisions have been made on whether to go forward and, if so, with what changes, then the program as a whole must be considered in the light of the department's capacity. Are the total manpower, money, facilities, and other needed resources available to do all the work? Or, must some of the lower priority items be dropped, delayed, or stretched out? Is there additional work which just must be done if the department's function is to be achieved, and, if so, are resources available to be applied to it, or must something else be dropped, delayed, or stretched out to accommodate it? Or are all programs of such importance that the problem is one of obtaining new resources to do the added work?

Competent financial and marketing specialists may be needed for advice on this point and for planning ways to obtain the required new resources. A small team of professionals may also need to be involved in defining the new program and blocking out its major outlines in enough detail to permit its description to those who must agree to its initiation.

MATCH RESOURCES WITH PRIORITIES

You will also want to take a last look at the way in which resources have been aligned with priorities in the new program. Sometimes resources are added to rescue a badly off-target program at a rate not merited by its importance to the overall business. It is helpful, therefore, to go back to the priority listing made earlier with its expected contribution and current and anticipated investment. For each program add specified time considerations, such as:

- approximate man-hours to be applied, both professional and supporting;
- rate of spending;

- quality of professional talent assigned; and
- priority given it for use of pooled talent or facilities.

Then make sure there is a reasonable relationship between expected contribution and total investment of resources.

FIGURE 6-1   Steps in Making Decisions About Work Program

---

1. Specify the department's function.

2. List current work programs in order of priority.

3. Evaluate the chances of success for each program and the actions needed to ensure success.

4. Substitute or add new programs as needed, with action plans to procure the required resources.

5. Compare the department's capacity with the total program.

6. Match resources with established priorities.

7. Make action plans for implementation.

DOES THE TOTAL PROGRAM MEET YOUR STANDARDS?

Finally, you will want to consider whether the total program adds up to your picture of the department's potential for contribution. Is the program bold enough to enhance the organization's plans? Will it provide the possibility of a striking competitive advantage? Will the work meet important needs? Assuming a highly competent group of professional workers, is the risk big enough to match this high level of competence?

PLANNING THE MEETING WITH YOUR MANAGER

When you have made your basic decisions and reached the point of recommendations, you need to prepare a clear, salesworthy presentation for your manager. It should certainly contain:

1. A comparison of your original agreement with him or her, together with your current recommendations
2. Your reasons for suggesting changes, if any

3. The specific changes proposed and what they mean in terms of the utilization and acquisition of resources
4. An evaluation of risks in and advantages of the new program as compared with the old
5. Burdens added to parts of the organization not under your control and the concurrence (or lack of it) of other managers who may be involved

INVOLVE KEY PROFESSIONALS

When you have put your materials together for such a presentation, you might consider a "dry run" with key employees. This practice has both advantages and disadvantages. Advantages are:

1. They are made a party to your decisions and become involved in their success.
2. What you as manager have been doing and thinking becomes visible to them.
3. They may well see points that you have overlooked, and make helpful suggestions.

Disadvantages are:

1. If changes proposed are important and involve obvious shifts in their responsibilities, they may be disturbed and the effect on work may be unfavorable.
2. One or more may disagree so strongly that they threaten to leave, and your own confidence may be undermined.
3. Word of what you are proposing may leak out before you have the agreement of your manager, and this may have a detrimental effect on work.
4. If you fail to sell your recommendations to your manager, your failure is exposed.

The advantages are so great in most cases that a few simple steps taken in advance to minimize the disadvantages are worthwhile. For example, it is desirable to hold a short private conversation outlining what his or her new responsibilities might be with anyone whose position has obviously been changed. Asking the assembled group to evolve a few simple precautions against the leakage of premature information may help prevent that occurrence. As for your own confidence, it is just as well to find out early where in your reasoning or arguments you are vulnerable than to discover it in a meeting with your manager or associates. And finally, it is helpful to warn your audience that the recommendations may not sell, and that if they do not you will tell them the reasons advanced for their nonacceptance or compromise so that all of you may learn from this experience.

MAKING YOUR RECOMMENDATIONS

Unless you are proposing only trivial changes, your meeting with your manager may take more than one session. Lay the groundwork for this in advance. Make sure that he or she understands the purpose of the meeting: tell your manager that you would like to bring him or her up to date, that you plan to review your conclusions about the work of the department, that some changes are involved, and that when these have been discussed, he or she might like to take some time to think over what you are suggesting and perhaps talk to some of your associates, even with an important customer in some cases, before final decisions are made.

At the meeting, present the facts as you have gathered them, showing charts and graphs and schedules as may be required to support your story. Whether it takes one meeting or two or more, whether you and your manager are able to make the decision alone or need the agreement of other involved department heads, whether he or she buys your suggestions wholly or in part or not at all, the objective will be accomplished when agreement is reached among all parties concerned. Your objective will be met when you have a "firm" list of work programs directed toward specific goals to be met by specific deadlines and there is clear understanding by all involved of where work now stands, what needs to be done according to what priority, and what resources are available with which to do it.

7

Organization and Staffing

When you and your manager have reached agreement on the key results expected of you, your first sensations are likely to be those of exhilaration and satisfaction. This is especially true if you have proposed major changes or have won additional resources. The second feeling is often one of urgency and occasionally panic. There is no question about it—your neck is out; your job is on the line.

On the way back to the office, inexperienced managers often begin to think about assigning certain work to certain individuals and making this or that change in organization structure. At the earliest possible moment, they call a meeting of individuals reporting to them, outline the work program agreed to, describe what the boss said, hand out the assignments, give a pep talk, and indicate "We're off and running." *This is just not good enough!*

Even though employees have contributed heavily to the plans, even though you explain very sensibly why certain recommendations were modified or not accepted, even though you hold forth at length on the importance of devoting full effort to accomplishing the new plans and discarding anything which does not contribute to them, *it is still not good enough.* The result, nine out of ten times, is almost certain to be the superimposing of the new work on the old, thus enlarging whatever problems and obstacles were present before. Instead of eliminating work now deemed nonessential, the pet projects of each person will somehow manage to be carried on, often to the detriment of more important work. The former duplications and gaps in work assignment will probably still exist. The barriers which prevented other departments from supplying information or materials or parts when needed will still be there.

When you, with the help of other professionals in your organization, made a detailed exploration of the status and probable outcome of your major work programs, you did so for a number of reasons. You needed, of course, to reach decisions about work based on sound information. You also needed to see how responsibilities and relationships could be clarified and how procedures and systems could be simplified. You needed to identify current and expected bottlenecks so that they could be eliminated wherever possible. Your full objective was to increase the possible contribution of the organization and enhance individual professional reputations while doing it. All these things demand as sound and systematic an approach to studying organization structure as you used in investigating and deciding about work programs.

THE ORGANIZING PROCESS

When managers decide to study their organizations, they frequently approach the matter like this: "Now let's see. Six people report to me. Five are pretty capable and the sixth is in the wrong job. She could, however, contribute quite valuably if she were doing 'this' kind of work. So I think I'll move her to 'this,' (still reporting to me, of course) and move Joe up to take over the vacant slot. Now, how can I divide up the work we need to do among these seven individuals?" This way of thinking can be disastrous over the years as more and more people are moved sideways because of nonperformance and take over pieces of work which they may be qualified to do and which may even be needed by the department.

The manager, however, finds himself with a larger and larger reporting group, giving him less time to devote to each person. Moreover, the added pieces of work frequently detract from the responsibilities of other parts of the organization, and more effort is required by all involved to mesh this work with related work. In addition, this kind of organization thinking tends to maintain old organization habits. How do you know you need even the *six* positions reporting to you? Maybe three or five would be more appropriate if you really looked at the work, its flow, and the decisions relating to it.

As a manager you owe employees the kind of clear, understandable organization which will leave them as free as possible to do needed professional work with a minimum of red tape.

A FEW BASIC PRINCIPLES

How to organize effectively has been the subject of considerable thought and experimentation.[1] The ability to organize is one of the basic skills every

---

[1]Suggested reading: Richard S. Hall, *Organizations: Structure & Process* (2d ed.; Englewood Cliffs, N.J.: Prentice-Hall, 1977); John M. Pfiffner and Frank P. Sherwood, *Administrative Organization* (Englewood Cliffs, N.J.: Prentice-Hall, 1960); H. Joseph Reitz, *Behavior in Organizations* (Homewood, Ill.: Richard D. Irwin, 1977); J. Clifton Williams, *Human Behavior in Organizations* (Cincinnati: South-Western, 1978).

manager should possess. While adequate coverage of the subject would be inappropriate here, the mention of a few basic principles would not be. These principles are listed in Figure 7-1.

FIGURE 7-1   A Few Ground Rules for Organizing

---

1. The work to be done should form the basis for organization structure.

2. Group work should share some important common factor.

3. Decision-making should be at the lowest organization level where full information is available.

4. Avoid over-organizing—set minimum structure.

Let Work Provide the Foundation for Overall Structure.   What the organization is striving to accomplish, what resources are available to accomplish it, and how much time is available in which to do it are the basic factors which determine how you should organize. You have already spent a great deal of thought on identifying the most suitable work programs, approaches to making them successful, and resources needed to accomplish them. Once you have factored in any modifications which have come out of the discussions with your manager, your understanding of the pieces of work which go into the total accomplishment should be reasonably complete.

Group Work Which Shares Something Important in Common.   Next, put together work which is basically similar. The most obvious similarity is *skill*. So, for example, in a hospital, nurses might be grouped under a director of nursing; in a bank, tellers under a supervisor; in an engineering organization, mechanical designers under a manager; in a laboratory, physical chemists under a senior physical chemist. But technical discipline is not the only basis for similarity. The *process* by which individuals go about doing their work may be an alternate. For example, in a technical organization, those who theoretically or experimentally investigate phenomena and produce data and the conditions under which the data will be accurate might be grouped in a Research Component. Those who take the data and use it to design new and improved products might be grouped in a Product Design Component.

The *customer* or client served forms a third alternate basis for grouping. In a personnel organization the recruiting, placement, and development of engineers and scientists might be separated from the same function for clerical and other office personnel and in turn from the same function performed for hourly employees. Or in an advertising agency, copywriters assigned to industrial accounts might be separated from those serving retail accounts and from those serving government installations.

Sometimes *geography* is the basic point of similarity which determines effective organization. Welfare workers might be grouped by area of the city to be served, a branch bank headed by its own manager established to serve a growing neighborhood, salesmen of all kinds assigned by geographic district.

Frequently, the most fundamental thing which work has in common is the ultimate *goal* or the result it is designed to achieve. If the work you manage has several important goals and will require a sufficiently large number of employees, you may wish to set up components by goals. These may be specific work projects or product lines to be developed, designed, and marketed.

For example, suppose one goal of a manager development organization in a major oil company is to establish an inventory of likely promotable managerial candidates for future openings. A project to do this might be established as a separate component within the Manager Development Organization. Or, suppose in a public agency a new method for handling unemployment insurance payments is to be installed. A separate organization component might well be established for this specific purpose.

The greatest use of the separate project or program concept has been in the defense business of the country. A major new aircraft is to be brought from pilot stage to full production. A manned space shot is planned to meet certain preestablished conditions by a certain date. Usually these major projects require optimum use of rare technical knowledge. As a result, a combination of components built around common skills is combined with a project structure. For example, the basic technological skills may be isolated functionally under functional managers. Each project may then be set up with a project or program manager reporting to the overall manager. Personnel in the project organization program the project, negotiate for the work required of each of the functional areas, expedite this work, provide the integrating or coordinating or systems thinking needed, keep track of progress, and so forth.

Push Decisions as Low in the Organization as There Is Adequate Information for Making Them. You want to do this in order to provide for the maximum professional growth of the individuals who report to you. You also want to do this to leave yourself as free as possible for the managing work which is your responsibility. To help yourself understand the effects of various forms of organization on decision making, pretend that the organization is functioning first on one basis, then on another. What decisions are likely to float up to you in each case? Suppose that you organize primarily around skills, for example, and the purpose of the organization is to design a new product. In all likelihood you will need to provide the systems thinking; that is, you will need to be sure that the electrical work and the mechanical work are meshed both in timing and in technical content.

Or, consider the program or project type of organization. It delegates the total responsibility for a specific result. It thus permits clearer delegation and pushes much of the decision making down a level in the organization. While it is preferred for this reason, it has the disadvantage of sometimes putting a variety of skills, technologies, and talents together. This implies ready availability of these talents matured to the point where the individuals are not dependent on the guidance and direction of a more senior technical individual in their own field. It is unlikely that the person responsible for a complex program or project will be current in all the skills needed in the program. This form of organization has an additional disadvantage because some reorganization is probably necessary after having attained the goal for which the project was formed.

Avoid Over-Organization. If you have done a good job analyzing needed work and the timetable for it and have reached some agreement with your manager on resources, you have at least a reasonable idea of the numbers and kinds of employees it will take to get the job done. Keep this in mind, and remember that most students of organization agree that a manager who devotes full time to managing is able to handle from five to twenty people, depending on the similarity and complexity of the work. But keep organization to a minimum. Every additional component and every "layer" of organization add to the difficulty of communication, increase the need for working time devoted to coordination, relationships, and information exchange, and add to the likelihood of a "not-invented-here" attitude if work moves from one component to another in the course of getting it done. All these things slow down accomplishment, add to cost, and make partnership relationships less likely. Since the purpose of organization is to establish an easy flow of work and facilitate its successful accomplishment, keep formal structure at a minimum.

POSITION DESIGN

Having made some decisions about the basic overall structure, you are ready to begin designing individual positions. Here again managers frequently do a rather hasty, sketchy job, preferring to let the incumbent work out "the details." It is true that professionals and other employees often contribute a great deal to the description of their own positions. The manager, however, can help himself significantly if he will incorporate a few fundamental concepts into each position. Use Figure 7-2 as a checklist.

Build "Whole" or "Complete" Positions. Write the position in terms of the sustained results expected. Where you can reasonably do so, give the incumbent all the decisions connected with achieving these results. Avoid like

FIGURE 7-2   Practical Suggestions for Position Design

1. Build "whole" or "complete" positions.
2. Build positions around long-term missions.
3. Design positions of equal complexity at the same reporting level.
4. Divide critical results among several positions.
5. Separate long-range from short-range work.

the plague your taking the complex, demanding part of the job and delegating the leg work and routine decisions. For example, if you are a market research manager, you might build a position reporting to you—"consumer research analyst." Give that person the survey method and content, the actual survey decisions and survey administration, and, finally, the analysis of data and recommendations based on it. This is, then, a solid piece of work, demanding professional skill and giving the incumbent an opportunity to influence the future course of the business. You may reserve the basic decisions for yourself—who will be surveyed, on what issues, and when—and delegate the preparation of survey questions, mailing surveys, and compilation of data. If you then take over again to make recommendations, you have a helper, not a professional partner. Most of the interest, growth possibility, and, hence, motivational impact has been designed out of the job.

Build Positions Around Long-Term Missions.   Occasionally, a situation so desperately needs saving that quite specific short-term jobs are set up. It is clear that once the immediate problems are solved a more stable organizational arrangement will be needed. Except in such emergencies, it is wise to build positions which allow for change and flexibility. The work in house today is not necessarily tomorrow's work. But relationships between people, particularly working relationships based on considerable give and take, are a long time building. To be effective, organization structure needs to be in place for a fairly long period of time. Employees are used to responsibilities being in a certain place; they know just whom to call when information is needed; they follow routines and procedures from habit. All these things require positions which are stated in terms of *general* results. The specifics can be taken care of at any point in time by the plans towards which employees are working.

Deliberately Design Positions Which Are Equally Complex.   This is a practical rather than a philosophical matter. When you fill these positions, you will want individuals of about the same capability so that you can work with them in about the same fashion and so that salaries will be roughly equal.

Occasionally a manager, considering this to be a relatively minor matter, establishes positions of quite different strength. As he holds group meetings, he finds it difficult to set levels of expectations for them as a group. The less experienced or less qualified people are sometimes unable to deal with the others as equals, to make the demands on them that their positions require. It *can* work, but it takes more of a manager's time and attention. Frequently is is an administrative position which is lower rated than the others. This is particularly disastrous since in most cases the normal give-and-take which is so important between functional work and administrative work is missing, and the administrative work of a component degenerates into a paper-shuffling job.

Divide Critical Results Among Several Positions. While presumably all work is essential, some is usually more urgent than others. Perhaps some results are needed sooner, perhaps certain projects are in serious trouble and need to be saved, perhaps the potential payoff in some is greater than others, and so on. It is simply good judgment to be sure that all critical programs do not end up as the responsibility of a single individual. It is wise to spread these heavier burdens among several people, even if it is at the expense of a more logically structured organization.

Separate Long-Range from Short-Range Work. If one kind of work is thoughtful, reflective, studious, creative work with payoff some time in the future, it is usually wise to separate it from the rush of day-to-day service work or from a project which is already late and involves a schedule designed to make up time, or from work which is of a busy short-cycle nature. Almost inevitably, if one person is doing *both* kinds of work, it is the busy work which is done and the longer-range work which is sacrificed. So if both kinds of work are essential, try to design them into different positions. If it is impossible to do this, you will need to work out a measuring system which reflects performance in both kinds of work and assigns the proper priority to each.

Finally, before you can be satisfied that you have an effective organization structure, you need to check two points: the delegation of work and the relationships between positions.

IS ALL THE WORK DELEGATED?

Go back over the commitments you have made to your manager and review the work it takes to meet them. Have you delegated all the functional work, leaving only the managerial part of the job for yourself? Are as many as possible of the decisions affecting that work incorporated in the positions reporting to you? Have you eliminated *yourself* as the bottleneck for work, yet made clear the few points on which your people need your approval?

RELATIONSHIPS BETWEEN POSITIONS

Finally, you need to analyze the relationships existing between the positions reporting to you and between any of these positions and other inside or outside departments. Are these realistic, and do they form some sort of reasonable pattern? Or, are several different positions faced with conflicting contact with other departments? Is work being transferred from one component to another likely to face "not-invented-here" problems and confused accountability for results? Correct these situations, if you can, by centralizing some contacts or restructuring some positions. If all cannot be eliminated, you can still make the organization function if you anticipate problems and deliberately employ devices to help minimize them.

For example, if conflicting requests will be made of other departments, you can establish the priority on which such requests are to be handled and how this priority will be reviewed and updated from time to time. If a "not-invented-here" attitude is likely to be present when responsibility for a piece of work moves from one component to another, you can reach an understanding in advance that some or all individuals working on that project will move either permanently or temporarily when the work moves. Or, the group which will take over the work can begin to assign manpower to the project a little ahead of the scheduled moving date to provide for a smooth transition. But these *are* devices, and they do cost something in time, talent, or feelings of responsibility. The objective, therefore, is to make each position as independent of other parts of the organization as is consistent with the economic attainment of results.

SYSTEMS AND PROCEDURES

The flow of work within and between organization components should be as easy and natural as is consistent with the results you are trying to achieve. It may be, however, that if the organization is large, certain formal procedures may be laid out and certain paper-work systems prescribed. The objective of such systems should be to facilitate work, to permit more efficient transmission of information to all who need it. While it is far too elaborate a subject for discussion here, you should concern yourself with three things: (1) that whatever systems and procedures are devised and implemented, they *reinforce* in a positive way the working relationships which you wish to have among positions and organization components, (2) that they are in agreement with whatever related policies and procedures exist in the overall organization and, finally, (3) that they are not overdone. The more natural and informal procedures are, the more likely they are to be observed and to facilitate work. Over-procedurizing and over-systematizing can be stifling to creative effort and can cost more in time and effort than they buy in economic results.

In working out your organization structure, you should go no further than structuring the positions reporting to you and at most sketching out key work below that level. When the incumbents are chosen, they will wish to devise whatever structure seems warranted below them, and you will want them to do this so that there is a match with their personal managing style. The list of responsibilities and relationships of each position provides the context for individual job descriptions which will, in turn, serve as springboards for planning and evaluating work. It forms the basis for negotiating partnership agreements with those who will undertake the assignments.

STAFFING

You are now ready to undertake critical staffing decisions. It is too easy to slot those who have been reporting to you in the new positions you have designed. Take a few rather simple precautions to prevent this sort of automatic thinking.

First of all, pretend that you own the firm and have decided to add partners to expand the potential of the organization. This state of mind should help you think rather critically about the capabilities you want to add and the kinds of individuals for whose work you are willing to assume liability. Remember that in a true partnership arrangement you share the profit or credit for the results of *all* contributions, but you also individually assume liability for organization failure. This state of affairs probably does not factually hold true for the institution in which you will all be, after all, employees. But the concept is a good one to help yourself make sound staffing decisions.

Next, take a critical, third-party look at yourself. Considering the business you are in and the direction in which you would like it to go, what basic talents would you like to add to the organization? There may be some that you do not possess at all, or possess in only a minor way, or they may be contacts or knowledge of certain processes or of other business or functions which would be highly desirable to have in house for improving short- or long-range results. Make a list of these.

Next, take the list of results, responsibilities, and needed relationships that you established for each position reporting to you. Think of all the individuals you know who have already demonstrated abilities to get these results or carry out these responsibilities or who seem to possess the potential to do so. If any one of them possesses one or more of the additional

talents you listed earlier, enter these after his or her name. Now, ask yourself this question about each person listed: Has he or she so completely
demonstrated his ability to do this work that there would be little or no
challenge or personal growth in the position? If the answer to this is an
affirmative one, and there is no special reason why these individuals might
find the work rewarding, cross out their names unless, of course, they are
already in this position reporting to you. If the latter is true, you have an
additional problem for later resolution—how to help them to more developmental positions.

Finally, take the names remaining for each position and put them in rank
order of their qualifications, with the leading candidate at the top. Is there a
good candidate for each position? Or do you need recruiting help from the
personnel department? Is your manager in a position to suggest candidates?
On the whole, how many of the skills and talents you would like to add to the
department are represented? Do you need to augment your candidate lists
to include more of them? How many of the candidates are within the department so that, while there may be delicate negotiations ahead, at least a
search is unnecessary? In how many cases does the candidate possess strong
qualifications for most requirements of the position, but some deficiencies
which are not likely to be overcome readily as far as other responsibilities are
concerned? In such cases, you may want to redesign some positions to take
this fact into account, making at least a mental note to reshape the position
should another person fill the job or the inadequacy be overcome with
experience.

"UN-STAFFING"

Now, let's look at the reverse side of the coin. Almost inevitably, one or
two individuals who have been in positions reporting to you will just not fit
the newly structured positions. These situations must be faced realistically.
Do they fit into lower-level jobs in the organization; that is, are their talents
still needed at the old reporting level? Or are they no longer needed? If the
latter is the case, what are the obligations of the organization because of
former contributions, long service, and so on? Has their work been marginal? Or have they been excellent performers, simply "reorganized out of a
job?" Are their skills and knowledge current and applicable to other parts of
the firm or agency, or have they allowed their information to fall behind the
times and their skills to become obsolete? Try to reach at least tentative
decisions about the kind of work each person is best capable of doing and
what, if any, action you must take to place that individual either inside or
outside the organization. Log all such situations for special planning, perhaps
with the help of personnel specialists.

DOES YOUR MANAGER AGREE?

Armed with basic recommendations concerning the organization structure, your proposed staffing plan, and arrangements for placing individuals whose work is no longer required, discuss your thoughts with your manager.

You will also want to take with you a rough timetable for implementing your proposals and any data on cost changes resulting from organization changes. Have you added positions that will make payroll costs higher? Will there be costs involved in placing surplus personnel, or have you strengthened positions so that they are worth a higher salary level? Have you effected savings by eliminating unnecessary work, parallel programs, and duplication? Are any additional costs warranted by increased efficiency and improved results?

Be prepared to substantiate your choices on staff selections with documented information regarding past and current performance. In cases of displacement, also be prepared to document both your decision and your tentative plans for handling the situation.

THINK AND MOVE QUICKLY

One note of caution: writing out in some detail just how to go about devising a suitable organization structure and manning it makes the process seem long and involved. It is. A manager faced with running a business or obtaining needed results (even when no profit is involved) cannot afford to let a long period of time elapse between his investigation of work status, his decision making about needed changes, and his implementation of them. Once the cycle has been initiated, the steps must move along very quickly so that final decisions are in place and the department functioning smoothly again within a very short time. The amount of time depends on the size of the group but even in very large departments four to six weeks is enough. A longer period devoted to what should be done, unless it applies only to establishing new work and is not likely to affect existing programs and people, will lower output and increase the concern of individuals for their own positions beyond the point where it is wise or thoughtful to do so. This period of getting organized, then, is one of concentrated effort for a manager, and both the quality *and* the timing of his decisions count.

Once your manager has agreed to your recommendations or you have modified your recommendations to the point where you have agreed, you are ready to implement your decisions.

8

Organization Changeover

When deciding what to do about work, organization, and resources, your emphasis was necessarily on determining the course of action most likely to succeed. You were concerned, in effect, with the correctness of your judgments.

ACCEPTANCE NEEDED

Now as you reach the implementation phase, the problem facing you has a new dimension. Your decisions must be *acceptable* to those who will, after all, be carrying them out.

Undoubtedly, each member of the organization has some vested interest in the work as it *has been* undertaken, the way it *was* organized, the responsibilities as they *were* assigned, and the resources as they *were* allocated. And so, regardless of the rightness or merits of your decisions, each person will weigh them differently. And if an individual feels, whether it is actually true or not, that he or she has lost something by the proposed change, you are not likely to obtain a whole-heartedly cooperative response.

Hopefully, the individual and group meetings in which you earlier involved key individuals to help study current and prospective work programs will have somewhat conditioned those who participated. But it would be ridiculous to make the assumption that all are "with you" on the changes you have in mind. In fact, the safest assumption you can make is that there will be resistance, and that the resistance may come from unexpected individuals over unexpected issues.

CRITICAL FACTORS IN REORGANIZING

So, starting from that assumption and recognizing also that you want to move in the direction of a true partnership with professional employees, implementation should be well thought through and planned with their understanding and acceptance as an important goal. There are a number of points to consider—speed, timing, the early involvement of key individuals, continuing communication both in person and in writing, and the control of work during the changeover.

Speed.   Anyone who has been through a reorganization knows that as soon as one person is aware of a coming change, information leaks and rumors fly. Small buzz sessions occur. Productivity drops. So speed is essential from the first move to the last. Once the machinery has been set in motion, each step should be taken according to a well-planned but nonetheless rapid timetable.

Timing.   There is no good time for an organization change. It always seems to affect someone or some work at precisely the wrong moment, so it is quite useless to wait for a "right" moment. If you are within days of completing an important piece of work, however, it is probably desirable to finish it before undertaking major change, even though you feel that particular piece of work will not be affected at all. Organization change is upsetting. It is like a virus; its first effect on just about everyone is adverse.

Involvement.   You will want to make it clear that many of your decisions stem from information supplied by the pros in the organization. In this sense they are already involved in the change. But you will also want to give each key person something active to do to help effect the change—some detailed planning, some materials to prepare, some piece of work needing special attention. Not only do you need this contribution, but it will help the employee to overcome whatever resistance to change that he or she feels.

More than this, you will want to clarify quickly the role each key individual will play in the new organization. Professionals, particularly able ones, have a way of becoming restless and seeking other employment whenever they feel left out or uncertain for even a short while.

Communication.   As soon as individuals affected by a change know about it and agree to it, put that part of the new structure in writing for all employees. Elaborate in some detail on its functions, the reasons for any change, and the disposition of work displaced or to be phased out.

This will need to be supplemented by group meetings where you can explain more fully and personally why you are doing what you are doing and your hopes and plans for the new arrangement. These meetings will also give you the opportunity to answer the many questions employees may have. By all means, invite those who helped study the situation and made recommendations to take part in the presentation, to answer questions on which they are the experts, and to provide information in specialized areas.

Control of Work During Changeover.   This can be critical. While admitting that there will be some productivity loss, as a new manager you want to avoid having the organization change mean a major set-back for the work for which you are responsible. During this period it is well worth while to list any major milestones scheduled for completion during, say, the next two months and negotiate these accomplishments. This may mean an interim appointment or two. Reviewing the status of each of these projects weekly pays off, even though organizationally you may be reaching below the usual reporting level and extending your work day.

Now let's go step by step through an organization change, assuming it to be a major one so that maximum problems are confronted and, hopefully, solved. Obviously there is no one good way to make an effective changeover, but the suggestions which follow should help you overcome the more formidable hazards.

ESTABLISH A PERSONNEL PLANNER

Organization change triggers anxieties and concerns even among the most competent and most needed professional contributors. It is, therefore, a wise first move to establish a "personnel center" during the changeover. If you have someone in the department who normally serves this function satisfactorily, he or she is probably your choice. If not, perhaps the firm's personnel organization is able to lend you a capable individual. Another possibility is to select someone who seems to have management potential and ask that individual to undertake this work as a development assignment. Specifically include among his or her duties:

- ◆ publishing current organization charts as soon as major segments become firm;
- ◆ maintaining control lists of department employees so that at any given time exactly who has and has not been placed is known;
- ◆ working with displaced employees to develop plans for helping them to find new assignments;
- ◆ working with managers and bringing to their attention available employees who might fill open positions; and
- ◆ giving special attention to unusual personnel situations.

For example, he or she may need to devise positions for employees to whom the organization has special obligations because of long service and past

He or She Has Been Reorganized Out of a Job. Perhaps an employee has been successful in getting needed results in the past, but his or her particular qualifications no longer are required, or fit one of the new jobs you have designed. In telling the individual this, you need to point out with great care just where you believe his or her strengths lie and the kinds of positions which probably require the worker's special capacities. It is essential here that you do not delude yourself or the other person. There have been so many instances in which non-performers have been designated as "organized out of a job" that both employee and manager have learned to suspect this situation.

Regardless of which of the three reasons applies, the critical steps to be taken are:

1. Acquaint the employee with the situation.
2. Review the employee's assets—the strengths on which he or she can build in a new job.
3. Describe the kinds of positions requiring their talents.
4. Work with the employee to develop sound plans for relocation either within or outside the firm or agency.

The last is by far the most important. Turn the person's attention from the past toward the future and show him or her by your helpful suggestions and actions just what support can be expected. Let him or her know that you will help make contacts and time available, enlist the help of the personnel planner and local consulting firms, and so on. Make clear exactly how much time the individual has to find a new position and what work you expect him or her to accomplish during this terminating period.

EARLY COMMUNICATION

As soon as all of the positions have been filled and individuals who have been displaced are either reassigned or working on relocation, all personnel in the department need to be acquainted with the new structure and basic work program decisions. You will want to make this a face-to-face communication so that you can explain the reasons for your decisions and answer questions. A meeting of *all* personnel is desirable; but if the group would be too large, at least all professional employees should be included.

This meeting is a unique opportunity to develop awareness of and loyalty to objectives of the firm and the way in which the department contributes to these. From this focus, then, the organization structure that you believe is required to help meet your share of requirements should be displayed in its broad outline, along with the names of individuals who will lead major segments. An appropriate word or two is in order about those who have been displaced. To ignore this point or to be vague about it only starts rumors and speculation which can be much more uncomfortable for the individuals involved than stating facts objectively. Since some of those present may also see that their jobs are affected, it is a good idea to present the plan for completing the changeover together with a rough timetable for doing it. It is also well to introduce the personnel planner and describe his or her function so that all are aware that this resource is available to them.

Open the meeting to questions and be quite candid in your replies. If most of the individuals present are engineers or scientists, they will not be satisfied with generalities for answers; they will want to know the data and assumptions on which you based your conclusions. Since this is one way of involving them in the objectives of the department, do not be dismayed by argument or disagreement. Your earlier program meetings should have brought out most of these, so you can be well prepared to describe the thought processes by which you reached certain conclusions. Or, if little information was available, and you made a choice pretty much on the basis of an educated guess, say so.

Finally, distribute the basic organization structure and names of key individuals to all present, with enough copies for distribution to any who may not have been able to attend. Put more than titles on this sheet: list the basic results expected of each key job. This will clarify the intent of the position.

REPEAT AT LOWER LEVELS

The process you went through of identifying key results, designing positions, listing qualified candidates in order of qualifications, negotiating to fill positions, and communicating fully should now be repeated by the individuals reporting to you, providing the department is large enough to require an additional level of supervision.

There is one major difference. You cannot outline the process, ask them to do it, and then sit back and watch. As manager, you have a teaching role which requires that you be sure they have the necessary knowledge and skill to carry out these processes. So review, either individually or in a group, the steps they should take. Hold discussions on how to take these steps skillfully (advance planning, cautions, practice, and so on). Moreover, at each point in the process, some reinforcement discussion is desirable. This period will be busy and full of the exchange of ideas about organization, job design, selection, displacement counseling, and so forth. The personnel planner will also be of invaluable assistance teaching or counseling managers as well as doing the planning, record keeping, and control activities.

As each major segment of the department is organized and manned, visit the group, meet as many as possible, and reiterate the goals of the department and their expected contribution to them. You will especially want to make yourself available on an individual and personal basis to anyone displaced or concerned by the course of events.

When the full organization is manned and in place, you may wish to meet again with all personnel of the department or at least with professional employees to focus attention on the relationships existing between segments of the organization. Invite comment and discussion, and urge anyone who discovers a problem resulting from the flow of work between sections to bring it immediately to the attention of appropriate managers so that it can be tackled and resolved as soon as possible.

"Final" organization charts should be distributed as soon as possible so that all see where responsibilities lie and are able to do their jobs with a minimum of confusion.

TIME SPAN

Individual decisions can take a long time. As you talk to each preferred candidate about the work that you would like him or her to do, each will probably want a little time to think it over. If all the actions discussed are taken in series, the time taken to man the organization and make its final structure and relationships known is likely to be much too long. Reorganization steps must be taken in parallel. A guideline about time may be helpful. In a small organization of approximately twenty professionals, a manager should be able to implement his or her organizational plans *and* be functioning on the new basis in about a week. In an organization with 300 professionals, four weeks might be necessary. But if the *planning* is done well and the action begun *only* when needed steps have been identified and prepared for, changeover time can be contracted, confusion minimized, and employee rumors and anxiety greatly reduced. So the important thing is to take the proper time to do sound planning and then carry out the implementation with dispatch.

YOUR PERSONAL ATTITUDE

Managers have a tendency to think that a new organization will solve all problems. Since it does nothing of the sort and is merely a facilitating device, your attitude through all this should be a questioning, exploring one. It is, perhaps, your first real product since taking on this managerial responsibility, and you need to watch it functioning to discover where theory and practice do not agree. Encourage professionals to bring any failures to your attention quickly. Make it clear that you expect some failures and that you are prepared to make adjustments when they occur. But you cannot do this task by yourself. You need the inputs of users—employees—to find the points for needed improvement.

Hold a frank discussion on the point that *any* organization can probably be made to work but that is not your goal. If the organization is not making it easier to get work done, if it is in fact requiring extra effort to make it function, you want to know this so that adjustments can be made quickly. Of course, change and newness always place additional demands for a short time, but if after a reasonable period this factor has not disappeared, corrective steps are necessary.

ORGANIZATION REVIEW

Even if your attitude is properly questioning and your discussion expresses your desire to find organization bottlenecks quickly, employees may fail to bring problem areas to your attention. It is a good idea to devote at least one staff meeting specifically to this subject. You are more likely to get useful information if you provide a little structure in advance. Figure 8-1 is one checklist you might suggest that the professionals use to identify organization deficiencies and bring them to your attention.

FIGURE 8-1   Checklist for Organization Review

If your replies to these questions indicate that any of the areas need action by someone other than yourself, asterisk the questions for group discussion.

1. Inside your own organization, have you uncovered:
   a. Unassigned areas of responsibility?
   b. Inadvertent overlapping of responsibility?
   c. Procedural difficulties between jobs?
   d. Fuzzy accountabilities?
   e. Fuzzy interfaces?

2. With respect to your *personal* contacts with other organizations, have you uncovered:
   a. Unassigned areas of responsibility?
   b. Inadvertent overlapping of responsibility?
   c. Procedural difficulties between jobs?
   d. Fuzzy accountabilities?
   e. Fuzzy interfaces?

3. With respect to contacts of employees with employees of other organizations, have you uncovered:
   a. Unassigned areas of responsibility?
   b. Inadvertent overlapping of responsibility?
   c. Procedural difficulties between jobs?
   d. Fuzzy accountabilities?
   e. Fuzzy interfaces.

4. With respect to your reporting relationship:
   a. Is the relationship between your work (or the work of the component which you manage) and overall organization goals clear?
   b. If you meet all of the results planned, will your full needed contribution to the overall organization be met economically?
   c. Are any of your responsibilities fuzzy?
   d. If your manager carries out the planned work, will you receive the full contribution needed from him or her?
   e. Is the information channel from and to higher organization levels adequate?

Your method of handling this review will be an important contribution to the development of those who participate. You should, therefore, work to get the problems out on the table with constructive suggestions for resolving them. When only two individuals are involved and policy is not affected, leave the resolution in the hands of the two parties. Most important of all, where decisions are needed from you, provide them, making clear the basis on which they are made and hearing whatever contrary arguments or protests there may be before finalizing them. The organization review is especially helpful now. It may also provide an insurance policy against deteriorating conditions later on. As such, it is a useful tool in your managing repertory.

9

The Groundwork
for Motivation

Your work programs are clearly defined. You are aware of their status and the difficulties anticipated in completing them successfully. You know most of the specialists in the organization and where their strengths lie. You have streamlined and simplified organization structure and have put qualified people in key positions. You have taken these decisions and actions, moreover, on the basis of factual analyses and thoughtful planning to which many capable individuals have contributed. Your manager and your associates are fully acquainted with what you have done and why, and you have their agreement on matters in which you are jointly involved. Any sense of strangeness in your managerial role should have passed. You should feel very much on top of your work.

BROADEN TRADITIONAL
JOB DESCRIPTION CONTENT

Your next step is to clarify even further the contribution of each employee who reports to you. The basic responsibilities of each position are already clear from the organization chart, but they need more detailed individualized translation to include the following elements:

1. The mission or purpose of the employee's job in broad terms
2. A list of specific responsibilities
3. Reservations of authority (such as committing the organization's funds or completing contractual arrangements with outside organizations)

4. A description of working relationships with other positions
5. Measures or standards for the work

So far these are traditional subjects for job description. To emphasize the desired partnership relationship among professionals, add the following:

6. The assets which the individual brings to the job, such as the body of knowledge and skill which is his or her functional specialty and with which he or she is expected to keep current, any useful contacts the employee brings to the organization and is expected to maintain and develop, and any specialized experience he or she has to offer and is expected to capitalize on. These represent the individual's personal investment in the organization.
7. The salary range of the position (and any other monetary features such as incentives or bonus) and the way in which both individual and organization accomplishment will be judged in determining them.
8. A statement of personal liability in the event of individual or organization failure, including the effect on salary, employment, and the probable future allocation of human and physical resources.

As the manager, your job description includes all of the same categories. It should state clearly the nature of your expected contribution to organization results—the information system you will put in place, evaluative and corrective actions to ensure an organization structure which continues to facilitate work, the method for filling open positions, the basis for allocating resources and awarding compensation increases, the planning and follow-up systems to ensure progress, and similar managing functions. It should make clear how your work will be measured and rewarded or affected by failure.

ENCOURAGE
CROSS-EXAMINATION OF JOBS

To reinforce the partnership concept, after all the descriptions have been prepared, exchange them with each other for the serious purpose of making each fully aware of the personal investments and expected contributions of his associates within the framework of common goals. This, of necessity, means spelling out any limitations placed on an individual by virtue of his or her association with others in a common venture. It also implies thoughtful evaluation by the individual of the general nature of the support which will be received from associates to be certain that he or she is able to carry out his or her share of the responsibility effectively.

Job descriptions should not require constant rewriting to reflect current conditions. In most cases, they should last for the life of the organization. They must, therefore, be somewhat general and serve primarily as the basis for agreement on each individual's role in meeting common goals.

SUPPLEMENT JOB DESCRIPTIONS WITH WORK PLANS

Though the individual work plans of each professional are based on job descriptions, they reflect current needs much more accurately. These should be far less formal, much more specific, and probably more subject to change. A good starting point for getting individual plans in place is a review with those who report to you. Go over the comments, suggestions, and objections which may have arisen in discussion with your manager and your associates when you were trying to sell your basic work program and organization structure. Supplement this with a written statement of the department's commitments, major milestones, and critical assumptions on which plans are based. With this information in hand, each person should put into writing the specifics of what his or her job will contribute to overall results, the timetable for doing it, and the specific resources he needs. It is a good idea to suggest that each assume the burden of checking with associates on inputs to and outputs for his work so that at least preliminary resolutions of scheduling problems will have taken place before you begin individual negotiation.

OBJECTIVES OF INDIVIDUAL NEGOTIATION

For the first round of discussions, set up *individual* meetings to reach agreement on work plans. Keep at least these objectives in mind:

1. To make certain that the planned contribution of each person meets organization needs and fulfills the mission of the position held
2. That the emphasis on different parts of the work is correct and that important day-to-day activities are neither ignored for more glamorous projects nor usurp the effort which should be devoted to longer-range matters
3. That the timing is sound, considering both overall aims and related work in other parts of the organization
4. That, as outlined, there are reasonable odds for successful accomplishment

5. That the plans contain one work improvement goal which will benefit the organization
6. That plans include work which challenges the full use of the talents of the employee involved
7. That the plans reflect an opportunity for the individual to grow—to develop his or her talents
8. That the individual who will carry out (or manage) the proposed work is thoroughly committed to its accomplishment

KEEP THE EMPLOYEE "IN CHARGE"

How do you do all of these things without giving the impression of being over-critical, over-detailed, over-involved in the work of a professional who is thoroughly qualified to do a job?

Have the Employee Present His or Her Plans to You. Make this a developmental occasion for the person. You made intensive preparations for meeting with your manager to "sell" your work plans and organization structure. Let the employee have a similar experience. Presenting and defending plans, proposing and considering alternatives in public situations are things almost every professional needs to do well. It is worth focusing a little attention on this important skill. So, watch the employee carefully. Make rough notes of any important observations. Is this an area of strength, or can this ability be improved upon?

Ask for His or Her Appraisal of the Plan. Ask for an overall evaluation of the adequacy of the plan. Ask where the greatest and least risks lie and what the alternatives are in the areas of greater risk. Ask where the schedule is tightest and what will happen if it slips. Test the resources that he or she requests by finding out what more the employee could do with more manpower or money or space—and what would be dropped or delayed otherwise.

Ask How He or She Plans to Evaluate Progress. Does the employee have a set of measures or standards for checking the accomplishment of day-to-day work and a system for collecting information on these points which will let him or her know that they are being done and how well they are being done? Are the worker's major projects programmed for a series of steps with due dates so that at key points along the way, there are clear indicators of how well the work is going and whether the end date is likely to be met?

PLAN FOR EMPLOYEE GROWTH

From the professional's description of his or her plans, his or her appraisal of the risks involved, and his or her method of evaluating progress, you should be able to meet your first five objectives. Meeting the next two related to employee talent and development requires more ingenuity and some preparation homework. Before the meeting, refresh your memory on the individual's performance strengths, the areas of heaviest past experience. Presumably in selecting the individual for this job you had two things in mind—a match between his or her talents and the requirements of the position, and growth opportunity for the worker.

As you listen to the person describe how he or she plans to reach desired goals does he or she appear to choose methods or routes which utilize personal strengths? Or, are there talents which you feel the worker possesses which are not being challenged? For example, will the individual make contacts personally if this is an area of strength? If not, does he or she plan to draw on the help of someone else who *is* strong, perhaps accompanying another to observe how a situation is handled?

When you have completed your discussion as far as possible by yourselves, discuss how you will work together from this point forward. Again, if you have planned this conversation, you may be able to make suggestions which will increase the probability of the employee's growth. For example, in the past he might have shown signs of being a "loner"—very capable, very dedicated, but somewhat unwilling to draw on others' talents or to let others know where personal work stands even when it affects them. In this case, you might suggest that from now on progress reviews against plans will be held on a group basis so that all involved can learn first-hand what obstacles and problems there may be in the organization. Or, if the employee has a history of doing excellent work on time, but overrunning budgets, you might ask him or her to devise some special cost controls and keep you apprised on a weekly or biweekly basis of financial status. The point is that you are in an excellent position to create much of the climate in which the employee will work and by so doing stimulate his or her development along lines which appear desirable for both of you.

In addition, with respect to the development aspect of the worker's plans, if both of you have had discussions in the past about the individual's career interests and desires for self-improvement, you might very well suggest one improvement goal which will represent straightforward growth or improvement for the employee *and a plus for the organization.*

HOW TO ENSURE
INDIVIDUAL COMMITMENT

Your last objective—to be sure the employee is dedicated to achieving results on time—is critical. The odds, however, favor commitment at this point. The person has been involved in the total planning of the organization. He or she has just accepted a position or at least renewed acceptance of it. There is a sense of beginning or starting over. All these things favor the employee's interest and desire to do the job. So, at most, you probably need only to be on the lookout for negative signs, such as ignoring certain work even though it is clearly a responsibility, or hesitating to set a due date by arguing about unknown factors that prevent making a time commitment.

There are at least three significant planning errors which either indicate a lack of commitment or, if due to inexperience, will later reduce the sense of urgency needed for a true results drive. The first is a formula plan—one which plans to plan, so to speak. The employee says, for example, that his or her goal is to establish a complaint service which will so restore customers' confidence that they will wish to continue to buy the firm's products. Steps are presented to meet this goal:

1. Analyze complaints to determine the most frequent sources of problems.
2. Devise and install effective routines for handling those more frequently encountered.
3. Train personnel who come into contact with customers.
4. Periodically reevaluate customer reaction.

This is not really a plan worthy of the name. This is the kind of activity involved in problem solving of any sort, translated into customer service language. A plan worthy of your joint consideration is possible only when the complaint analysis has been done and the specific courses of action likely to improve the situation identified. To view this as a legitimate plan is about equivalent to going before the board of directors of a small company to ask for funds for a new product development and presenting the following:

1. Do market research to determine customer needs.
2. Establish a research program to provide needed information.
3. Develop a product.
4. Outline an advertising campaign.

You know how unlikely it would be that the board would provide funds on any such basis! Not only is this a poor plan, but an employee is unlikely to feel committed to so general an outline. Commitment is much more probable if specific work content for specific results is delineated.

A second fundamental planning error—one which inhibits both creative work and commitment—is the plan aimed at activity rather than result. For example, the training director of an insurance firm gives as a goal "to enroll 90 percent of the clerical employees in training courses given on their own time." Undoubtedly the motive is good in setting this target, but the inevitable result is to focus attention on the volume of registrations rather than on benefit to the company as a result of the training. The manager to whom such a target is presented should ask "Why? Why? Why?" until the result expected from the training is clear. When that is spelled out, it is probable that the training will not solve the problem completely. For example, suppose that the reasons for emphasis on clerical training is that there has been an increasing volume of arithmetic errors in billing. This has caused the company considerable embarrassment. Policy holders have been annoyed. Work has had to be redone. The training director plans courses in number typing and in simple arithmetic in an effort to reduce such errors. With this understanding of the problem that the courses are designed to solve, the manager is in a position to evaluate the adequacy of the proposed actions and work toward a more meaningful program. Training may well be one step. A system for checking each other's work may also be effective. Improved access to desk calculators may be helpful. And problem-solving conferences with the clerks may suggest even better ways. The point is that an *activity* may look sound, but its true adequacy can only be determined in the light of the total *result* needed. Fortunately, too, employee commitment is much more likely to be generated when there is a clear tie to an important organization need.

A third fundamental planning error which minimizes commitment and the likelihood of obtaining needed results is a general, measureless goal such as "Maintain excellent relationships with customers." Due Date: "Continuing." This kind of goal usually brings very little result. The manager to whom such a "plan" is presented should acknowledge the soundness of the idea of having good relationships with customers. He or she should then ask the employee to identify one or two customers who may have decreased their buying lately or who are known to be on the verge of placing a large order with someone else. The goal can then be reworked to state the results to be obtained from these customers and the actions, tactics, and timing likely to produce these results. You can help the employee move from the general to the more specific by asking, "How will you know if you have succeeded in maintaining good customer relationships?" If the first reply indicates something quite long-range, add: "Will there be any earlier indications of this? We probably shouldn't wait that long to know whether our efforts are paying off."

Summarizing, then, sound planning will contribute to an employee's commitment provided that he or she has sufficiently analyzed what needs to be done so that the plan represents a factual, specific approach to reaching the goal; the employee has thought through how it will contribute to the overall organization and is prepared to judge its success based on the contribution to organization needs rather than the mere performance of his or her part of the activity; and he or she spells out plans with sufficient specificity that make it possible to know both ultimately and at interim points whether the work is producing the desired result.

YOUR BEHAVIOR CONTRIBUTES
TO COMMITMENT

Supplementing what the planning process can do to assure commitment, here are five important *don'ts* when reviewing an employee's plans:

1. Don't ask for plans and then, when the employee presents them to you, act as if they were unacceptable compared with those you already had in mind.
2. Don't insist that the employee go about reaching his or her goals the way you would if you had that job.
3. Don't "rubber stamp" the employee's plans.
4. Don't pretend to know how easy or how difficult they are to meet if you have no basis for this evaluation.
5. Don't change dates arbitrarily so as to appear to be a "tough" manager.

Let's look at each and try to understand why and how to avoid it.

You Had Something Different in Mind. If you have done a reasonable job of matching the employee's talents with the position, his or her understanding of what needs to be done and how to do it should be adequate—*providing* you have done your job of supplying that individual with basic information about the overall business or agency and its plans and any limitations on resources. In order to get an intelligent contribution from the employee you do have to contribute your share of these inputs and, clearly, for best result this must be done *in advance* of his or her thoughtful planning.

Contributing your share of input does not mean, of course, that the employee will submit plans which give the same emphasis that you feel is desirable. When this happens, center your discussion around the information that each of you considers relevant and try to find reasons for your disagreement. Usually, this exchange of facts and interpretations permits you to find common ground for agreement. This does not mean that you should yield on matters where neither of you really has any choice. In any planning situation, some things cannot be changed. There is, for example, just so much money. Or the timing of a particular program is fixed by other events—if it is earlier or later, much of the potential accomplishment is lost. Get such factors out in the open and, if possible, do so before the employee is ready to present his or her plans. If you literally forgot to mention something ahead of time, admit it. If new incidents have occurred which change the situation, say so. Then let the employee adjust his or her plans to accommodate the new information.

You Have Your Ways—The Employee Does Too.   It is sometimes hard to resist insisting that an employee do something "your" way. This is especially true if you have held the job before that person and were quite pleased with the success you achieved by following a certain course of action. But keep in mind that each of you possesses certain talents and past experiences. Your most important consideration is to help the employee do his or her work in a way which capitalizes on *his or her* strengths. Does this mean you should withhold your own experience? No. By all means help the person consider several different ways of reaching the desired result. Tell him or her what you did and *why* and what was good about it from your point of view. But in the end let your employee choose the course of action about which he or she feels most confident, providing it is within the established framework of resources, time, and similar factors.

Don't Rubber Stamp Your Employee's Plans.   A great interest-dampener is scanning plans which have been thoughtfully worked out and agreeing with them in a sort of offhand manner. This cavalier attitude is a slap in the face to a professional who has carefully collected facts, analyzed data, estimated risks, considered alternatives, and finally reached a decision on what needs to be done and the most successful and economical way of doing it. It indicates that you consider this an unimportant part of the professional's job and somehow unworthy of any more of your attention. Even when the reason for your treatment stems from your confidence in the worker, your attitude still fails to reward the employee's efforts adequately.

So ask for a better definition of expected results, discuss alternatives considered, add some thoughts from personal experience. Talk about the assumptions on which the plans are based so that as professionals you can track these assumptions to be sure of their accuracy and adjust plans if some do not prove out. Identify "points of no return," times beyond which the need for resources will increase substantially so that the size of investment makes it almost impossible to turn back. Log these in your own plans so that you and he or she can review progress at these points to be sure that the additional resources are warranted.

Don't Evaluate What You Don't Understand.   Sometimes you may feel that you do not know enough about the details of a specialized field to evaluate the adequacy of an employee's plans. This is all the more reason to define results clearly, probe for courses of action considered and reasons for choice so that both of you know what to expect, what risks are involved, and how to measure the extent to which results are being obtained.

You may not appreciate the ease or difficulty of doing the technical or functional work involved. If so, do not pretend that you do. Congratulating a pro on a piece of work which he or she feels is second-rate is worse than no recognition at all. As a manager, the thing you *must* be able to evaluate is the worthwhileness of the proposed result to the organization's goals. So work at understanding this by asking, "Why this action? What are its implications? What will we do if we get this result?" and "What will we do if we fail to get this result? What will be the demands on others in the organization? What further investment will be required if we are successful? Unsuccessful?"

If after your discussion you still feel inadequate to judge the soundness of the plan, use a qualified consultant to help you or ask the employee to bring his or her associates to a meeting to discuss pros and cons. The ideas of the group may provide you with needed inputs. And do not hesitate to ask for a self-evaluation. There are certainly times when an individual is so personally involved that objectivity is lost, although in the early stages of planning one can usually back away from the work and make an unprejudiced evaluation.

What About Due Dates?. Sometimes a manager feels that he or she should change estimated completion dates to speed up results, perhaps believing that this shows toughness. Unless a result *must* be obtained by a certain point in time, and the plan as presented will not do it, or the meshing of schedules with others in the organization requires a time change, or you have some other very good reason, *do not do it.* Particularly the first time around, let the employee name the time that appears reasonable. If experience shows that there is water in the schedule, it can be taken out at later reviews. For the most part, professional workers overestimate how much they can do in a given time period. If dates are made even tighter and appear unrealistic to the employee, motivation to achieve them may be dampened and the worker may, in fact, be moved to prove how unreasonable the dates are. Dates that are "given," that are requirements, should be discussed in advance so that the plan represents the employee's best effort to reach results in the specified time. If new information comes which requires a change of date, let the employee think through his or her plan again to see if a shortcut can be found.

Integrate Plans Across Organization. When you have worked with all employees individually to get their position responsibilities crystal clear and to get on paper the specific results that you are counting on each to achieve, the next step is to make certain that all individual and component plans mesh with each other. This will mean at least one meeting in which the plans of all components are laid out for scrutiny by everyone. If the organization is large, some staff work may be necessary to identify the interfaces and ensure coordination at these points. This can be an excellent developmental assignment for some individual or, if there are administrative personnel specifically designated, one or more may be asked to look at meshing problems. In small organizations, individuals can iron out disparities for themselves if they have access to each others' plans.

What Happened to the Partnership Relationship?   In looking at individual plans and working to make them more incisive, more innovative, and more likely to reach organization goals, it is easy to slip into a superior-subordinate relationship or assume a power role which may prove harmful to the long-term joint venture relationship you have been trying to establish. Avoiding this is a rather subtle and delicate thing to do. On the next page are a few do's and don't's to help you.

Let Employees Review Your Plans.   Finally, *do* have a set of plans which you propose for carrying out your responsibilities and contributing to the accomplishment of their work. Ask for their review and contribution to them; ask for their evaluation of your plan's adequacy as far as they are concerned. Include such items as provision for pooled services such as recruiting, computer service, drafting, or purchasing; plans for obtaining resources which they cannot provide for themselves—space, investment funds, and similar items; coordination with your manager and your associates particularly where their positive support is needed; provision for information exchange and feedback which will help them know the status of expenditures, inventory, head count, and other needed operating data. Include also your plan for integrating, reviewing, and recycling the work of the department. Remember that you have embarked on a joint venture. Your contributions are different, but they should meet each other's needs so that together they produce the result that you are seeking.

Do	*Don't*
Do ask, "How are *we* going to do this? What can I contribute to this effort? How will *we* use this result?" thus implying your joint stake in the work and results.	Don't imply that it is the employees' total responsibility, that they hang alone if they fail. Individual failure *means organization* failure.
Do use an interested, exploring manner, asking questions designed to bring out factual information.	Don't play the part of an interrogator, firing questions as rapidly as they can be answered and usually requiring only a "yes" or "no" reply.
Do keep the analysis and evaluation as much in the employees' hands as possible by asking for their best judgment on various issues.	Don't listen to what they present and then sum up your reaction on an emotional basis.
Do present facts about organization needs, commitments, strategy, and so on, which permit them to improve and interest them in improving what they propose to do.	Don't demand a change or improvement in a peremptory tone of voice or on what appears to be an arbitrary basis.

Do ask them to investigate or analyze further if you feel that they have overlooked some points or overemphasized others and to return with their plans after factoring these items in.

Don't take their planning papers and cross out, change dates, or mark "no good" next to certain activities.

Don't redo their plans for them unless their repeated efforts show no improvement.

10

Sustaining Motivation Toward Organization Goals

You have laid the groundwork for a high level of commitment in the organization. Your objective now is to sustain and, if possible, increase it. Your chances of doing this are good if:

1. You establish sound information and feedback systems.
2. You reinforce and renew commitment to work goals, keeping planning current.
3. You help each employee plan for personal growth through his or her work.
4. You reward and recognize accomplishment appropriately.

INFORMATION SYSTEMS—FEEDBACK

Few things discourage enthusiasm more than devoting a great deal of thought and discussion to the formulation of a plan of action—to argue, weigh, protest, defend, and finally agree on what will be done—only to find that silence follows. An employee starts out with keen interest, knowing what is to be done. It has been promised by a certain date. As time progresses and there is no feedback, the individual experiences a sense of uneasiness. Is he or she the only one carrying out the plans? The worker begins to query associates: "Say, how are things going anyway? Are you working on Project X? What's happening?" Inevitably, the employee discovers that at least one associate is embarked on a different course of action than he thought was agreed to. Another person has found a shortcut and is gleefully pursuing it.

Most are running behind schedule, held up by this or that unanticipated occurrence. The individual tells associate B what A is doing. B is amazed. Both then corner C to tell what they have discovered. And so it goes. The employee returns to his or her own work or to his or her component's work with considerably less than the original dedication. This hesitancy shows itself in what the worker does and is felt by others. The importance of the work is lessened. The urgency to meet agreed-upon dates is reduced. The employee feels let down.

This is not the time to drop the ball. Do not fall into the trap of believing that because work has been carefully planned and each person knows what is expected, you have done all that is necessary. Nothing could be farther from the truth. First of all, you need a good information system—not just for yourself but for every employee in the organization. As a minimum, you should confirm basic plans in writing and secure understanding and involvement at lower organization levels.

Confirm Basic Plans in Writing. Put on paper, or ask someone to do it for you, the broad plans agreed to. Include critical activities and dates, points of no return, and major milestones so that all are in a position to know whether work is on target. Almost inevitably in doing this you will find some member of the organization who did not fully realize what was decided or who misinterpreted the agreement. This provides the opportunity to resolve the misunderstanding before effort is misdirected.

Gain Understanding and Involvement at Lower Organization Levels. Make certain that organization and component goals and courses of action are communicated to employees who do not report directly to you. You need their understanding, acceptance, and active involvement in order to accomplish planned work.

IS YOUR EXAMPLE BEING FOLLOWED?

You took great care to involve each member of your staff in planning needed work which capitalized on individual talent and interest. You negotiated with each person to the point where the result to be obtained was clear and measurable. If managers report to you, have they followed your example? *Every* employee should see the relationship of his or her work to the whole, should be involved insofar as this is possible in choosing an economic course of action, and should associate personal progress with organization progress.

So make certain that individual negotiation is in every manager's work plans, discuss good ways of doing it, and review how it was done. The amount of choice available tends generally to be less at lower organization levels, but a sincere manager and an interested employee will usually find some measure of freedom. Encourage the search, and reward it when it is successful.

Establish Minimum Basic Reports. Work with those who report to you to identify the key items that will let them know how things are going. The kind of organization and the work they do determine the content. For example, in an industrial manufacturing component, such things as shipments against schedule, waste, rework, and various inspection reports are essential. Marketing personnel probably need information on such things as sales against quotas, by customer and product, along with comparative inventories, customer complaints, and service required. On an overall basis, everyone will want to know about business, forecasts, actual and backlogged orders, the status of performance against contracts, and expenditures against budget. If a mechanical system such as PERT is in place, PERT charts should be accessible so that at least all professional workers can see where work stands and where holdups exist. The other side of this coin is not to overburden employees with making and reading unnecessary reports. No reports for the sake of reports! If you keep in mind your objective of providing timely and useful information so that all can react quickly and incorporate it into their work in a suitable fashion, you will find the right balance.

Use Face-to-Face Discussions. Reports have their place and can provide useful feedback on an individual or group basis, but do not rely on the written word to generate action. Most employees frankly admit that they procrastinate when it comes to reading long, dry, technical accounts of events. The written report of expenditure against budget arrives, and the superintendent puts it aside for later study while he or she goes off to tackle the problem of inadequate materials or an archaic purchasing system. The PERT charts are updated and made available to all engineering personnel, but the engineer is involved in a tricky design which has him or her totally absorbed for the time being. The engineer decides to study the PERT diagrams just as soon as immediate problems are solved. So, recognize the need to arouse interest. Regular or irregular meetings with those who report to you may serve this purpose, particularly if you designate individuals as "centers for analysis" of various kinds of information. They may report to the group only if it is their feeling that there is a special reason to do so or, if you prefer more regular attention, may simply review highlights of whatever new data are available. One caution: if such oral group reviews are likely to point to a failure on someone's part, you must avoid the appearance of a public accusation by giving the individual time to make recommendations for correcting the situation or insist that the reporter and the individuals involved get together ahead of time for this purpose. In this way the meeting tone remains constructive and forward-looking.

Continue Program Reviews. Earlier discussions described how you could gain an understanding of the status and prognosis for each major work program or project underway. Continue such reviews as frequently as progress or changes in the situation make them desirable.

Skip-a-level employee meetings are also a very important and useful device. They permit you to get to know the back-up people better, and they give employees the chance to get a first-hand feeling for your personal philosophy and vision of the organization's purpose and strategy. In order to keep relationships on a sound basis, you will often want the people who report directly to you to take an active part in such meetings by describing some special aspect of the component's work or anticipated problems or by highlighting a few major milestones ahead. These represent opportunities for you to pinpoint serious coordination problems in the department, drawing the implications for cooperative effort across organization lines. Be as specific as possible in doing this, giving examples which individuals can apply to their personal working behavior.

Such occasions provide an opportunity to discuss limitations on resources. Certain skills may be in very short supply in the organization. Pointing this out, together with plans to conserve their usage, does two things. It helps employees understand and, therefore, cooperate with certain burdensome restrictions. It also helps some employees see how they might increase their value to the organization by learning these skills or refreshing their knowledge of them.

It may be that financial resources are limited, but it is not enough just to say this. Show how limited they are, for what reasons, and how you and those who report to you are preparing to meet this limitation. Frank discussion will also ensure greater cooperative effort and elicit suggestions for economies. If space is inadequate, point out the effort it would take to correct the matter now and how it would affect the progress of the business. This will probably make the situation somewhat more acceptable to employees, although it may not prevent the usual gripes. In your desire to win acceptance, though, do not promise correction of any restrictions unless they are really within your control. Nothing generates poorer confidence in managers than repeated, unkept promises.

Do not worry about organization levels in these meetings. Invite all whose work is such that they should speak for themselves. Encourage and reward frankness; draw out differences of opinion so that they can be factored into whatever decisions are made.

Invite First-Hand Client, Customer, or Associate Contracts. At irregular intervals bring in customers, clients, associates, your manager, or other officers of the firm or institution you serve. Such individuals are a great spur to improved performance. Comments from a pilot or service mechanic about the airplane you build help focus attention on real-world problems.

Student reaction to library facilities, policy-holders, feelings about adjusters' methods, even patients' responses to hospital facilities can be constructively used. It requires a clear display of interest on your part and your interpretation too, to prevent any personal biases from over-influencing the course of future work programs and to minimize the rather natural defensive reaction of employees to criticism. Well-chosen comments by your manager at an occasional meeting may give a better understanding of the role of the department in the total firm or agency. An associate whose work is meshed with yours might explain from his or her viewpoint some of the problems which are experienced in dealing with your organization. If this is followed by a discussion to the point where helpful decisions can be made by both sides, it may be that work can move across organization lines with much less difficulty in the future.

Such a program of full information displays to employees your determination that the organization's work programs should be completed successfully. It cannot help but add to individual alertness and interest. Use Figure 10-1 as a check list for developing the information system in your organization.

FIGURE 10-1   Elements of a Sound Information System

---

1. Confirm basic work plans in writing.

2. Get understanding and involvement in organization goals at lower organization levels.

3. Establish a minimum system of reports.

4. Hold face-to-face discussions with employees.

5. Continue work program reviews as needed.

6. Invite first-hand client, customer, or associate feedback.

RENEW COMMITMENT
TO WORK GOALS AND PLAN
FOR INDIVIDUAL GROWTH

Even though an employee sees the relevance of his or her work to the organization's goals, has personally contributed to these goals, and wants very much to help achieve them, conditions probably are not sufficient to ensure sustained motivation. The employee needs, in addition, to feel that in achieving organization goals, personal goals are reached. The employee's dedication is likely to depend on the degree to which this is understood. Since growth is an individual matter, much of your work here will be on an individualized basis.

There are, of course, a wide variety of tools and approaches available to you.[1] In general, however, the steps are to understand the individual's own aims, identify at least one important goal towards which he or she is able to work while on the present job, evolve an action plan, and set up feedback devices to indicate success. Your first reaction to this concept may be that this is the employee's business, that you do not want to stand in his or her way, but you certainly do not wish to interfere. Unfortunately, to keep motivation toward organization results at a high level, you need to make a more positive contribution. This must be done in such a way that the employee will regard it as a display of interest on your part. This is possible if the employee shares personal goals with you, you appraise them as realistic, the two of you are able to put together a sound plan for reaching the goals, and his or her current position will accommodate the planned activity. Let's look at a sound approach for accomplishing these requisites.

MAKE ADEQUATE PREPARATION

When you were first given the job of managing the work of this organization, you sat down with each professional and reviewed their work and interests. Later, when you staffed the restructured positions, you again spent considerable time on the abilities, career objectives, attitudes, and motivations of the candidates. Begin by reviewing your notes from these occasions. Then reflect on the performances, attitudes, and interests displayed since that time. Note the consistencies and inconsistencies in the two. These are probably accurate and can be factored into development planning. They raise questions to be resolved through discussion with the employee or with others who know them. A month or two after reaching agreement on individual work plans, schedule a second round of discussions. By this time, there should be some significant progress to report, perhaps some significant obstacles as well. In any event, enough should have occurred that plans for the following few months need review and revision. Presumably, too, your work as manager merits discussion. Are you meeting the employee's needs? Does he or she have suggestions for changes or additions to make to you?

LET THE EMPLOYEE
BRIEF YOU ON PROGRESS

Either the employee does the work or it is the result of a group effort. Be sure, therefore, that you are briefed on what has been done since your original agreement. Some news will be good, some bad. The important thing

---

[1]For a complete review of these, see Marion S. Kellogg, *Closing the Performance Gap* (New York: American Management Association, 1967).

is to deemphasize the backward look except as a base for analysis of what should be done in the future. Again, as in the original agreement, keep the ball very much in the employee's hands. He or she is the specialist on this work. You may have thoughts or ideas or information or relevant experience which you will want to share with the employee, but as before, do this as an information service for them.

Questions such as the following are helpful: "What could we have done differently that might have worked out better? Have we learned something from this to use the next time we face the problem?" And even more important, "What is the best thing to do now? What can I contribute? Will this action be enough to rescue the situation?" And, "What other things could we do? Is there anyone else in the organization who could help us? That's a good point" (when he or she makes a suggestion) "Is there something *more* we could do?" In this manner, the employee's responsibility to retrieve what has been lost, to make up for schedule lags, to devise reasonable courses of action is kept in his or her hands. The resources of the organization are available. *You* are interested, helpful, sympathetic, inquiring, exploring, listening. You will provide any managerial service needed. But you are not a savior. You cannot do your employee's thinking or work. You expect to achieve what appears reasonable and what is needed by the organization, all matters considered.

KEEP THE FOCUS ON THE FUTURE

Having looked at the past and considered needed retrieval actions, examine carefully how well the individual has thought through what is likely to occur in the next few months. Has he or she investigated the current performance of those who are scheduled to supply them with information, materials, or designs? Will these people be able to meet their commitments? Or, if during the next few months they are trying out a new idea, is there an alternative in mind in case it doesn't live up to expectations? In other words, is the employee doing his or her share of the job of looking ahead to anticipate obstacles and to work around them or solve them in advance?

Equally important, of course, have you reviewed all that you know about the course of future events—changes in business strategy, likely Congressional action which might affect the agency, or economic or social changes of significance to the work of the organization? Have *you* thought them through and discussed them sufficiently so that the employee is able to adjust work accordingly? In all probability, this forward-looking part of the discussion should take the largest share of your meeting time, thus emphasizing that progress to date is the base on which to build future action. It is how the employee handles their work from this point forward which is critical to the organization.

MANAGERIAL OPTION

As you discuss the future, you must use your judgment in exercising an option. You had two purposes in mind in setting up this meeting. The first was to review and revise work plans and renew commitment to them. The second was to learn about the employee's personal goals so that they could be factored into the work. The nature of your option is whether to move on to the issue of career goals now, set the stage for a future meeting, or delay the subject indefinitely. The reason why you must use judgment on this is clear. If the employee's work is foundering, if it is so badly off schedule that it will require every ounce of personal effort and ingenuity to get it back on target, this is hardly the moment to suggest additional effort for personal growth.

You should also be alert to signs of antagonism, defensiveness, or hostility in the employee. If he or she appears to feel "put upon," claims to have been sold a false bill of goods, or shows resentment at giving a progress report so soon; if he or she counters your probing about future plans by saying "Just leave me alone"; if the person reacts to your suggestions by stating, "You don't understand the situation"; go no further. Such reactions clearly indicate that this is not the moment to try to examine career targets together. Under these conditions, or more subtle ones which you sense as precluding further discussion, close the meeting.

GROUND RULES
FOR GROWTH DISCUSSION

On the other hand, if the briefing indicates that the individual has made good solid progress, and he or she discusses future work with interest and in a constructive manner, raise the issue either for immediate examination or for a meeting in the near future. There are a few minimum ground rules.

Give Enough Advance Notice. Most of us like a little warning if we are expected to discuss our long-term career objectives. Under the most favorable conditions, we need time to decide what we are willing to expose of ourselves, how much to discuss, where to put emphasis, and so on. At worst, we may not have identified career targets for ourselves or have only vague notions of likes and dislikes. We need to think through how to explain this without appearing naive.

Explain Why You Are Asking. Say that you believe that people who give their best to meeting organization goals should feel that they are benefiting from work, and that the work reflects personal value. Point out that your intention is not to pry into personal areas, but merely to be sure that the work capitalizes on each employee's unique capabilities and interests.

Keep the Focus on the Present Job.   Make it clear that you are considering how to adapt the goals and methods of the present job to encourage the employee's development and that you are not suggesting a change of position. This is important for two reasons: you do not wish to raise false hopes of a promotion, and you want to keep him or her dedicated toward current position goals which represent organization needs.

Identify the Extent of Employee Interest in Managing.   Even if employees are very unsure of their ultimate target, they probably know whether they wish to stay in or get into management. This makes a good starting point for discussion. Does the employee see him or herself in the near future managing a large organization, a small organization, or depending mainly on personal effort?

Identify a "Next" Function.   How does the individual feel about the function (engineering, manufacturing, marketing, and so on) in which he or she works? Does he or she feel that the current one is appropriate or that another would be better? Does the employee know what he or she would like to try or experiment with?

Identify a "Next" Specialty Within the Function.   Does the employee feel at this time that he or she wants to go into more depth in this current specialty or is the person growing stale and wishes to shift to a new area in due time? If the person is in advertising, would a switch to direct selling or consumer research be satisfying? If in employment, does a move into compensation seem desirable?

Ask for a Self-Appraisal.   Considering the employee's best evaluation of what the next career step is likely to be, what does he or she see as gaps in knowledge or skill which require special reading, training, or experience? It is during this self-evaluation that your preparation pays off. Do these current thoughts agree with earlier statements? Are they consistent with performance? Do former managers agree with the employee's evaluation, or are there additional points which they make consistently which need to be factored in? Most important of all, does his or her self-evaluation agree with your personal observations during the time you have been associated? If you find significant inconsistencies, you may wish to delay completion of the discussion until you have had time for further reflection or professional advice. If, as is more likely, the total pattern is roughly consistent and his or her thoughts for next assignments or direction of growth jibe pretty well with other evidence, you can move on to goal setting.

HOW TO FACTOR DEVELOPMENT
GOALS INTO CURRENT WORK

Start by selecting what appears to be an important gap in knowledge, skill, or behavior. There are two critical points: the employee must have the ability to fill the gap, and the current work must be adaptable to it without unusual contriving.

How to do this is best shown by example. Suppose the employee, Tom, is an engineer and currently an individual worker. He would like to manage the work of five or six other professionals. You might point out that on the first phase of a certain technical program, inputs from six or eight specialists are needed to design a particular component properly. The employee might take a leadership role for this design and set a goal of developing relationships with each of these specialists so that they function as a small professional organization or team during the design period. He could make specific plans for giving them advance information on the overall system, the component specifications, and his design strategy. He might (on a very informal basis) review with each one just what his plans are for producing needed data. As a vehicle for doing these things, he might initiate once-a-week luncheon discussions to clarify each person's role and progress. From your point of view, this little plan may pay off in better design of a critical component. From the employee's point of view, there is an opportunity to focus some extra attention on developing interpersonal skills and trying them out. If he runs into difficulties with the other professionals, you have the chance to review with him just how he has gone about this effort and what changes he might make in his approach next time. You can help him approach the problem of relationships with other specialists on a systematic basis, keep track of what he says and does, get feedback, and discuss it with you as honestly and objectively as he can. He is, in effect, experimenting with the behavior he would need to acquire in order to manage the work of a small organization successfully.

Or, to take another example, suppose the employee, Laura, is a promotion specialist in a charitable fund-raising outfit. Her desire is to obtain a job similar to yours as head of an agency. She has had little experience, however, in *organizing* a major effort. As a beginning, you might suggest a book or two to read and propose that when her "door-to-door" campaign is ready for implementation, she might organize the volunteer effort in her home city. This, from your point of view, might give her valuable, first-hand feedback on the adequacy of the materials which she prepares as part of her current work. From her point of view, it would give her the opportunity to try out a few organizing principles and test herself in one of the most difficult of all situations—structuring the work of volunteers over whom she has no authority. Again, in this situation as with the engineer, there is opportunity for continuing interaction between you and the employee to your mutual benefit.

Efforts to develop skills such as those described do require an investment of time on both your part and that of the employee. They can, however, mean the difference between continuing drive to reach needed results and a fall-off of interest accompanied by a more pedestrian effort.

PLANNING DEVELOPMENTAL ACTION ON A GROUP BASIS

Not all actions pinpointed as "developmental" need to be designed specifically for and implemented by a single employee. While each person has a unique combination of talent and interest, while each may be willing to devote a different amount of effort to personal growth, and while each may respond differently to your developmental efforts, there are a number of things that you can do on a group basis. Are there, as one possibility, some experiences which you feel would be helpful to the work of the organization but which seem to be missing from almost everyone's record? If so, you might raise the thought at a meeting, point out one or two ways in which you feel this knowledge would pay off, and ask for suggestions of things that might be done as a group to improve overall know-how in the deficient area.

For example, perhaps a better understanding of accounting practices would help in bidding on contracts or requesting investment funds. Plans might include lectures by an economist from a local college to lay the groundwork for better understanding and a series of presentations by members of the firm's financial organization. If such actions are timed to precede an important decision or action requiring better financial information, whatever is learned will be reinforced by actual use.

A second possibility for group developmental action involves the improvement of interpersonal skills. It may well be that certain individuals need to improve their presentation-making, defense of their ideas or proposals, conference leadership, ability to contribute more to group discussion, listening habits, or similar human skills involving other people. If you will select assignments which require them to use the desired skill at a scheduled group meeting, provide some advance information or suggestions, and supplement their performance with feedback from you, it may help them considerably. When relationships among individuals are particularly strong and more than one individual is trying to improve a group skill, the members of the group can often provide constructive feedback.

REWARD THROUGH INTERNAL
SATISFACTION

We come now to a critical factor in the motivation cycle: the differential recognition of excellent, mediocre, and poor performance and the handling of rewards so as to maximize their motivational impact.

The matter of reward and recognition is complex at best. It is especially so for professionals. If you are associated with mature professionals who have developed a set of work standards primarily connected with the objective demands of problem solution, much of their sense of reward is internal. To have set a challenging goal and found a way (preferably innovative) of meeting it within specified conditions brings an enormous sense of self-satisfaction. One proviso, of course, is that the goal must have been challenging. If professionals know that almost anyone could have accomplished a given piece of work, their satisfaction is lowered. Another proviso is that they must feel that the conditions imposed on them were necessary. If speed was required because of anticipated competitive moves, if funds were in short supply, if critical manpower shortages really existed, they will accept these things as part of the challenge, and this will add to their satisfaction if they achieve the result in spite of the shortages. But if they feel that cost-cutting is a whim of the moment and its application to their work is unjust, if they feel that the schedule is arbitrary and forces incomplete, sloppy work, they may grudgingly try for the result anyway. But their dedication is usually lessened and their satisfaction in accomplishment reduced.

There is clearly a perceptual problem here. Perhaps viewed from a manager's vantage point certain conditions appear necessary, but from the individual's viewpoint they do not appear so. Whenever possible, such differences should be brought out and resolved in the planning stage.

It is also true that a sense of internal satisfaction may be short-lived. The professional worker may see the accomplishment of one goal as a part of another, larger problem. The discrepancy between his or her accomplishment and the bigger goal may trigger a whole new planning and working cycle. You, as manager, need to be alert to this possibility. If you feel that a worker's efforts would be better directed toward the solution of another problem, you may need to begin providing information and ideas about it before the old goal has been completely achieved. Timing is important—too soon and the professional will think that you have lost interest in the old goal; too late and he or she will already be embarked on phase two.

EXTERNAL REWARD
IS ALSO NECESSARY

While internal satisfaction with accomplishment is necessary, it needs to be supplemented by external reward and recognition. When you filled the positions reporting to you, you spelled out the compensation arrangements as part of your agreement. The value of the work and the way you administer increases have therefore been discussed and agreed to. It is essential to follow this agreement to the letter. It represents the professional's expectations; any deviation in a direction viewed as unfavorable is likely to have a demotivating effect. If you agreed on joint appraisal sessions every 12 months, hold them in 12 months; don't let them slip to 13 or 14. If salaries were to be reviewed at stated intervals and increases awarded on specified bases, follow these guidelines. And be prepared to describe and defend your decisions to the employee, who deserves this information even if he or she fails to raise the question at all.

Seek other forms of recognition. A luncheon of a few carefully chosen associates to honor a piece of distinguished work, a letter of commendation for a job which involved a great deal of personal time, a party for an organization that went over the top on a difficult fund-raising campaign, a trip to Hawaii for the contest winner of a major sales competition—all are marks of recognition and, when deserved, have a positive impact on performance.

REWARDS MUST BE CONGRUENT WITH ACCOMPLISHMENT

Almost everyone agrees that reward and recognition are necessary. There is however, an additional and very fundamental point. Compensation should follow the pattern agreed to in advance. But the more informal recognition—the unexpected praise, compliment, or honor—should *fit* the accomplishment. Lavish praise for something which the individual views as routine or a special award for results that the specialist feels are inconclusive may backfire. The feeling that relatively minor or marginal work receives as much recognition as the successful completion of a complex task brings with it the feeling that neither is understood nor appreciated. When this happens, it is difficult for a professional employee to align his or her personal goals with those of an organization which somehow seems substandard. In time, this conflict may show itself in lessened interest in the work undertaken.

And so we return to a point made many times. It is so important however, its repetition is worthwhile. As the manager of work performed by specialists whose individual knowledge of their respective fields must inevitably surpass your own, you need sound information on which to base your evaluations. This is only likely to be available to you if the result each was to attain for the organization was clearly specified in advance and updated frequently to match changing conditions. Then, in the final analysis, when work has been completed, you can judge whether it did or did not achieve this result.

Lay the groundwork, therefore, for sound motivation toward organization goals by involving the individual in planning for the organization and formulating specific goals for his or her work which meet organization needs. Sustain motivation through a continuing updating of these goals, thus reinforcing their importance and contribution to the whole. Ensure the flow of relevant information in the organization. Contribute to individual growth by the deliberate injection of work which requires the addition of knowledge or skill and leads the individual in the direction of personal career interests. Follow compensation agreements to the letter. Finally, match your reward and recognition to the value of the contribution.

11

Fighting
Obsolescence

It is an unfortunate fact of life that as we grow older we become more set in our ways. We learn to reduce as much of our work as possible to sensible routines. We become more efficient. Unfortunately, we do not always become more effective. Innovation means change. Discovery flows from difference—a different approach, a different application, a breaking away from past habits and practices. Professional workers presumably strive to add to knowledge, to push aside information barriers. Much of their satisfaction and recognition comes from advancing the state of the art. But invention takes mental alertness and energy, an inquiring and open-minded spirit, and an honest stake in the future. These are qualities normally associated with young people.

There are, fortunately, enough examples of extraordinary creativity in middle-aged and older individuals to show us that it is not the exclusive property of the chronologically young. It is possible to fight rigidity, sameness, routine, and efficiency for its own sake. As a manager of professional work probably performed by individuals in a variety of age groups, you must improve output through continuous battle against obsolescence. As in most efforts, it is easier to prevent it than to change it once it has occurred. Preventing obsolescence is a disciplinary process; it is a continuous process; it is a planned effort on your part requiring people to do things that make them uncomfortable. Because it is these things, it is difficult to do. It suffers from a lack of drama; you get little credit for doing it, but failure to do it shows itself in deteriorating, non-competitive work.

FIGHT OBSOLESCENCE IN YOURSELF

Fighting obsolescence is not just a matter of preventing it in other people. The battle begins with you. You must find personal dissatisfaction with the state of your own knowledge, with your almost automatic way of tackling problems. You must watch for signs of closed-mindedness in yourself, such as sudden irritation if someone questions an assumption or a principle which you consider well established, a tendency to let your mind wander during the explanation of a new theory or idea, or hearing yourself say: "Here we go again!" when a directive which you disliked earlier in your career reappears,

Fight these tendencies by a deliberate search for at least one idea that you can put to use in every suggestion, every presentation, every "discovery." Make doubly sure that the situation you are attempting to deal with is indeed the situation in fact. Are you, for example, remembering an employee or an associate as they were five or ten years ago and making judgments about his abilities today? Are you focusing attention on results needed six months ago without checking to make certain that the same result is needed now? Are you providing services for clients or customers based on incorrect assumptions about their needs or desires? Are you attempting to work with your own manager in a way which no longer fits his or her managing methods or style?

There are quite a few specific things you can do to counter obsolescence in yourself and in the organization as a whole.

SELECTING NEW EMPLOYEES

As positions open in the organization, make a deliberate effort to hire new employees who come from different backgrounds. This is not to say that it does not matter whether they are competent to do the work, but merely that you upgrade a requirement. Ask that they *add* something or bring some change in thinking to the organization. Personnel experts have long pointed out that managers tend to hire in their own image, that the strengths and deficiencies of a given manager are reflected right down the line. The best managers, the most successful ones, those who are determined to push back knowledge frontiers, do not do this. They look for the competent *and* unusual person. They look for the person whose value system is different from their own, whose experiences have been different, who comes from different disciplines, and who is accustomed to using different techniques in his work.

This is harder to do, and it takes more courage. It means questioning what you are doing and why you are doing it that way. This can be annoying and time-consuming. But it is this kind of constructive re-examination which fights obsolescence, staleness, and ingrown habits, and permits use of the best of each one's ideas. So determine to fill open jobs with people from other disciplines or other functions, or bring in a new person who is fresh from college or graduate school and encourage this individual to acquaint all of you with the things he or she knows. The learning experience should be a reciprocal one.

UPGRADE KNOWLEDGE
AND KEEP AN OPEN MIND

The second battleground for fighting obsolescence is in the knowledge or information area. You need to be sure that up-to-date information in the forefront of knowledge is available to and used by the professionals whose work involves its application. Encourage taking and giving courses, discussion seminars, individual or team research, and papers requiring the exposition of new ideas. Bring in current theorists occasionally for consultation. Introduce proponents of concepts different from those of the organization's professionals to stimulate and, hopefully, upgrade thinking. Keep yourself abreast in a general way of what is going on in fields of work which you manage so that you can ask whether current thinking has at least been considered and incorporated or discarded on rational grounds.

Keep asking your associates: "Hasn't *anything* new or better been discovered? What are *others* doing in this field?" There is no implication that the latest is always the best or that it is likely to apply to your goals and problems. The intent is to emphasize that awareness of all the choices available permits a sounder decision.

Apply this to your own work. Ask yourself: "Am I aware of the current management thinking? Have I investigated different management practices? Am I changing my style to fit current needs? Am I improving as a manager?"

Seeking or providing up-to-date information is only one phase of the learning process. It is equally critical to maintain an open mind so that the experiences of others can be transmitted to us meaningfully and so that we can make use of them without undergoing each experience for ourselves. It takes a similar openness of mind to allow us to capitalize on our own new experiences fully by grasping and grappling with them and wringing the learning from them. It is a real asset to have a reflective ability which lets you calmly think back over various happenings in your lifetime, observe trends, interpret changes, and adjust and adapt accordingly.

G-2 INTELLIGENCE

Competition is a great stimulator. Make the assumption that someone somewhere is doing what your organization is doing and doing it much better. Keep lines of communication out to know what is going on. If you are in a government agency or bureau, what is going on in industry? If you are in a hospital, what are the best hospitals in the country doing? If you are in a foundation, how do others function? Systematically reporting this kind of intelligence may be useful as development for a number of different employees and provide stimulation for the entire group. When substantial differences in approach or results are uncovered, the debate or devil's advocate approach can encourage re-examination of the issues so that current courses of action can be continued or abandoned based on a rational decision.

DON'T KEEP EMPLOYEES
IN THE SAME JOB TOO LONG

Most growing, expanding organizations are concerned because there is so much mobility that no one becomes really expert at his or her job. This situation, however, has more advantages than the fixed organization. There is certainly some amateurism, some error because of inexperience. But there are also excitement, enthusiasm, and interest, coupled with complaints, impatience, and short temper. All these are signs of dedication and determination to reach a result. The stable organization settles, becomes more efficient in doing what it is doing. Interest may wear thin and desire to do something better may almost disappear. There is a staleness, almost a resignation.

If you are in this state, do *something!* Reorganize, play musical chairs, bring in a consultant with a totally different viewpoint. Get some fights and arguments going. Shorten time schedules or cut the budget. Do something to rouse employees from the routine of their jobs. Get them focused on effective goals and new methods of reaching them. There is no rule for determining how long individuals should remain on their jobs. So much depends on the complexity of the work, how quickly they learn, adapt, what kind of a manager you are, how dynamic the whole organization picture is. Probably, however, in the early working years you should begin to think seriously of a change when an employee has been on the same work for two years. Later, five is probably a better figure. Much beyond that, and something deliberate and conscious should be done to inject new life into the position if you cannot arrange a change.

WATCH OUT FOR INDIVIDUAL
OVER-INVOLVEMENT

Staying on a job too long seems an obvious hazard. Less obvious, but almost as serious for the organization is staying with a certain piece of work or a certain course of action past the point of probable payoff. When a professional is engaged in work which he or she feels is important and necessary, when the person involves him- or herself in this work so thoroughly that full creative energies and interests are absorbed, he or she may suffer from another form of obsolescence. One may not be able to abandon it at a reasonable point in time and start over with a fresh approach. The professional is convinced to make just one more try, that the next investigation will pay off. For the doctor, teacher, or psychologist, this willingness to keep working with a patient, student, or client is laudatory. The human being is worth the one more try, the extra effort, providing others who also need help are not slighted in the process. But in working with products, data, programs, or campaigns, the professional needs a little help to tear away from the low-probability-of-payoff program, to step back, take a few deep mental breaths, and tackle the problem from a new perspective.

The manager's maxim, of course, is that the earlier unproductive work is stopped, the sooner more challenging, more promising work can be started, and the less waste there will be. Knowing when work should be stopped, however, is difficult. There are just enough instances of rewarding results after everyone else had given up to make a manager uneasy about dictating closure. Group approaches—discussions, reviews, debates—are enormously helpful in getting facts out on the table to permit a more realistic look at effort versus likelihood of payoff. Sometimes a vacation, the distraction of a task force devoted to another subject, or attending a technical meeting will help the professional "break set." Or a totally different problem presented for urgent attention may be the answer. The important points are for you as manager to recognize the danger and take counteraction soon enough. Learn to praise the individual who knows that work must be put aside because it is stagnating.

MAKE SURE YOUR
ASSUMPTIONS ARE VALID

Another danger, especially for long-term work, is that the situation may change in unexpected ways. If your planning was based on assumptions about what customers are likely to want, what money Congress will appropriate, or what strategists predict will be our line of defense, you must keep abreast of these situational factors so that you can change direction rapidly if one or several of these predictions should prove incorrect. Failure to do this accounts for loss of a great deal of productive effort. Suppose that a result is produced. Under certain conditions, it would be most useful or salable. Under actual conditions, it is not—it costs more than the consumer is willing to pay or a substitute service beats it to the marketplace. We cannot insure the rightness of our predictions, but we can track influencing factors and adjust our efforts toward a reasonable outcome.

AN IMPROVEMENT GOAL
IN EVERY WORK PLAN

One good managing practice is to be sure that all professionals have improvement goals in their work plans. Regardless of how "busy" their job is, some routines can be simplified, some preventive action taken against recurring problems, some paperwork system streamlined. This means keeping track of what is taking excessive time to pinpoint activity which should be handled differently to achieve the same result with less effort. Engineers, for example, who normally carry their work through to drawings, might learn to sketch and let draftsmen take over at that point. An agenda planned and distributed in advance might cut down on meeting time. A speed reading course might help the technical writer digest source reports more quickly. Mechanized personnel data might contribute to improved upgrading systems in the employment office.

The individuals may be so involved in their work that they are unable to see the opportunity for improving it. They may link greater output only with greater effort. You as manager have the opportunity and responsibility to work with them to identify needed improvements. This may mean walking with them—figuratively speaking—through a typical day or encouraging them to keep track of their time in some detail for a number of days so that you can study it together. Often, the opportunity for improvement may cut across the work of several people, and a small task force can be helpful in identifying needed changes in procedure to reduce time or make the process more productive for the organization.

HOW YOU DO IT COUNTS

The way you go about getting an improvement goal incorporated into each professional worker's plans is of considerable importance. You need the employee's acceptance that this is an important goal and that it will contribute to better performance. You need to instill the feeling that it is possible to accomplish the goal, and that the work on it *now* is reasonable. How can you go about generating these attitudes?

First, involve workers in the formulation of goals. If they point out the need for something and the desirability of working on it, their acceptance is guaranteed. So begin by asking what they feel their improvement goals should be. Or ask them to study relevant data and recommend corrective actions. If the actions involve them, they have set their own improvement goals.

Second, show considerable thoughtfulness and interest regarding the amount of time needed to make the study and to incorporate their decisions into their work. If the employees feel that you are asking them to add this to an already full day, the reaction is very likely to be resentment. So if you can agree on some activity which can be carried at a minimal level or delayed until the improvement project is completed, you will show how important you feel that this kind of investment is, and the employees are more likely to see their efforts as reasonable.

Third, examine the worthwhileness of the goal with great care. If something else will be dropped or delayed to accommodate this work in the schedule, it deserves rather thoughtful evaluation to ensure that it is of higher priority. That is, will it have a higher payoff than the dropped or delayed item? You do this by asking questions to get a better definition of the expected result and to determine what time and resources are needed to achieve it, to clarify how it will be done.

Fourth, key it, if possible, to the employees' career interests with respect to this job or future advancement. Will they learn something which will make them more valuable? Will this project save enough time to devote toward a major effort which should result in added stature for them?

FIGURE 11-1   How to Gain Acceptance of the Improvement Goal

---

1. Involve the employee in formulating the goal.

2. Concern yourself with the source of time for goal accomplishment.

3. Make sure that the goal is more worthwhile than work it may replace.

4. Key it to the employee's career interests.

5. Make improvement goals a way of life in the organization.

Fifth, make "an improvement goal in every work plan" a way of life in the organization. Make all employees aware of the idea so that they expect to set a new improvement goal as soon as one has been reached. This way employees do not feel singled out in any unfavorable way by the process.

DON'T LET THE IMPROVEMENT GOALS
BECOME REPETITIOUS

You can give constructive help if you will prevent inertia from taking over in the selection of new improvement goals. After working on one or two goals, it is easy for the professional to select goals which do indeed represent improvement in his or her work but which channel the improvement along certain lines. The employee, for example, may continuously select projects involving the computerization of data or reports. After one or two such achievements, additions to personal knowledge become smaller and smaller. If your objective is literally to fight obsolescence as well as add to organization results, you need to help the employee "break set," explore less-known areas, and expose oneself to unfamiliar functions and concepts. You can do this by presenting several acceptable alternatives for the person to consider before he or she has chosen or by asking the employee to suggest a number of "next" goals which do not involve the well-used idea. In ways such as these his or her selection is limited to those that lead away from well-trodden paths, and the employee's self-determination will remain high.

YOUR PERSONAL VISIBILITY

All your efforts to help employees fight obsolescence are likely to be viewed with skepticism unless you demonstrate in your personal planning your determination to fight this in your own thinking and behavior. You need, therefore, in your personal work plans an improvement goal toward which you are also conspicuously working. If your manager is willing to help you in selecting it, you may avoid some of the more obvious pitfalls. But whether he is or not, a few general rules will help you select sound targets toward which the professionals in the organization will be willing to help you work.

Focus on an Improvement Contributing to the Results of the Organization, Not Merely Your Own Career. A growth or improvement target which readies you for a higher, more important position might interest you, but it will hardly be greeted with enthusiasm by other professionals. Instead, take a look at your managing work. Where do you spend most of your time? In meetings? In hiring new employees? In reviewing work progress? Pick an area that consumes a great deal of time, and assume there must be a better way of doing it. Talk to your manager. Talk to your associates. How do they do it? Pick up a current management book or article. Is there an idea there that could be modified to fit your needs?

Talk Over Your Goal with Employees. At a convenient meeting, tell them what you have been thinking about, what others are doing, what the literature says. How do they feel about your present method? Has anyone reported to another manager who had a different and better way? Get their ideas. You need their help to carry out any plans which involve them and to explain observable changes in your style or methods. In addition, your discussion may have a development effect, particularly if they are managers. You may in fact find their ideas quite useful. Above all, letting them work with you in this way emphasizes your interest in keeping current, in using the best practices known. It says clearly that upgrading competence is not something which is good for everyone else. You believe in it for yourself. You practice it. It is your way of life, too.

Put Your Experimentation on Display and Relay Feedback as You Get It. When you have finally decided on your improvement goal, let employees know what it is and the activities you plan to reach it. As you try new ideas and begin to find out how and under what conditions they work for you, tell them about it. If they were involved, by all means seek their reactions. Do not be hesitant about describing what did not work and why you think it did not. This openness on your part should provide a reasonable model for them with respect to their own improvement goals. Make it clear that you and they are not correcting deficiencies in any personal sense; you are all working to keep yourselves up to date.

RECYCLE THE WORK OF THE ORGANIZATION

Fighting obsolescence is a defensive mission. Recycling the work of the organization to meet changing conditions and influencing change itself are positive, forward-looking endeavors. To accomplish this recycling effectively, you need to devote considerable energy and personal creative ability to stimulate the innovative talents of the other professionals with whom you work.

When, as a group, you first developed your plans, there was a great deal of interpersonal stimulation. Each expressed his or her pet ideas, and they seemed new to the others. Through a process of information pooling, a great many ideas were elicited and argued. You were probably spurred on by this interaction, and when you finally made your decisions, you undoubtedly felt a sense of elation. When it was presented to higher levels of management and they eventually agreed, your enthusiasm was conveyed to your associates and carried over into the beginning of the work.

Two things happened, then, as work progressed. First of all, some of the limitations of the plans became apparent. Not everything went along smoothly or satisfactorily. Perhaps major clients or customers changed their minds or their specifications or shifted the focus of their interest. Perhaps competitors made unanticipated moves or another agency or institution announced a course of action which sounded better than yours. These events have a dampening effect. Second, as you work together more, the ideas you express lose their quality of newness. You have heard most of them before, so your interchange becomes less stimulating.

You must, however, redo the organization's plans. You must repeat the analysis of the value of your programs to current objectives. You must be sure that the department's goals reflect the firm's or agency's needs and that resources are allocated to match priorities. And you will not have a whole new staff each time the review is made. Here are a few suggestions for keeping your planning meetings out of the doldrums.

Assign Information Sources in Advance of the Recycling Meeting. Make a checklist, possibly with the help of the other professionals, of the information that you need to determine the continuing soundness of your programs. Identify the sources of such information. If the source is an individual outside your management area but within the firm or agency, invite that person to present the information to the group. The difference in his or her language and way of expressing things may trigger a different thought process. Differences in viewpoint may refresh the group. Do some switching of function to obtain information. Put the finance person, for example, on a manufacturing problem or the case-worker on a semi-legal problem or the copywriter on a layout problem. Assign individuals to information procurement duties prior to the meeting so that they come prepared to describe what they have learned.

Vary the Agenda of the Meeting. Think theater or drama. A "formula" for a meeting usually results in lack of interest. A participant tends to decide when it will be his or her turn and then "tunes out" to prepare that part.

Use Participative Devices. As a minimum, call on individuals to express their opinions, supply information, or report an event or finding. Deliberately set up debates to present opposing viewpoints. Assign the devil's advocate role to various individuals, giving them sufficient notice to prepare their positions thoroughly.

Use Feedback Devices. Once in a while, ask the participants to view the meeting as a process. Ask them to examine rather critically whether the objective was clear, whether it was met, how various members contributed, and how the meeting might have reached its objective more quickly.

Rotate the Chairmanship.   Become a participant occasionally. When a particular work program or topic is especially relevant to one individual's work, ask him or her to chair the meeting. You can still supply management inputs in the role of participant. Moreover, you might gain insights needed to improve your decision-making. In addition, of course, you provide a development experience for the chairperson, and you have the opportunity to observe that individual in a leadership role.

Rotate the Job of Recorder.   The recorder should keep track of questions at issue and final decisions made. Perhaps he or she can summarize on a blackboard or easel pad where the meeting stands—what has been agreed to, what assumptions have been made, what decisions are left hanging. This visible record focuses attention on cliff-hanging items and provides some sense of accomplishment as decisions are completed. If, following the meeting, the recorder issues a final summary to all in attendance and others who need to know, it serves a necessary communication purpose.

Match Your Manner, Speech, and the Pace of Meeting to the Urgency of the Problem.   If you want a thoughtful, quiet, reflective meeting, a fairly slow pace with adequate time for individual thinking and writing will help make it so. If you want a brisk, crisp affair and faster delivery, more urgency of manner will convey the message. If you have asked someone else to chair the meeting and feel that he or she is doing a reasonable job of it, try to match their mood or style. If you behave quite differently, the group will find itself in conflict over whose signals are to prevail.

Stop an Unproductive Meeting.   If, in spite of your best efforts, it becomes apparent that the meeting will not be productive, cut it off and schedule it for another date, if possible. Unproductive meetings can happen for a variety of reasons—lack of preparation, misunderstanding about objectives, a dull day, loss of spark or leadership from a key individual. Marathon meetings under the circumstances usually have rather low payoff. Participants grow weary. If the chairperson insists on staying in session until a decision is made, one will eventually be made, perhaps out of desperation. It is very likely to be regretted, reviewed, and remade at a later date after unnecessary expenditure of resources.

EXPRESS POSITIVE ATTITUDES
ABOUT CHANGE

Formal planning sessions devoted to recycling the work of the organization can only be held once or twice a year. During intervening periods, you must count on individuals to adjust their work appropriately. To encourage this, talk with enthusiasm about looking for change and keeping pace with it. Talk about creating conditions in which your product or service will be most welcome. Reward employees who have the courage to report that certain assumptions have not materialized or that they foresee obstacles and have worked out corrective plans. Give special recognition to those who quickly report competitor moves or leadership actions by others when these affect what you are doing. Keep track of how well you are able to outguess future events or how successfully you took early steps to create a favorable climate for your product or service. Help employees see the excitement of knowing objectively and precisely where work stands against plans and improve group problem-solving skills to translate this information into sounder plans for the future. You always have two objectives: to get off-schedule work which is still needed back on schedule and to do a better planning job, or better still to plan a better result for the organization to achieve if you can find an economic way to do it.

There is, of course, risk in encouraging change. But there is also risk in not changing—the risk that someone else will beat you, that the service will not be adequate, that the timing will be off. As manager, you may ask, "Is there *enough* risk?" and "Is it worth *this* risk?" Your judgment of the proper balance between the two will ultimately be tested by the responses of the customers, clients, or patients you serve.

II

RELATIONSHIPS
WITH
INDIVIDUALS

12

How to Help
the Beginner

Sooner or later in your managing career you will hire a beginner. In these days of emphasis on higher education, he or she will probably have a degree in a chosen field, and may even have a doctorate. The individual may have studied under a distinguished specialist and done independent research related to the work he hopes to do. In the best of all possible situations, your new employee has had a summer job in your firm or a similar outfit. Such prospects come equipped with basic knowledge, with apparent self-confidence, and with great enthusiasm for their work. Pre-employment psychological tests probably showed the person to be bright enough to handle complex problems and the pre-employment interviews probably indicated considerable drive and interest in this career. The beginner has not had time, of course, to establish a superb record of accomplishment, but his or her grades are good, he or she has had some campus leadership roles, and has managed to hold a part-time job to help with college expenses. This individual seems pleasant, warm with other people, and not easily offended. In short, he or she seems to have everything. You are pleased to have this new employee in the organization, and this new employee appears pleased to have joined it.

In a case such as this, and this one is deliberately over-drawn, you may be tempted to assume that you need to do little more for employees of such obvious potential than to give some "orientation." This usually means introducing the new workers to associates, pointing out the rest rooms, cafeteria, library and other facilities they may wish to use, and reviewing the organization structure in some detail. Then you can begin giving assignments.

A FIRST JOB IS CRITICAL

While such things are recommended in all the manuals on supervision, they are woefully inadequate to help a beginner make a rapid and successful transition to *professional* working life. Summer assignments are at best introductory and designed to get some needed things done or to substitute in a stop-gap way for those on vacations. More and more, they are a lure for the prospective college graduate who will shortly be available for employment. They almost never give the individual any sense of *organized* effort, of the meaning of individual responsibility within the framework of a complex working system, of the importance of relationships or the intricate meshing of one human being's work with another. In fact, in all likelihood, the beginning professional comes with a number of inaccurate preconceptions about the institution or agency which he is joining. These need to be supplanted with accurate information on which he may then make his own judgments.

Psychologists tell us that the basic personality of a child is formed during the first half-dozen years or so. Lifetime working attitudes and habits are also frequently formed during the first six months of "permanent" work. So it is worthwhile to give your attention to the problem of the beginning professional. What can you do to help this person begin building an early record of satisfying achievement? You have a personal stake in this too, since the contribution of each employee increases the total accomplishment of the organization and reflects favorably on your capability as a manager.

THE CASE OF ANTHONY MICHEL

An example makes it a little easier to get down to specifics. Later, general concepts can be drawn. Let's take the imaginary case of Anthony Michel, employed as a management trainee in Bank X. Tony has a Master's degree in Business Administration from a large, well-known university. His grades are excellent, and he is well recommended by his professors. As an undergraduate he majored in finance and minored in personnel administration. He deliberately chose this combination to prepare himself for a banking career, and he would like eventually to be a bank manager. He worked two summers as a teller in another organization. His first assignment is in the personnel office as an interviewer. While he will have this post only four months, he is pleased because he especially liked his personnel courses, and because he took an undergraduate interviewing course in which he got an "A."

When he reports for work, he attends the bank's one-day orientation program. He is given a presentation on the bank's purposes, its functions, and its major customers. He tours headquarters and is told about the branches and their locations. He learns about the benefit programs available to him and signs up for them. The president gives him a taste of the longer-range business objectives, and he is exposed to some of the other officers who explain their various responsibilities. He is given an overview of the kinds of assignments he will have on the training program and a rather general picture of probable opportunities for permanent placement.

GIVING THE FIRST ASSIGNMENT

The following morning he reports to his manager, who explains the function of the personnel office and assigns him to employment interviewing as his first experience. In an effort to be sure he knows what to do, he walks Tony through the first interview situation. He begins by reviewing the opening for which there are candidates to be interviewed. He suggests that rather than relying on the job specification form submitted by the supervisor, he should visit the individual, discuss the job in detail, look at equipment which the employee will use, meet some of the people with whom he will be working, and, in general, get a more complete picture of what is involved in the job. In this way, the interview will be more valuable. Tony does this. The next step the manager takes is to sit down with him and review the applications that have been submitted. Together they read through one or two, and the manager asks Tony whether the applicant is worth seeing or not and the basis for his evaluation.

When he is satisfied that Tony is able to do a reasonable job of screening resumes, he suggests that he call the applicants who appear most promising and arrange an interview with each. He recommends that early in the game Tony will want to allow about two hours for each interview. Later he can shorten this time, but he should not rush his first evaluations. He also makes a point of suggesting that Tony check with the hiring supervisor to be sure that this latter individual will be available if the candidate appears to be well qualified.

Prior to the first interview, the manager reviews with Tony the kind of information that the interview should provide and the way it should be recorded. Since Tony has had interview training, he lets him conduct the interview on his own. He does, however, review his findings and the completed paper work for the record.

Let's look at what the manager has done so far. He has given Tony a specific assignment. He has carefully filled him in on the information he needs for it, and he has done it step by step so that Tony is able to put it to use fairly quickly. Following each step, he has set up an immediate review of Tony's performance so that he can tell whether or not Tony has understood. If something is not clear, there is an opportunity to explain again and prevent further error. The manager is quite directive on matters where Tony is without experience. All these things make clear to Tony what the content and procedures of his job are. They do not, of course, help him develop the desire for achievement nor the ability to set professional standards for his work.

The inexperienced employee has no useful frame of reference for judging the quantity and quality of his or her work. Homework in school is usually assigned on the basis of what is reasonable to do before the next class. College courses may teach the student to try for "excellence" in terms of high grades. But what is "excellence" on the job? The first manager has the responsibility of helping the employee acquire realistic professional values on these points. Moreover, he or she must find a way to do this which will not build dependency on a manager but free the employee to set these for him or herself and to be dissatisfied unless he meets them. Returning to the story of Tony Michel, let's see how to do this.

INTRODUCE SOUND PLANNING CONCEPTS

Once the manager is convinced that Tony understands his basic work and does it with reasonable competence, he will want to initiate a discussion on standards of quality and quantity of work. He might begin something like this:

> "Tony, I think you've taken on your responsibilities very well. I, and perhaps more important, the people with whom you've been doing business have been very pleased with the way you've taken hold and with your sincere desire to be helpful. Those are valuable qualities in the banking business, regardless of your job.
>
> "So now I think you ought to begin to plan for things you can accomplish during the few months you will be in this job. It is too easy to settle into a daily routine in which you do as much as you can each day. You see, in business there is no professional job in which everything that needs to be done can be done. So the individual tackles this problem in the only sensible way possible. He takes a look at everything that is needed, estimates roughly how much effort is involved in each item, and then sets some priorities or decides what comes first or to what extent he should devote his effort in each area. It usually happens that if he really looks for it he can find some improvements he can make in the *way* he is doing things—some streamlining which cuts unnecessary time off some things and gives him a little more time for others."

GET THE EMPLOYEE'S SUGGESTIONS

> "I thought today we ought to talk about your job from that point of view. As a newcomer, you probably see things you feel should be changed which we who've been around awhile just take for granted. There may be good reasons for some of these things, but others may be just bad habits we've fallen into."

Notice that the manager has done two things here. He introduced the thought that it is both necessary and desirable to plan work so that the most important things receive the most attention and have a reasonable chance of getting done. He has also presented the thought that Tony, new as he is, is expected to contribute to the planning of his own work and to find ways for improving it. A new employee, even though professionally trained, is not expected to make the substantive contribution of a more mature, experienced person. But the concept of contributing to whatever plans are ultimately agreed upon needs early introduction.

SET PROPER PRIORITIES

The manager continues:

> "Let me start by saying that we have no choice about working to fill open jobs. This is one of the main reasons for our existence in the organization, and open requests are particularly heavy now because of the new computer installation with its requirements for programmers. I made a survey just six weeks ago to see what the recruiting load looked like for us, and here's what the bank supervisors said they needed."

He gives Tony the report with the figures and various categories of open positions. Tony studies it for a few moments and then says:

> "Some of these have been filled by now. Do we know where we stand at the moment?"
> "No, not exactly; you see we've also had some turnover, and I'm not sure just what the status is right now."
> Tony says slowly: "Well, one of the first things we ought to do is find that out and develop a method of keeping it current. . . . And some of these figures don't look reasonable to me. Since I've been here, we've only hired one programmer, and I see they're asking for 15 to 20 over the summer months. We either have to work out a more aggressive recruiting campaign or start an internal training program or maybe both."

This is excellent. Tony understood the manager's comments and is responding as an interested, intelligent employee.

> "Good. You're right about this. But programmers may not be the only critical manpower shortage. Perhaps you could see if there are others and work out special plans for taking care of them in some way. Training programs aren't in your bailiwick, you understand; you'd have to talk to George Heisel, the training director, about them. He might take some persuading because his budget is already tight. But if you develop your ideas as carefully for your sales pitch to him as you do for planning your work, I think you would be able to convince him."

Notice, the manager has introduced another idea—that of organizational relationships and the fact that frequently a *result* which the business needs is not obtainable by one individual's efforts. There are areas of specialization within an organization and the most desirable and most effective way of achieving a result is to make use of all the special knowledge, experience, and resources available within it.

TRY FOR IMPROVEMENT IN METHODS

"Are there any other things you've noticed that need improvement?"

Tony smiles. "Well, I think we're losing some good candidates because of the way we're handling them. When a person applies for a job and fills out the application blank, we send him away until we decide whether we have a suitable opening and whether there is a supervisor willing to talk to him. He sometimes walks right out of here and into another office and is hired. I know, because when I call to arrange for a full interview, I find he's no longer available."

"But if you saw every applicant right away, wouldn't that overload your time with interviewing so that you couldn't do some of the other things that need attention?"

"It might, but I think I could handle it by shortening the interview as soon as I realized he didn't have the qualifications. Of course, I'd have to be more familiar with the openings than I am right now. But with a little extra effort I think I could get over that hurdle. Anyway, I think it would make such an improvement in our hiring rate that it would be worth it."

Now the manager has generated some special interest in achieving a particular result, and it is one that the business badly needs—open jobs filled more quickly. He did it by a little mild questioning of Tony's suggestion, and the fact that Tony had to defend it to prove he is right has whetted his appetite. Things have really progressed quite well. Tony has moved from the mere attempt to learn what his duties are to the point of beginning to plan ahead and put first things first. He has developed a personal interest in what he is doing and how he is doing it.

The dialogue continues, covering other aspects of Tony's work, until it is apparent that there are indeed more things to be done than Tony is able to do or has the time and money to do. This is a critical point. Tony is willing to commit himself to more than his manager feels is realistic. If he throws cold water on Tony's enthusiasm, some of it may be lost. Yet the manager wants him to have enough success that he is encouraged to continue to work toward worthwhile, even though difficult, goals. Let us see what the manager does at this point.

KEEP THE RESPONSIBILITY
IN THE EMPLOYEE'S HANDS

"Tony, I hope you see now what I meant when I said earlier that practically every professional job has more to be done than is possible to do with our current resources. Rather than trying to make decisions right now, why don't you spend two or three days putting the various thoughts we've discussed on paper, figuring out about how much time each would take, and then come back with some recommendations of what things seem reasonable to tackle right away. Other items can be wait-listed for the time being. Just keep in mind that what the organization needs most from you is well-qualified candidates for open positions."

Tony agrees and goes off muttering: "And we didn't even talk about learning more about the qualifications of candidates!"

This is a good way to handle it. The manager has kept the responsibility in the employee's hands, although they had enough discussion to be sure that Tony has not overlooked any major items. Tony has the opportunity to make a thoughtful reevaluation of the total picture in the cold light of another day. Moreover, the manager's parting words remind him that plans must fit the needs of the organization and not merely represent what Tony feels would be "good" to do.

SECOND MEETING—MEASUREMENT: FRIEND OR FOE?

A few days later, Tony comes back to present his plans to his manager. After a little prompting, he begins:

"Since filling our open jobs is our most important function, I still think we should try to see applicants right away and see if it brings about the improvement I expect. So I suggest we do this for about three weeks to a month and see what happens."

"All right, Tony. I'll buy that. How will we decide whether or not it should be continued?"

Tony thinks for a minute. "Well, the number of offers we make per applicant ought to go up."

"How much greater do you think it should be?"

"I don't know, frankly, and I really don't know yet how much increased interviewing time there will be as a result of doing this. As I see it, offers have to increase enough to make the extra interviewing time worthwhile."

"Not offers, Tony, the numbers of hires has to go up or the length of time it takes to fill positions needs to decrease enough to make it worthwhile. I don't think we should set a target for ourselves until we've tracked the new system for a while and have some data. But could we agree that it wouldn't be worth doing if the extra interviewing didn't produce at least as many hires proportionately as the current interviewing does?"

"That sounds all right, but there are other factors, too. I'd guess I interview about 20 hours now for each job that's filled. I think under the new system there'll be wasted interviewing. But there'll be less wasted *advertising* and faster filling of jobs. Those two things ought to count."

"You have a good point, Tony. We both know what we're trying to do, and if it isn't working I know you'll try something else. So will you collect data for a couple of weeks and then we'll take another look? Even then the hiring data won't be complete, but we'll know more than we do now."

The manager has introduced the concept of measurement—not as a way of "ranging" the employee for poor work but as a way to *improve* work. He has also made it clear that while measurement of results is necessary, there is no sound way of setting a standard for Tony which would indicate when he has been successful. There is just not enough information and no past experience on which to make a judgment. Out of repeated looks at measurement data which reflect the situation, standards will gradually evolve.

REINFORCE THE NEED FOR MEASUREMENT

"Have you thought at all about the problem of improving the *quality* of the hires, Tony?"

"That's a rough one. I've thought about it, but I haven't reached any conclusion."

The manager makes a suggestion: "In the past, the number of new employees who have quit because they didn't like their jobs or who were transferred or fired for poor performance has run about 4 in 100. Using that same basis for measuring, could you try to get the number down to, say, 3 in 100?"

"I could try it, but I don't think that three or four months is long enough to tell. I'd be gone before you know whether I'd done it or not."

"That's true. Well, could you take an informal poll of supervisors whose openings you filled to see how well qualified they feel the new employees are?"

Tony is clearly interested and adds: "And another poll of the new employees to see whether the jobs are what they expected them to be?"

"That's a good idea."

"I do want to try some things to get better information about candidates, and I'd like to know how well they work."

"Well, don't forget to put the polls in your work plans, then. Getting supervisors to agree to fill out forms, working out the questionnaire, and finally sorting and compiling replies will all take time."

The manager has brought out the point that an employee wants a measure of what he accomplishes for his own satisfaction. He has also made it clear that measures and standards are often negotiable and that the employee is expected and should want to contribute to them. This is not always possible. Sometimes, the standard is "given" and no negotiating can be done except on how to reach it. Let's look at that situation.

WORK MUST MEET BUSINESS NEEDS

"Now about the programmers. What do you propose?"

Tony outlines his plans. The manager suggests some alternatives in a couple of instances. Finally, they reach agreement.

"Tony, you understand that we absolutely *must add* 15 programmers by the end of August. The bank won't be realizing its investment in the new, larger capacity computer if we don't."

Tony indicates that he understands but says: "You should know that we'll only make it, though, if we have all kinds of luck."

"I'm afraid there's no room for luck on this one, Tony. We'll accept any that comes, but it's really up to us to think of enough things to do to *insure* absolutely that number of additional programmers. Since this is so critical and we're so uncertain of the adequacy of our plans, let's look at progress on this project every week. If we're not making real inroads, we'll call in some other people for ideas and keep revising our plans until we're there."

Tony asks, "What happens if I don't make it?"

"What do you think?" his manager asks with a smile.

"I'm a failure."

"Well, Tony, *we're* a failure to be more exact. More important, the *bank* is the loser. So don't try to do this alone. Enlist the aid of everyone who will listen and even a few who won't."

"Will I be fired if I miss?"

"No, Tony, but you will have let the organization down badly."

"It seems unfair—there just aren't enough trained programmers, you know."

"Reality isn't always fair, you'll find. But when a result is needed by a business, it is part of the challenge and fun to figure out how to get that result on time. The important thing here is that you aren't asked to do the impossible. There is just about no limitation placed on the money or help you can have on this program. You are merely asked to develop a good plan, organize to get it done, and ask for what you need. It'll take some ingenuity and very careful following of the results of all the actions you take. We'll all help. Are you willing to try for the hard one?"

Tony says yes somewhat dubiously and leaves with the statement that he'd "better start working on the programming thing right away."

Notice that the manager didn't soften the result or imply that since Tony was a beginner, no one would expect him to meet the goal and the standard set for it. If he accepts responsibility for the result, he must take responsibility for the success or failure that goes with it. Tony's job, you may be sure, has now assumed new dimensions. He no longer thinks of it as one in which he comes in at 9:00, does his work, and goes home at the end of the day. Suddenly he is keeping track of data which describe what he is doing and what results he gets. He has, in effect, put himself under self-observation. He has some long-range work to prepare for an end-of-assignment survey which will tell him and the world how well he did in recommending candidates for openings. (He had better brush up on his interviewing and reference checking techniques, because now they are suddenly "for real.") And he has the responsibility for the success of the programmer recruiting which is urgent.

From these discussions, Tony should have grasped the importance of planning work, focusing on organization needs, and on better ways of doing work. He should understand the use of measuring the effect of his actions in order to improve them the next time. He does not, of course, understand all of the implications, but his feet are wet. His manager should try now to reinforce the point about using specialized talent wherever it is in the organization. And he should help Tony be objective, interested, and fearless in looking at results against plans. The latter is difficult, but if it can be done, the manager will have given Tony one of the most valuable gifts that a professional employee can have.

THIRD MEETING—PROGRESS REPORTING

The manager meets with Tony the following Monday morning. It is the first review of action against the programmer recruiting plan. He knows that no startling results can possibly have been reached in a week's time. Having suggested that the matter is urgent enough to review on a weekly basis, however, he wants to follow through as discussed. In addition, he wants to use this meeting and those that follow to establish an interaction pattern between himself and Tony which will reinforce the basic concepts that he has already put forth. He wants to help Tony see how to use them in practice. He also wants to give him the benefit of his personal experience in similar situations. Even more important, he wants to create a climate for reviewing work which will be developmental for Tony and help him acquire sound attitudes about planning, accomplishment, and anticipatory problem-solving—that is, the ability to foresee obstacles and plan how to get around them or minimize them.

ENCOURAGE CANDOR

Tony comes to the meeting bringing papers and charts. He is by himself. His manager expected this, but it is one of the things that he hopes to change. He wants Tony to learn that he cannot obtain the needed result by himself and, therefore, must involve others in its accomplishment.

> The manager prompts: "How's it going?"
> Tony begins by giving a fairly elaborate account of what he has done in the past week—additional advertising in local newspapers, discussion with the training specialist, intensive review of job requirements.
> "Of course, it's too soon to expect any results yet."
> "What's your estimate, Tony, of the results these actions will bring us eventually?"
> "To be honest, I'm not sure they're going to help very much," he says after a moment. "You see, the supply is just so small that there aren't enough qualified people to go around. There's no real *reason* why a programmer looking for a job should come to us. We have no more to offer than the next guy. And unless I increase the number of applicants to be interviewed, knowing the job requirements won't help me."
> "That's good reasoning, Tony. I don't have to tell you that I'm not delighted to hear that we've spent time and money with only a small hope of progress.

But I *am* pleased to learn you've thought the problem through to the point where you can make an accurate evaluation, *and* you've done it soon enough that it isn't past repair."

Notice that what the manager says *encourages* Tony to make an accurate judgment about what he has done, even though it represents bad news for the organization. At this point in Tony's development, criticism of his ineffective efforts, perhaps justifiable in the case of a more experienced employee, would probably keep Tony from making such frank evaluations in the future. His manager gains more by rewarding the frankness.

ENGAGE THE EMPLOYEE IN PROBLEM-SOLVING

Tony has presented a problem. This is the moment for his manager to help him learn how to recognize it is there and work objectively toward its solution.

> "You raise an interesting point. You say we have nothing more to offer than any other establishment. I wonder if we shouldn't talk this thought over with the Manager of Computer Operations. If she understood the issue, perhaps we could work out something that would make us more attractive to applicants. Shall I ask her to join us?"

Tony agrees and the Computer Manager comes into the meeting. Out of the ensuing discussion a training program leading to broadening assignments and possible advancement is developed for new recruits. As the three talk, they realize that they know very little about potential applicants. They really do not know what represents "opportunity for advancement" to such employees. It is clear, too, they need to know more about sources of employees, what they like and dislike about their jobs, what appeals are likely to hit home.

> The manager suggests: "Tony, I'm wondering if our advertising agency could help us investigate some of these problems. Could you spend some time with agency personnel this week to find out what they might do for us? If they have some ideas, you might ask one of their representatives to join us next week to tell us about them."
> Tony agrees. "Even so," he says, "chances are still not good for hiring enough experienced people. I still think we ought to select some promising employees already working in our bank and train them."

There is general agreement on this, and the manager asks the training specialist to come in to discuss the matter. He comes in, and it is clear that he is somewhat reluctant to add to his programs. Yes, Tony has already talked to him about this, but who is to do the training, and how are they to know who are trainable, and the whole thing is too expensive! The Computer Manager then has an excellent idea.

> "I'm sure the computer manufacturer has run into this before. Perhaps he has training programs and some selection devices. Let's talk to the service rep and see what we can find out from him."

The meeting breaks up on this note.

OBJECTIVE ANALYSIS PERMITS CHANGE IN ACTION

The manager wants to reinforce a couple of ideas with Tony.

> "I hope you realize that it was because you took such an objective look at the problem and reported your unfavorable evaluation so frankly that we were able to develop new courses of action that show much greater promise than the original plans. I hope you see too, Tony, how many good things happen when a number of people become actively involved in a problem. This doesn't mean that we should avoid doing our own thinking or use other people's talents carelessly. It is often the case, though, that a result is only obtainable through the efforts of a number of people, and each of us needs to learn to organize the efforts of others effectively—even when they don't report to us. The Computer Manager is probably the person most interested in the bank getting enough good programmers. Yet she might easily have sat back and blamed 'personnel' for failing to recruit. Actively involving her in the problem helps her contribute to her own success."

The weekly program review meetings continue. Tony automatically invites those who are contributing to results to attend. If they cannot, he gets information from them and reports it. His manager continues to reinforce the idea of measuring results objectively. This leads to the improved identification of problem areas, which in turn sparks sounder future courses of action.

The story has progressed far enough to illustrate how a manager might work with a new employee. The points to keep in mind when working with an individual who hopes to build a professional career are:

1. Show the need for sound plans which meet key organization needs.
2. From the beginning, encourage contributions to the formulation of plans and the measurement of progress against them.
3. Help make commitments of quality and timing which are realistic and match organization needs.
4. Help evaluate progress objectively and accurately by building measurement devices into the original plans.

5. Show how to use measurement to work out solutions *in advance*, and to change the course of action to bring about improved results.
6. Explain the importance of getting needed contributions from others and how to involve them in obtaining important results.

You do these things through your interaction with the beginner, questions which expose problems more clearly, your receptive attitude, your insistence on obtaining recommendations and evaluations, and your "give-and-take" discussions which force the employee to question what you say and defend what he or she says in an effort to reach a sounder agreement and generate greater dedication.

With an inexperienced employee, you probably have to give more information, make more suggestions, and do a little more "paving the way." The net effect, however, should be rapid learning for the employee and improved results for the organization.

13

Over the Hill?
What to Do
About It

Some day you will find that you have inherited or unwittingly hired a professional who seems to have retired mentally. The employee may be any chronological age; past records hopefully show some solid accomplishment and some experience which the organization needs. He or she is probably an individual worker, but also may be a manager, in which case the situation has additional complications. That this person presents you with a number of problems is an understatement. The apparent marginal involvement and commitment to work makes it likely (or at least makes you suspect) that output is below standard. The professional's negative attitude unfavorably affects the attitudes of associates, including you. Failure to give wholehearted support to organization efforts, "let-well-enough-alone" ideas, and failure to contribute from personal experience in group discussions (except perhaps to point out why something cannot be done) infuriate some coworkers, dampen the enthusiasm of others, and result in his or her exclusion from informal decision-making conferences and spur-of-the-moment work discussions. This, in turn, reinforces the lone wolf tendency and leaves the individual in the position of working without the informal information so valuable to good team effort.

If this employee totally failed to meet assigned goals the problem would be almost simple: dismissal. But no such black-and-white situation exists. The professional has the ability and experience to do the work and does it passably. Frequently, deficiencies in output can be directly traced to the fact that he did not have needed information. And this can be traced to the fact that the individual *was* excluded from an informal discussion at which certain work decisions were reached which everyone forgot to report. You under-

140

stand why he or she was not included and feel that it is mainly his or her fault. But to talk this over with the employee would involve you in personality and attitude considerations which you are not sure you can handle and which you feel might make matters worse.

You could, of course, refer this person to the personnel office for counseling or to an outside consultant. This may well be the best thing to do in the long run. But meanwhile you want to be sure that you are taking reasonable managerial actions to encourage participation as a full member of the organization and complete use of talent.

In an effort to analyze, understand, and find ways of coping with this almost universal problem, let's take an example and work out some specific discussions and actions you might take to help such an individual.[1] From this we can draw some general principles and recommend sound practices which you will find useful when faced with this problem.

THE STORY OF HARRY ANDERSON

Let's call the employee Harry Anderson. Harry works for an electronics firm. He is 56 years old, a mechanical engineering graduate and, except for his Army service, he has always worked for this company. After a short time in engineering, he made the switch to manufacturing and has remained in this function ever since. By most standards he has been reasonably successful. Early in his career in manufacturing he redesigned some critical factory equipment. His design is still in use, and it has been very satisfactory from the standpoints of improving component quality and cutting the cost of manufacture. His later manufacturing engineering efforts continued to show inventiveness of a very practical kind. Moreover, he ran the shop for eleven years, and while some of his old performance ratings indicate that his relationships with hourly employees were not as good as they might have been, he does have an excellent record of meeting commitments.

When top management placed increased emphasis on product reliability, he was given this assignment for some of the key product lines. He dug into this field, went back to school to brush up on his math, and took several statistics courses. The statistical approach was not, in his opinion, fully satisfactory, and he showed considerable ingenuity in devising component and product tests which rounded out reliability information. Also during this period he was credited with important contributions to the design of test equipment. A small group of professional employees reported to him when

[1]For an excellent description of the effects of age and how the unfavorable ones can be minimized, while the favorable ones are capitalized on, see the pamphlet. "The Older Director—His Limitations and Advantages," published in 1960 by the Institute of Directors, 10 Belgrave Square, London, S.W. 1, England.

he managed the reliability function, and the record shows no problem in the human relationships area.

Eventually, defense production was cut back drastically, and the firm's emphasis switched to greater development of new products. There was a corresponding drop-off in reliability work, and Harry was asked to return to manufacturing engineering. There were two other engineers in the group and Harry had the title of "manager," although the greater part of his effort was devoted to engineering work connected with making the new products more producible. After he had been on this job for about six years, he moved to his present position which is also manufacturing engineering. The responsibilities are not too different, but the situation represents quite a change.

HERE IS THE SITUATION

Harry's new manager is Ken Stone. He is a product manager responsible for piloting a hot new product through its design, development, and early manufacturing stages. A few months ago Ken needed someone with Harry's experience. When he saw Harry's resume, he felt that it matched needed qualifications almost perfectly. Ken's discussion with Harry confirmed that he had exactly the know-how required. Former managers corroborated his accomplishment. There was no indication of "poor personality" or "bad fit" or "low motivation." Ken's organization is small; its members are young and enthusiastic about the new product, but they are relatively inexperienced. Ken feels that Harry will be a good balance and will bring mature, practical thinking to the organization.

Ken is not a new manager. He is, however, very anxious to advance, and this job is his first chance at running all aspects of a business. So it is quite a testing period in his career. At his first meeting with the newly formed group, he presents the market forecast for the new product and discusses in some detail what needs to be done to make this forecast come true. This includes the urgency of getting the product on the market ahead of the competition and at an attractive price. He feels some uneasiness when Harry takes very little part in the discussions and is distressed to hear him say to one of his associates on the way out of the meeting:

> "Here we go again! How many times have I heard the same pitch. We'll never be able to make that product for that price with all the overhead we have to carry in this company. Oh, well, they'll find out."

During the next month, Ken's uneasiness turns into discouragement. When he asks for reports or information, Harry's is always the last to come in. Two of the men complain that Harry's work schedule will delay introduction of the product. When Ken asks Harry if he can tighten up his timetable, Harry says "Sure, we can do anything on *paper*."

One night, about five minutes after quitting time, Ken goes out to talk to Harry at his desk, but he has left for the day. It is very clear that he is not giving up any personal time for his work!

Harry looks like a hiring mistake. But because Harry has so much experience to offer, a good record of accomplishment, and so much seniority with the company, his manager really cannot in good conscience fire him. Moreover, to find a replacement now would mean automatic delays that would hurt the product program. What can Ken do?

If you are in this or a similar situation, you should recognize the difficulty of the problem you are facing. In some cases, there may actually be physical changes which limit the employee. In the case being discussed, the man seems too young for this, and the problem is more likely his attitude. But changing attitudes is also an area in which managerial tools are weak and odds for improvement are not high.

While facing the fact that he may not be successful, it is certainly worth the manager's intelligent effort to take reasonable steps to help the employee become more productive. The material which follows describes one approach he might use.

EXPLORATION—GET THE FACTS

First of all, the manager needs more facts. While it is possible "to change overnight," it is unlikely. Current attitudes and work habits probably have been developing gradually. Since former managers mentioned nothing about lack of enthusiasm, unwillingness to work with others, and similar characteristics which have been so prominent since Harry took the new job, Ken needs to explore these behavioral points to find out if they did, in fact, exist earlier or whether something has happened to Harry in his personal life which has caused the change or whether something about the new position has been responsible.

He begins with two or three phone calls to former managers or associates.

> "We have our work pretty well planned for the next few months, and now I'm giving some thought to individuals in the organization—what their career interests are, what opportunities they have for improving the effectiveness of their work, and what things I might do to help them. You know Harry Anderson as well as anyone does, and I wonder if you could give me your thoughts about him from this point of view."

Notice how the manager handled his inquiry. It would be very easy for word to spread that he is dissatisfied with the employee's performance. This could hurt the employee's future career, and, if the word got back to him, which is probable, would make the manager's chances of working with him to correct the situation much poorer. He, therefore, states the problem truthfully but in a way that will not hurt the man and is likely to please him if he hears about it. Moreover, asked this question in this way, almost any self-respecting ex-manager would do his best to give the requested information.

It is important to work a little on the technique of getting information. If the ex-manager comes up with no areas for improvement or none close to things you have been observing, you ought to have a laundry list of questions ready for him which cover the specific negative points that you have observed. In our example the manager might be prepared to ask: What about his relationships with associates? What about his willingness to give his full talent to his work? Does he express his opinions clearly and openly so that he makes a sound contribution to technical and administrative decisions? Did you find that he was willing to give personal time when necessary to get his part of the work done?

Then, in an effort to get information about specific things you might do to encourage better performance, you should have a set of questions ready about how the former manager worked with him. Again, illustrating from Harry Anderson's case, they might be something like this: Was it necessary to give him any special attention? How did you handle the situation if you needed a tighter schedule than he proposed? How did you keep him informed of all the decisions that affected his work? Did you give him any special responsibilities of a prestige type?

Back to Harry Anderson and his manager . . .

After careful, planned discussions with former managers, Ken Stone goes over the information he obtained. There are very few new things—his preemployment checking had given him most of the same information. Harry had not been a prima donna. His work was good. He cooperated well. He fit in with the organizations in which he worked. He had given fully of his personal time—in fact, had been a leader in employee off-job activities. He was an ardent golfer and had chaired a number of employee outings. He had done his share in the community, too—had been chairman of the plant's United Fund Campaign one year. These last *are* changes. Since coming to the new organization he has not participated in after-hours events.

One other new and important piece of information came from a former manager. Five years after the reliability organization was folded back into the inspection set-up, Harry was considered for promotion. He was a candidate for the Production Manager's job.

"He was a good candidate, too. Lost out mainly because of his age. I talked to him afterwards myself. Gave him the facts and he took them well and went back on the Manufacturing Engineering assignment. Shortly after that your opening turned up. He took it and, well, you know the rest."

This conversation makes Ken stop and think. Why did Harry take this job? It did not represent an upward move to the company, and at his salary, it did not even mean more money for him right away. Ken had assumed that the idea of launching a new product would be exciting to Harry. On thinking it over he realizes that this may not be true. For Ken it is a "first"—not so for Harry. For Ken it represents a way to advance his career dramatically—not necessarily so for Harry.

Ken should not fall into the trap of trying to be a psychologist and draw conclusions from the limited information he has. About all he really knows at this point is that Harry *has* changed, and that the change is recent. He knows that Harry was not promoted and was told that it was primarily because of his age. He is not even sure that Harry wanted the Production Manager job. He needs a lot more information, and Harry is probably the only reasonable source for it.

ASK HARRY

Ken's problem is to ask Harry how he felt about losing the promotion without having him withdraw even more. He *could* hold a performance appraisal discussion with him and give him a frank evaluation of his performance so far. But this would force him to point out all the things that have been wrong and might well put Harry on the defensive. Ken needs a more constructive approach than that. He decides that a career planning session might be sound, providing it avoided the implication that he wanted Harry out of the organization.

Ken's decision is sound. A well-handled career planning discussion implies that the manager sees a career ahead for the employee. If a man is truly concerned about his age, this should be a constructive move. The important thing is to set up the session so that the employee sees it as an honest effort on his manager's part to be of help in working out career advancement plans. It usually takes several meetings to get at and begin to solve any problem as important and deeply personal as choosing effective career action. This is even more likely to be true when there are fewer than ten years of career to plan for. It is hardly an idealistic exercise at this point. This has its advantages of course. The fact of its reality makes it more likely to be productive.

SESSION ONE—SET THE STAGE

Ken goes out of his way to bump into Harry in the hall.

> "Say, Harry, I've been wanting to get together with you for a few minutes. Do you have time now?"
>
> He has, and they go off to the manager's office.

Ken begins: "Harry, I feel a very special responsibility in your case, taking you off an important and relatively secure job and bringing you into this slot. As you know, we need you desperately, but if we fail to make the product launching on time, we may both be looking for another assignment."

Harry: "Well, I can always retire early if I have to, so don't worry about me."

"I'm not worried about you in that sense. It's just that when a company has a man with as much experience as you, who has made as many solid gold contributions as you, it's awfully important to find ways of maintaining that contribution level for the company's benefit. For the others here, just about everything they're doing is new, and so it takes everything they've got to keep their heads above water. But for you it's old hat for the most part. So I thought we ought to get to know each other a little better and have some plans for your work which incorporate some of the things *you* want out of life as well as the commitments you know I need for the organization. If we make a date now to discuss it, would you give some thought to your personal objectives for, say, the next two to three years and how they might be incorporated into your work? I realize you may not be able to be very specific. Most of us don't really have very clear ideas of what we want out of life. On the other hand, you've been around this company a while, and you may have some definite ideas. Anyway, let's talk about them."

Harry agrees and they set the date.

You may think that the manager introduced the idea of the session pretty quickly and did not give the man much opportunity to discuss the matter. The point is that the employee will react much more soundly on this subject *after* he has had time to think it over. So just make certain that he understands what the discussion will cover and gets a general impression of good intention and personal interest. The reaction, discussion, and interaction can come later. Notice that the manager asked for recommendations covering the next two to three years, thus keeping the focus on the short term. That is important; it adds to the likelihood of reality.

SESSION TWO—TIGHTROPE WALKING

In this session, Ken wants to find out what Harry expects of himself and his work during the next few years, to learn the reason for his change in attitude and interest in his job, and to reconcile the two and begin to identify ways of restoring his old level of contribution. Since neither of the men knows the other very well, they have no reason to expect a frank, open discussion. Tightrope walking is likely to be the order of the day. For Ken, this means more preparation, more careful phrasing of questions, more reflection before replying to Harry's questions, and careful observation of his reactions. Any signals that he is hurt, withdrawing further, or covering up may suggest postponing the remainder of the discussion to a more favorable time. The important target is to get the problems out on the table so both parties understand them and can go to work on them.

Ken begins: "To set the record straight so that you know how I feel about it, I've been giving quite a bit of thought to the job you're on. I want to make sure that it uses every bit of the know-how you've developed over the years. As nearly as I can tell, it does capitalize very well on your experience. Maybe it over-capitalizes! By that I mean that there are a few elements in the job that you haven't done many times before. How do you see it?"

Harry: "I agree. I've done it all before. Of course that doesn't mean it's easy or that it doesn't take a lot of thought to make it come out right, but basically I can anticipate most of the troubles we're apt to have. And some are certain to happen no matter what we do. I guess that discourages me a little. Somehow it seems as if we ought to be able to prevent more failures."

"I agree with you on both these points, Harry. Moreover, I think we *can* prevent more from happening today than we could a few years ago. I'm really counting on you on that score. But since the work isn't new to you, Harry, I feel we should deliberately plot to introduce some new twists in it so that you keep your good reputation—even add to it. Do you have any thoughts on how to do that?"

"Yes, I have. And at my age, I think I ought to be able to look forward to retirement and plan for things I can do when I'm on pension."

"I don't think that's a bad idea at any age, Harry, but unless you really have early retirement in mind, it probably isn't the *only* thing to plan for. You know if we're successful with our new product, you'll really have your hands full. We'll need far better production facilities and more automated equipment and a much larger planning staff. You'll have to work much more closely with engineering, too, so that our designs are realistic. You'll need inventory controls and warehousing arrangements and quality checks and refinements that right now with our handmade operation seem unnecessary."

Harry laughs. "If all that happens, you'll want a younger man in the job."

"Harry, age isn't important; but doing things right *is*. So everything depends on your contribution up to that point. You're here because you have the know-how we need. Why all this talk about age and retirement as if you were over the hill? If you feel you are, that's something we'd better talk about. How *do* you feel about it?

Harry: "I never felt anything at all about it until I missed out on that Production Manager's job. That was a job I really wanted, but they said I was too old for it. I wouldn't have minded so much, perhaps, but then they put me back on a job I'd done years ago. It started me thinking that I better look after myself, spend more time with my family, enjoy life a little more."

"And have you?"

"Well, I've taken more time for myself, but I can't honestly say I've enjoyed things more. My wife says I'm a crab since I took this job, and I guess the other fellows think so too, because they leave me out of things."

"You seem to have dropped some of your extracurricular activities, too."

"Well, with a new job I thought I should, and then maybe I ought to be giving the younger men a crack at some of those things."

Ken doesn't quite know what to say and is quiet. Harry continues:

"I guess they were right about my being too old, you know. Since I joined this organization, I've realized just how right they were. I simply don't fit any more. These young fellows have so much energy, and they're so optimistic. I just can't seem to go along with them."

More silence, but nothing further is volunteered. Ken says rather slowly: "Harry, I don't agree with your analysis of your situation. You've built a case for yourself around a few thoughtless words and actions. As a fine, practical engineer you know how dangerous and misleading that can be. Now that I know how you feel, let me do a little thinking, and you do a little more too. Let's get together again on Thursday. The thing I want to make clear right now is that I have no such pessimistic view of you or your work. As a matter of fact, I feel your *best* contribution can be made during the next few years if you want it that way. This is the time for you to capitalize on all your experience.

Let's look at the discussion so far. The manager was lucky. With a minimum of probing Harry seemed to open up. It could equally well have developed that the employee refused to talk, sparred with his manager, or said the "right" things in order to deflect further probing. Any of these would have reduced the likelihood of improved attitude. Notice that the manager did not try to cover too much ground at one time. He states his case in positive terms. He wants the present job to challenge Harry, and he sees growth opportunities ahead. But he is also factual in pointing out what is required of Harry for the better job. As soon as Harry expresses his feelings, he closes the meeting. This is sound. Such a "confession" is likely to have been very difficult; it is enough for one day. But he sends the man away on a clear note of confidence.

SESSION THREE—WHAT CAN WE DO?

Now that at least one problem is out on the table, Ken needs to consider it objectively. The man has been told that he is too old for a certain promotion. This has undermined his confidence; he interprets everything that happens as reinforcing the idea that his age impairs his value to an organization. He viewed the return to a job done earlier in his career in this way. He feels the difference in his approach to his responsibilities from that of his present associates stems from the same issue. Fortunately, his change in attitude is relatively recent, so the chances of minimizing it are probably better.

Ken is sure that the work builds on Harry's strengths—on the knowledge and the skill he has demonstrated in the past. He recognizes that he needs to change the present work situation so that it will no longer appear to reinforce age as a negative factor. He also has a confidence-rebuilding job ahead of him. When he meets Harry again, he is ready.

> "Harry, I'm convinced that your evaluation of your status for contribution and growth in this company is way off base. It is premature to say the least. I asked you to join us *because* you have had the tremendous experience you've had. The age goes along with that. You know that you couldn't get the same experience in half the years. As I told you the other day, I don't believe this is a dead-end job for you. If you get the pilot line operating successfully, there's a much bigger job ahead. I can't promise you that job. After all, maybe the new product will be a flop, or maybe someone will decide *I'm* a flop, and I won't be around to keep a promise. But the opportunity is there, and it's a real one.

Maybe you don't want it; I realize that. But I'd like to ask you to think through what you do want. I don't mean to eliminate all thoughts of your retirement period. Instead, I want to help you get a better focus on them. How does that sound to you?"

"It sounds fine. But you know maybe I really am too old. . . ."

"Well, let's find out, Harry. Just to be on the safe side, why not have a thorough physical by your own doctor or our company doctor? Let's see about your physical condition. It wouldn't do any harm either for you to sit down with a professional counselor to talk about the changes you can expect in yourself. Maybe the thought doesn't appeal to you, but let's hear what a counselor has to say. Let's get some facts to work with and less speculation. What do you say?"

Ken has been watching Harry's reaction closely. He seems to be buying, and Ken is relieved when Harry agrees.

"Now about retirement . . . I don't think too many people stop one career and plunge into something totally different. I think it sort of evolves from the things they've been doing. And I don't think you're the sort of man who could just stop everything and sit in a rocking chair."

Harry smiles. "I guess not."

"Do you have any ideas about what you might do? Would you, for instance, like to teach or write a book or two that young graduates could read and learn some of the things you've learned the hard way?"

Harry smiles even more broadly. "No, I'm not the academic type. I really don't believe I'd be any good at teaching—just wouldn't have the patience. As for writing, that's the hardest and worst thing I do. You ought to know that just from my poor reports that are never on time."

"Well, then, think about some things—what you want to be in this company during the next few years and some beginning retirement plans—for working, I mean, not for leisure."

This session has been pretty directive. The manager is taking a risk that the advice of the doctor or psychologist may be negative. But he feels that the man should take steps to inform himself on the effects of age on his work and activity level so that whatever decision he makes is based on reason rather than emotion. He is also in danger of Harry's becoming overly interested in retirement. But the manager counts on Harry's maturity and practical nature to balance out company and personal interests.

SESSION FOUR—SOME SPECIFICS

By the time Ken and Harry meet again, there has already been a noticeable change for the better. The doctor has given Harry a clean bill of health with a few warnings about diet and exercise. The counselor has been quite frank in pointing out probable slower learning and reaction time, both of which are counterbalanced by his high experience level.

This time, Harry starts off the conversation.

"First of all I *want* that better job with this organization if it opens up. And I've been thinking about the longer range future, too. Does it sound ridiculous to think about working for the government to help some underdeveloped nations improve their manufacturing capacity? I understand it's one of their major problems, and it's something I surely know. It wouldn't take a lot of extra effort. In my spare time I could read up on these countries—what they're like, and so on. What do you think?"

"It sounds great *and* it sounds practical to me. Moreover, I suspect that what you're doing with us now is pretty close to what you'd be doing with them later. By all means look into it further."

Things are looking up. The manager may be tempted to think that the problem is solved. In reality, it may only be partly identified. The steps he and Harry take from here will determine whether Harry's contribution can be bought up to the needed level and whether he will be better accepted by his associates.

SPECIFIC FOLLOW-UP ACTIONS TO TAKE

The manager must now help Harry focus on improving his output and his teamwork. Ken needs to provide a climate which will reinforce Harry's renewed confidence in himself, but not at the expense of relationships with other employees. These are major tasks and require added investment of Ken's personal managing time.

Step one would clearly seem to be the redefinition of Harry's work goals. They should be redefined in such a way that he contributes to them and accepts what is ultimately decided upon as worth doing and realistic of accomplishment. Ken realizes that planning with his associates—the way it was done the first time—produced defensiveness and withdrawal, so this time he and Harry should do their negotiation in private. When they are both proud of Harry's plans, they can be exposed to the rest of the organization.

Next, since Ken wants to increase Harry's interest and desire to meet his commitments, he should limit the detailed scheduling to relatively short-term activities of about two- to three-months' duration and work out frequent views of progress, possibly bi-weekly or monthly. In this way, he and Harry keep in close touch, and Ken has the opportunity to watch how things are going.

These steps are likely to keep the work on target, but they may not help the relationships problem. If Harry is to be a strong, independent team worker again, this must also be solved without confiding Harry's personal problems to his associates. There are several solutions Ken might consider to improve the relationships angle. Since Harry has had so much more experience than the others, he might be asked to report at occasional meetings on problems previously encountered in similar situations. He might describe how they were tackled and the extent to which they were solved. The group might then be asked to analyze these experiences to see if they contain ideas and thoughts that might be useful now. This clear indication of the manager's respect for Harry's past experience may give him a little needed prestige with the group.

A second possibility, if his work status permits it, is to team Harry with one of his associates on a special, important assignment. As he works with his partner closely, respect may increase and a warmer feeling may develop between them.

A third possibility is to capitalize on Harry's golfing interest and get him involved again in the firm's ladder matches. It is possible that the more relaxed atmosphere may generate friendly give-and-take, thus making it possible for Harry to bridge the gap into the work situation.

Or, thinking of the job that may develop if the product is successful, Harry might be asked to be part of a team effort to develop a series of plans for expansion from pilot line to full scale production. There is at least a reasonable chance that in a different situation, with different associates and a high stake in the result, Harry may respond in his old way and eventually make the transference to his normal work.

It may be hard for Harry to change his behavior with associates, having once committed himself to a lone-wolf pattern. Yet, chances are reasonable for gradual improvement, if his manager will have both the patience and ingenuity to find ways for: 1) showing associates that Harry has an excellent contribution to make; 2) letting individual associates know him better in a variety of different situations which call for teamwork to which Harry can contribute; and 3) giving Harry opportunity (and reinforcement) to suggest ideas and thoughts in group discussions on topics where he is knowledgeable.

The point, of course, is that identification of the problem does not automatically remove it, and considerable effort on the part of all involved will probably be required before the total problem is solved.

SUMMARY AND IMPLICATIONS

Harry's story is contrived to make certain points. In real life, any number of things might have gone wrong. Ken Stone might never have gotten the information that he needed from former managers or from Harry. The "care-less" attitude might have been an old one with much less likelihood of change. The physician's report might have indicated severe limitations on the work Harry could do. The counselor might have reported serious learning or memory deterioration which would have prevented many of the recommended actions from having a useful result. At any stage of the process, the manager might have encountered strong resistance.

If one or more of these things had happened so that the manager saw almost no possibility of success, he would have had to change course, help the employee find work he could do, and set out to choose a replacement.

In the absence of such a conclusion, however, three responsibilities lead him to pursue his "rescue" mission—his responsibility to himself as a manager, his responsibility to the employee because of his past service and contribution, and his responsibility to the organization which needs this man's talents.

Here, then, are some useful guides for working with the "older" employee who displays signs of retiring on the job:

1. Get as much information about the employee as possible—past experience and contribution, and interests. This means the careful probing of former managers, associates and the individual. Look for the point when a change in attitude or performance was first observed, and try to find out what caused it. Get as clear an understanding of the problem as possible.

2. Obtain the advice of professionals—physician, psychologist, professional counselor—so that an accurate picture of the employee's health and state of mind is available and the chances for improvement estimated.

3. Build the job as much as possible around talents which have already been displayed. Capitalize on past experience.

4. Keep work developmental so that there are at least moderate demands to add to know-how in the course of the job.

5. Support the worker's efforts. Display confidence in the individual and in ensuing results, but do not compromise needed results in order to do so. Keep informal contact level high.

6. In making work plans with the individual, build goals with scheduled completion dates in the *short range*—usually two to three months at most.

7. See the person frequently—perhaps monthly—to exchange information on the state of his or her work and factors affecting it.

8. Find ways of developing specific assignments which will emphasize the value of past experience and which, if successfully accomplished, will give the deserved prestige and recognition.

9. If the employee is close to retirement—three to five years away—and it is reasonable to do so, help the individual build some activity into the job which will be preparation for the kind of retirement life planned.

These actions will not guarantee success. They will, however, raise the odds substantially that the employee will again be a productive professional worker.

14

Challenging
the Promotable
Employee

At some time in your career a most promising employee will work for you. This employee will understand the job thoroughly and perform it with competence, will contribute to associates' results and be of more than usual help to you in carrying out your managing responsibilities.

Your first task is to recognize this individual. Your second is to make the challenge. Neither of these is easy. Here are some of the problems involved. First of all, it is easy to focus on the discrepancies in performance and to visualize how differently *you* might have done a piece of work. This may prevent you from seeing the employee's potential. It is also easy to be so concerned about your own advancement that you view this person as a competitor and almost unconsciously discredit any accomplishments. It is, moreover, distressingly simple to dampen the enthusiasm of a dedicated employee, to exclude him from informal channels of communication, to make it harder and less desirable to do the job well. Even beyond this, it is possible to "hide" a capable individual, so that opportunities to move to another part of the organization just do not present themselves. Many of these things are unconscious, of course, but this does not lessen their unfairness to the employee or the resulting loss of talent to the organization.

AIDS TO EVALUATING EMPLOYEE
POTENTIAL

As a manager, one of your major responsibilities is to discover ability and channel it toward greater contribution. If you are a new manager and have little basis for comparing one employee with another, you need a rational way to make judgments about individual capabilities. Here are a few suggestions to help you do this: First, make a habit of checking out the performance of all employees with their former managers. There will be differences in standards among them, but their comments in defense of their evaluations will give you an understanding about how other managers make their judgments.

Second, seek the counsel of a qualified personnel specialist if one is available within the organization or an experienced management consultant, if this is within your budget. Such a professional can teach you to observe on-the-job employee behavior and learning time and help you understand how much growth you are asking of employees in the normal performance of their work and how much you could ask of them.

Third, make a habit of developing specific work plans with employees so that you have objective data as you jointly evaluate progress.

Fourth, have the courage to experiment with psychological tests—both individual and group—but get qualified personnel to help you do this. These tests may give clues to potential not otherwise available to you.

Fifth, do not hesitate to ask the employees how they feel about their work and their prospects for and interest in promotion. Their comments may not always be reliable, but they will make you aware of what they want you to know on the subject. You will thus be in a better position to understand some of their motives and to seek professional advice if you feel you need it.

These steps will not ensure your accurate identification of an employee's potential, but they will improve the likelihood of your doing so. Let's suppose that you have taken some of these steps and have made honest appraisals. You conclude that at least one employee who reports to you is promotable. Then what? The obvious answer is to grant the promotion to him. And, if all the conditions are right, that is undoubtedly the thing to do. Usually, however, a "right" opportunity is not immediately available or, if you are new in your job, you may feel it necessary to delay the move temporarily, or the employee may be working on an important problem which must be solved before such a step is taken. Regardless of the reason, there is usually a period of time in which you are working together, and you need to do your best during this period to contribute to the employee's growth.

THE CASE OF THE PROMOTABLE ACCOUNT REPRESENTATIVE

Once again, let's take an imaginary case and work through some typical situations. The manager involved is Manager of National Accounts for a private, nonprofit health insurance organization. He works with private industry to develop employee group health insurance plans at a cost to employees which reflects the actual utilization of health benefits. In the organization is a young woman who handles several key accounts. No one reports directly to her, but she is expected to function as a leader to obtain new accounts, work out the details of their contracts, and serve them after they are in-house. In addition, she periodically reviews any problems encountered in administering the plan for them.

There are three Account Representatives reporting to the manager, so he can make direct comparisons of their work. By all objective standards, Helen is the most successful. She receives complimentary letters frequently. She is in demand to address employee groups to improve their understanding of available benefits. Her relationships within the organization are excellent, and she seems able to get that "extra" effort out of the computer staff.

The manager feels that she is an excellent prospect for eventual promotion and wants to be of help to her in the meantime. What are some of the things he can do?

FIRST STEP—EXPLORATION

Since the manager is new to the organization, he decides to begin by finding out everything he can about Helen's qualifications. What was her education? What experience has she had? What do previous managers say about her? Do her personnel records corroborate past excellent performance? How much of her present job did she build and how much did she inherit from the previous incumbent? How long has she held the position? Does her salary reflect her performance to the extent permitted by current policies? What are her career interests? Does she want to remain in the health field? What other more responsible jobs might she hold? Are there gaps in her education or experience which ought to be closed or additional skills she ought to acquire?

Personnel records show that Helen is 33, single, a liberal arts graduate in mathematics with a minor in economics. She had one year of graduate work and began her career in accounting in a department store. She left after two years, giving as her reason "no opportunity to advance." Her next position was as supervisor of clerical personnel for a well-known charitable fund-raising organization for about three years. She joined this organization about five years ago, beginning as a statistical analyst. Because of her good work and excellent personal qualities, she was selected for the Management Training Program. After a series of assignments on this Program, she was hired by the National Accounts Department and promoted to the position of Account Representative about a year ago.

What Helen's Former Managers Say. The manager decides to do a little informal telephoning to get some off-the-record comments from former managers. The man who hired her changed jobs after only a few months. He remembers Helen very well and felt at the time that she showed considerable promise.

"Of course, our business was so new to her then that I couldn't tell how well she was going to like the work or how she would fit into it. I hired her as a statistical analyst. But she soon showed that she was also good at putting together visual presentations of the data and at making very persuasive explanations which often got other people to take long overdue actions. She's pretty convincing, you know, and yet not at all overbearing. She just makes certain conclusions inescapable."

Her present manager had observed this same skill, and he is pleased to have his appraisal confirmed. The manager asks for knowledge or experience needs that Helen might work on, but the ex-manager is at a loss. "I think she has everything she needs," he finally says.

The administrator of the Management Training Program emphasizes another aspect. He stresses how well Helen worked with others on all her assignments. He feels that her relationships with associates, with top management, and with servicing personnel were all unusually fine.

"She is always welcome, no matter whom she visits or on what difficult mission. The problem is that I don't really see a step for her. She's in one of our best jobs now, and to take over as manager of one of the units, well, there's never been a woman in a job like that, and the competition would frankly be pretty tough."

This comment reinforces the manager's awareness of his responsibilities. He owes the organization and Helen his best effort to sustain her growth and contribution and to help her realize progress toward her personal career goals. He realizes that he does not know what these are and that only Helen can give him this information. He therefore schedules a discussion with her:

"I just want to review your feelings about your job, Helen, and chat with you a little about your interests and your future. Don't make any great preparation. Just think about it a little and we'll discuss it very informally."

FIRST DISCUSSION—HOW HELEN
FEELS ABOUT HER JOB

The manager begins by letting Helen know how pleased he is with her work and that the others with whom she deals in servicing her accounts feel that same way.

Notice the manager does not open the discussion by giving Helen an appraisal of her strengths and weaknesses. If you are in a similar situation, give praise where it is deserved; be quite specific in giving examples, and avoid that great managerial sin of following the praise with a "but." Let your recognition of accomplishment and good personal qualities be honest and wholehearted.

"Helen, with someone in the organization doing as effective work as you, I like to take special pains to be sure that I'm contributing enough to your progress. That's, frankly, the reason for our discussion this morning. So I wonder if you would be good enough to talk to me about your job, how you see it, whether it's satisfying, and whether there are enough new things in it that you're still learning as you go along. Don't hesitate to say so if you feel that everything is pretty well under control and there are very few new problems to tackle. All of us try to get our jobs boiled down to a routine so that we can control results better. Yet when we've done it, the routine can get pretty boring."

"I'm not bored, Mr. Frankel." Helen laughs. "There is enough variety that that isn't possible. I never really know in the morning when I come to work just what I'll be doing that day. I may have it all planned, but then a phone call comes in from one of our accounts and the plan goes out the window."

"I'm glad you're not bored, but what about the more important question, are there opportunities to learn substantial new things about the health field?"

Helen thinks a minute. "No. I guess if I'm honest with myself and with you I'd have to say no. There *are* new problems, of course, but they're mainly variations of the old. It hasn't particularly bothered me because it's only recently that I've been through the whole cycle of developing a new account, working out the detail, setting up the system, and then servicing and reporting on it. This happened with the XYZ Company, and it was the first time through from beginning to end. The other accounts were all in different states when I took this job."

The manager thinks for a moment and says: "I guess there is still quite a bit to be learned from going through the cycle more than once. But we ought to begin, at least, to think about ways of broadening your knowledge."

"I'd like that, Mr. Frankel."

"Well, I feel I need to know a little more about you, Helen, and what you want from your working life. I'm told it's always a delicate matter to ask a woman about her career plans, but I don't see how you and I can do anything sensible together unless you help me set the compass in the general direction in which you want to go."

What are Helen's career interests?

"Ever since you mentioned you wanted to talk about that, I've been thinking about it very hard. And I guess I'll have to say I'm not sure. If I were to stay with this organization I know I'd like a managerial job, but I can't narrow it down more than that. I was a supervisor before, you know. I liked it very much and felt I was quite successful. That's perhaps one of the few things I miss here. But I also realize I may not be able to stay here and advance as rapidly as I'd like. The openings at higher levels aren't very frequent, and there are quite a few others eligible for them. I think I'm good, but I'm not so egotistical that I think I'm better than everyone else who might be eligible. That's pretty frank. I hope you don't mind."

"No. I'm glad you're realistic, Helen. I hope opportunities develop here for you, and if they do I'll certainly see that you're considered. But you're right— there is strong competition."

Helen continues: "You know that I work pretty closely with my assigned companies and every once in a while an opening occurs in one of these firms that I think I could fill. The ABC Company hired a Benefits Manager the other day, and if I just knew a little more about pension plans, I could do that job well. Of course, I don't know whether a job like that would be an advancement for me. I have no idea what they pay. But it *is* a managerial job."

"That's a good thought, and our organization would still be the winner in such a move, Helen. With your understanding of how we operate, you'd be an excellent 'customer.' But don't think I'm even remotely encouraging you to make such a move. You're doing a fine job for us, and we need you badly. Our organization will be expanding over the next few years, too. The main thing I wanted to learn was enough about your general interests that I could be sure your present job is rewarding for you and is helping you grow. Now that I have some idea of what's in your mind, let's try to develop some assignments that might teach you more about management. But let's face it. To make it worthwhile for both of us, whatever we come up with should add to the contribution you're already making as well as help you toward your career targets. We'll try to work something out the next time we review your accounts. Okay?"

Helen agrees and the discussion is closed on the thought that each will give this some attention before the next meeting.

Notice that the manager does not mislead Helen about her chances for advancement, even though he very much wants her to stay with the Agency. There is a strong temptation to overstate the likely future opportunities in a case of this sort in the hope that the employee will remain. This, of course, creates later and more serious problems if a promotion is not forthcoming within a reasonable period. Making it clear that positions are awarded on a competitive basis so that the employee faces that fact realistically and prepares himself to meet the competition is the soundest thing the manager can do. He balances his fairly tough appraisal of the promotional situation by his sincere display of interest in helping the employee learn and grow, and he keys the direction of growth toward the employee's own interests. He carefully plants the seed that this will entail an addition to her present work.

SECOND DISCUSSION— STANDARDS OF EXCELLENCE

When the manager next reviews Helen's accounts with her, he has two objectives in mind. He wants first of all, to be sure that he is expecting enough of her, that she knows that he expects excellent results, and that her own standards for her work likewise demand excellence. Second, he wants to introduce something new into her work plans which both agree will add to her accomplishment record and will advance her career interests.

Helen begins the review by making her usual clear, objective analysis of the status of the accounts she services. She pinpoints a few problems that she is experiencing and the action she proposes to take in order to minimize them.

The manager leads the discussion toward higher standards by asking:

"Helen, the problem with the ABC Company is not a new one, is it? I seem to recall a similar one with FG Inc. not so long ago."

"That's true. We frequently run into it. Companies that have been self-insured for a long period of time have developed certain practices of their own. They're so accustomed to them that they forget to mention them when we're working out the terms of our contract. Then a claim is placed. Under their former plan, they would have paid. Their employees know this and expect payment. Yet in our contract there is no provision for such payment. We get together with the firm and determine what is best to do. We are usually able to iron it out very satisfactorily. So it isn't a big problem, really."

Set an improvement goal.

"Yes, but only after the claimant is temporarily inconvenienced and feels that he has suffered as a result of his company's decision to insure with us."

"That's true, Mr. Frankel, but you must realize how *few* individuals we're talking about."

"I know that, Helen, but I really believe that we should eventually be able to reduce this kind of dissatisfaction sharply. Of course, we can't totally eliminate it. Some claims are unreasonable. To cover them would add too much to everybody's costs. So we have to display judgment and responsibility in such matters and encourage our accounts to do likewise. But within that general framework we need every insured employee on our side if we're going to grow and perform the service to the community that is possible."

"Well, I'm perfectly willing to try, but I really don't see how we can do much more." Helen is a little annoyed at what she obviously considers a rather minor matter.

"As a start, you could go back over your records and those of the other Account Representatives and make a list of cases of the sort you described with the ABC Co. Surely there are a limited number of these items, and eventually we might be able to build a checklist to review with new clients in advance. If you like, I'll tell the others that I've asked you to make this little survey. . . . But that's only one thing to do. Can you think of anything else?"

Helen thinks for a minute. "Well, with new accounts I could review their claims for the preceding two years to see if I could spot anything unusual in their practices." Some of her annoyance disappears as she becomes absorbed in the problem.

"Would that take a great deal of time?"

"I just don't know, and I don't know whether going back two years would be long enough either."

"Well, perhaps you could try it with one company to see if it's worth the time."

"All right, on the very next case I'll try it."

"Good. That gives us *two* things to do. Can you think of anything else?"

Helen thinks for a moment or two (by this time all trace of annoyance has disappeared) and then says: "You know, maybe we're going at this the hard way. Maybe for new accounts we should just review each claim we plan to refuse with the Benefits Manager. We could do this for the first six or eight months. In that way, before we say 'no' on anything we're sure the company agrees or at least understands why we think the claim is unreasonable."

"Helen, that's a much better idea." The manager shows his pleasure. "Let's do that instead of the long claims study. I'd rather we anticipated these problems and got them straight in advance."

Helen: "Yes, that's why I think the checklist would still be a good idea and when we see what kinds of claims are on that list, we'll have a chance to involve some other parts of the organization, too. The group that works on improving our health plans would be interested, I think. And, of course, the people who write our manuals. Maybe there are others as well."

"Good. Let's add a goal then to what you had already planned for the next quarter: to reduce embarrassment to or unfavorable reaction of employees in member companies. That's a good target anyway. And the analysis and checklist and prior discussion of claims not to be paid will be the first steps. When we've completed them, let's try to think of other things we can do along the same lines. And let's not forget to involve the rest of the organization in helping us with this project."

The manager has accomplished a number of things so far. First, he has made a start toward higher standards for Helen's work. He has introduced her to the concept of at least one improvement goal in every work plan—one target which represents streamlining work or better performance of certain parts of the work. If you reread their discussion, you will see how skillfully he got her to contribute to the content of the work she would do. He presented his view of a problem, and when Helen appeared somewhat defensive, he made a suggestion which they discussed. He then asked her for a suggestion and rewarded her verbally when she made one, but he did not settle for her first idea. Instead, he asked for another, until she became quite involved in the problem and was thinking very constructively. The little plan on which they eventually agreed was made up of inputs from both of them, and the door is open for additional effort in the future.

Put Something New in the Job.   The manager still has to introduce the "newness" concept to Helen—the deliberate addition of some new work or application or method which will provide a substantial opportunity for Helen to grow while doing her job.

"Did you give any thought to ways of putting things into your job that would help you grow as a manager even though for the moment you have no one reporting directly to you?"

"Yes, I did. It seems to me that the biggest thing I haven't done is fill an opening—hire someone whose work I don't know, make an evaluation of whether he could do the job, and start him doing it. Probably that's not a very good idea because no positions report to me. . . ."

"Well, let's see." The manager thinks for a minute. "Helen, I'd be willing to do this: As you know, we're going to expand the National Accounts Department during the next six months. If you feel you have the time and it wouldn't detract from your regular responsibilities, I'd be very happy to have you work with the Personnel Department to line up candidates, interview them, and check out their records. When you think you've got two or three qualified individuals, let me take a look at them. The final decision would have to be mine. I'm sure you understand that. But I would count on you for everything else. Then, too, I've been trying to think of how to bring new people in with the least disturbance. Maybe a good way to do it would be to assign each new person to work with one of the experienced Account Representatives. In this way he could learn about the current accounts and gradually take them over. This would give you the chance to orient and train at least one new person so you would get the entire experience you feel you need.

Helen is really enthusiastic. "That would be just wonderful! It's more than I hoped."

"Fine. I have to point out, Helen, that you'll need to plan your own work a little more carefully so that nothing slips because you're doing these extra things. You see there's a risk here—risk because you're trying something new, and you may not do it as well as older parts of the job where you're experienced. And then there's the risk that you'll over-emphasize the new effort at the expense of the old. We can't afford that. I suggest we get together a little more frequently when you begin some of these new activities. Maybe I can be of help. Incidentially, on this selection business, we have a little time. Why don't you ask the personnel people to recommend some good reading for you as a start? Then as soon as I get the first authorization to add a new person, I'll let you know."

The manager accomplished quite a lot in this meeting. He and Helen agreed that she would try to achieve certain improvements in her work. He demonstrated his serious interest in helping her advance by devising a special assignment for her which fits her career ambitions and which will be of real help to the overall organization. He pointed out the risks involved in these courses of action, made it clear that he felt that they were reasonable ones, and took steps to reduce the risk by setting up more frequent discussions of progress. Through it all, she was in the goal-setting position for herself, and he was clearly supportive in his suggestions and attitude.

The Manager Does Some Self-Analysis.   The steps which the manager has taken so far have been toward very specific targets—work needed that he felt Helen had overlooked or new experience which might be of use in another, better position. Often, however, the changes which a manager feels would help most are not of such a tangible nature. They are more attitudinal, more personality-based, more a matter of perspective and outlook. Such changes are necessarily more difficult to encourage. The material which follows is constructed to illustrate this kind of situation and show at least one managerial approach to laying the groundwork for less tangible change.

Helen and her manager have been getting together almost every week to see how her work is progressing. The manager is pleased with the way she has taken hold. In the benefits area, the checklist has been developed, and certain types of problems are indeed recurring—mainly with respect to dependent coverage. A plan is in place to remedy this situation. In the selection and training area, the first new account assistant has just been hired. The man appears to have excellent potential, and the manager is delighted with the choice. Helen has taken on each of these responsibilities most capably. However, she has not suggested new improvement activities. Instead, she has put each completed item aside as if crossing it off a list of things to be done. The manager is chagrined. He feels that she is waiting for him to point out new directions for her efforts rather than finding them for herself. Perhaps his way of working with her has encouraged her dependence on him. He thinks back about the way he has been managing—what his relationships have been not only with Helen but with other members of the organization as well. He concludes that he has not really been sharing much of his personal experience with them. In addition, a number of changes are occurring in the health field, and the overall organization is undertaking important new work. There are implications for the National Accounts Department. These need to be discussed and explored thoroughly so that they will have strong plans ready for implementation at the right time.

The manager makes some resolutions. He decides to ask the members of the Department to contribute more to the organization's total plans. He feels that this will have a number of desirable effects: Their motivation to achieve decided-upon results will be higher. Their understanding of the relationship of their personal work to the total will be greater. They will be better able to make work choices if they see the overall picture. They will realize how their work affects each other.

For Helen, it will be especially helpful. It will give her a frame of reference for her work and permit her to see needed improvements. From her current perspective, this may not be possible.

The manager is wise enough to realize that a sudden change in the way he is doing things is likely to create surprise and suspicion, and that he must lay the groundwork. He decides to do this at the next regular staff meeting.

When the usual business has been completed, the manager explains that a number of new ideas are entering the health field, that they will affect the overall organization, and that he, therefore, wants everyone to be familiar with the thinking that is going on. He outlines some of the anticipated changes and the reasons for them. He discusses in some detail the implications which he envisions for the National Accounts Department. He goes on to describe the series of planning and discussion meetings which he proposes to initiate in addition to the regular staff meetings. He asks that each person contribute his best thoughts and experience in these sessions so that the department formulates a set of plans for itself that will really meet the new objectives. He sets the date and topic for the first meeting and asks certain individuals to undertake exploratory assignments in preparation. The reaction of the group is good. They appear interested and anxious to contribute.

How Frank Should the Manager Be with Helen?   Now the manager faces a difficult decision. Should he or should he not discuss with Helen what he expects of her in these meetings? Will it make it easier or harder for her if she knows her participation is being watched closely? Based on her frankness and earlier cooperation, the manager decides that she will benefit by advance warning.

THIRD DISCUSSION—TOWARD GREATER INDEPENDENCE

The manager asks Helen to stop by his office for a moment. When she arrives, he says:

"Helen, I've been very pleased at the way you've set about accomplishing the extras we put in your work plans. I certainly hope you'll continue to work on the problem of improving understanding with our member companies. I'm counting on you to find a second addition to the staff. He won't be helping with your work, of course, but if you would do the screening for us again, I'd appreciate it. Tell me—how did you feel about your experience the first time? Did you feel you learned what you wanted?"

"Oh, yes." Helen is enthusiastic. "But I know I need more practice."

"Good. We're both gaining by this arrangement then."

The manager pauses, then adds: "It seems to me, Helen, we've accomplished a great deal so far. Are you willing to push on a little further?" As Helen nods, he continues: "I'd like now to work on something else with you. Something a little more intangible. One of the qualities I've observed in those at the top of organizations is that they're always looking for opportunities to improve things. They're never satisfied with what is being accomplished. They seem convinced that better ways can be found and bigger targets sought. I'd like you to develop this attitude, if that's what it is, in yourself. I'd like you to feel more dissatisfaction with results, to look for improvements in what you do and what the Department does. I'm afraid I can't tell you how to generate this feeling. But perhaps it would help if you would put yourself in the shoes of our Division Vice President, try to envision where you think the National Accounts Department ought to be heading and try to figure out ways of influencing us in that direction."

Helen is silent. Finally she says, "I wouldn't even know where to begin."

"If that's true, Helen, it's because you haven't had any reason to think along these lines before. This probably means that I haven't been discussing overall plans and strategy and problems enough with all of you. The sort of thinking I'm suggesting requires interest *and* information and then, of course, skill in presenting your ideas. I know you're able to do that and I'm determined that the meetings we're planning will supply you with the information. Can you generate the interest?"

"I'm a little floored by the whole thing, Mr. Frankel, but I'm certainly willing to try. . . . How shall I handle it—if I have an idea, I mean? Should I come to you with it?"

"No. Not unless there's something personal about it. Otherwise, bring it out in our group planning meetings. Let everybody kick it around a little. You may find some ideas get a little bruised that way, but usually an even better course of action comes to mind. Do you think you can take that kind of criticism? It's different from having plenty of time to analyze things and come to a sound conclusion. Lots of ideas that grow out of group discussion are unusually good, even though at that moment the person who suggested them probably couldn't defend them with facts if his life depended on it. We don't dash into action on the basis of that kind of spontaneous idea. But we do discuss it and try to bring out as many pros and cons and desirable modifications as we can think of. Then we assign people to investigate thoroughly. If, after all that, it still looks good, we put it into our plans."

It is clear from Helen's expression that this is a whole new world for her. It is also clear that she understands what her manager is asking of her and that she finds the new world attractive, even if it is a little frightening.

Only time will tell if Helen is able to respond to the situation, adjust her thinking and her behavior in ways the manager feels are desirable for advancement in the organization. The points for you to recognize are these. In his discussion, the manager did not try to solve his problem by telling Helen he was disappointed that a "take charge attitude" had not shown itself or that she had not come up with new improvement goals. Instead of focusing on her deficiencies, he first decided to alter his managing style and some of his practices. In so doing, he created a situation in which she could behave differently, and it would appear natural for her to do so. He carefully described the situation in which she would find herself and suggested how she could handle it effectively. So that she would understand very clearly, he explained why he wanted her to act in a certain way and the benefits from her actions. All these things improve the likelihood of a favorable employee response.

He would probably not undertake this plan if it would benefit only one employee. But he sees benefits to the entire staff. He is making more total information available and making many of his problems visible to employees. He is helping them to participate meaningfully in the decision-making for the department. He is, of course, encouraging them to function better as a team. At the same time, by careful assignment of the investigation and analysis of the pros and cons of issues, he has a vehicle for contributing to the individual development of employees, taking into account each person's unique combination of talent, experience, and interest.

Setting up such a growth situation is an important step. As the meetings proceed, however, the manager must be alert to observe the behavior and contribution of all who participate. When he sees change occurring in a favorable direction, he needs to reinforce it; in an unfavorable direction, to provide corrective feedback. With Helen, specifically, he will be careful to compliment her good suggestions for needed improvements or changes in direction of the organization. If he finds her failing to participate in longer-range thinking, he will deliberately seek ways to draw her out.

THE MANAGER'S RESPONSIBILITY
FOR PROMOTION

It was noted earlier that a manager is responsible for recognizing ability when he sees it and for challenging the individual to continue to grow. A third responsibility clearly follows.

If Helen responds to developmental efforts and makes herself capable of bigger contributions, the manager must take positive actions to seek better opportunities for which she is considered.

He must make sure that his manager and his associates are aware of her accomplishments and potential. He may contrive situations in which they will meet her personally. If a lateral transfer would be a good investment for her to broaden her knowledge of the organization or further education in public administration or the health field generally, he will recommend it to her. The point is, of course, that he must be active in promoting her consideration for more responsible positions which she is qualified to fill. It goes without saying that she must compete for such a position. That the manager must sponsor her for consideration should be as clearly understood.

SUMMARY

To summarize then: the presence of a strong, promotable employee in the organization brings unusual responsibilities both to the institution and to the individual. Your responsibilities are of a dual nature—to provide a useful direction for development and to accelerate growth so that the employee is able to make an increased contribution now and in the future. Key ways to fulfill these responsibilities are:

1. To help the employees set progressively higher standards of performance so that they continue to demonstrate unusual competence and contribution.
2. To ensure enough *new* work elements in the job that they are required to add substantively to acquired knowledge and skill in ways the organization can use and which will also take them in the direction of their career interests.
3. Through your managing style and practices, to provide a working climate which permits and encourages the employees' growth.
4. To contribute as much information about the purpose, plans, and strategy of the total organization as is reasonable so that the employees are better able to make sound choices in their work and with respect to their careers.

5. To expose employees to the work, decisions, and problems of your position so that they have first-hand information about differences in requirements at the next higher organization level.

6. To reward successful development efforts appropriately.

15

The Excellent
But Nonpromotable
Specialist

The relationship between two people, one of whom controls some essential elements of the life of the other, is never simple. It seems to be more than usually complex between a manager and a competent, but probably not organizationally promotable, specialist.

The specialist has certain knowledge and skills which far surpass those of the manager. He or she may even be world-recognized for a tremendous talent and contribution to mankind. Professional work may earn a promotion or salary increase for the manager. Yet the specialist may not have even minimum administrative or managerial ability. He may or may not recognize this, and, if he does not, the situation is made more difficult. Such employees may or may not be interested in advancing up the managerial ladder, but if they are, the manager's problems and responsibilities for solving them are at least doubled. They may feel that the material rewards for their efforts do not match their contribution and they are very likely to be right about this. Any expressed desire to become a manager may stem from this fact rather than from any real wish to change the nature of the work. Or they may feel that the information which they possess is not given adequate consideration when important decisions are made, and the determination to manage may grow from a desire to have greater influence on the future course of the institution in which they work.

THE SPECIALIST IS NEEDED

Most organizations have such individuals although the extent and maturity of their talents vary widely. Their contribution is very much needed. It is their innovative ideas which condition and permit progress. But their satisfaction with their total working situation is in delicate balance. To encourage their continuing productive effort, it is not enough to give lip service to their importance or to dole out small pay increases at sufficiently frequent intervals that they are lulled into accepting the status quo. Neither is it enough to say in effect: "Well, you've reached the top of our pay scale, and there's no future for you here. Try someplace else to see if they'll do better by you." What usually follows is that discontented Specialist A is traded for discontented Specialist B; who serves for a time, and the cycle is repeated. It is true that a specialist dedicated to a particular field may leave one organization for another if the specialty has more value to the second. But that is a different problem. The one considered here is how a manager can sustain the productivity and encourage increased contribution and growth on the part of the specialist, recognizing that managerial advancement is very unlikely.

THE CASE OF THE VIBRATION SPECIALIST

In order to come to grips with the specifics of this problem, let's take an illustrative example and develop at least one sound approach in the hope that it will add to your insight and permit you to deal effectively with similar situations.

Let's take the case of an aerodynamics laboratory located in one of the government's technical agencies. Engineers and scientists within the laboratory are for the most part highly specialized professional workers who evaluate the proposals of private industry, establish standards for technical work performed under government contract, serve as high level troubleshooters to help solve unexpected problems which arise in major defense programs, and, in addition, do research and development work on their own in-house programs. Activity is, therefore, quite diverse although largely organized around technical fields. The organization structure of this laboratory is quite similar to that of R&D laboratories in private industry. The "span of control" is perhaps a little smaller, averaging four or five individuals reporting to the same manager. The same informality and rather loose disciplinary control exists as in counterpart laboratories in industry.

Within this organization is a vibration specialist, David Kurwitz. David is both talented and experienced. He has his doctorate in mechanical engineering from a well-known West Coast university. He joined this agency directly upon graduation. David is essentially an experimentalist. He is perfectly capable of doing a sound piece of mathematical analysis, of course, but his first move to solve a problem is usually to get out in the field or in the laboratory and try to measure the vibration in the blade or the mounting or wherever it may be. He is extraordinarily ingenious both in designing the instruments which he needs for measurement and in getting accurate data on size and cause of vibration. The latter frequently involves his getting into mechanic's clothes and crawling around the equipment to place the measuring instruments for himself and take readings. Armed with these data, he is then able to make recommendations for modifying equipment design or assembly in order to damp the offensive vibration successfully. He has shown himself, in addition, to be far more cost conscious than the usual lab man is thought to be. He really works at coming up with alternative suggestions until he finds one that is not prohibitive because of cost or time delay. This work is extraordinarily valuable and is, moreover, needed in almost every phase of the government's broad, technical defense program.

David has been in his present job for eight years. His salary has increased at a steady, moderate rate. However, he is at his maximum, and there are no more increases in sight for him for the foreseeable future. His ratings document his outstanding technical competence and a rather frank, brusque personality which occasionally rubs people the wrong way. This is usually forgotten or overlooked after someone has worked with David long enough to understand how much expertise he supplies. His ratings also indicate, however, that he has few qualities which would help him succeed as a manager. He is impatient with those who are slow to grasp a point. He is completely disinterested in administrative matters. His monthly activity reports are hand-scribbled, almost meaningless notes. His attendance at staff meetings is marked by foot-tapping and finger-drumming unless the topic under discussion is a serious technical one.

THE PROBLEM

Recommendations of his former and his present managers are to retain David in a specialist capacity and not to dilute his vibration work with direct management responsibilities. This seems right, but a number of things are making his manager uneasy. Two of David's associates have been made managers in the last year, one in another part of the agency, the other within the laboratory. With their new status came a promotion in grade, and their pay now exceeds David's. His manager feels certain that David is aware of this. Second, David's important experience is not being transmitted to less experienced men. David has been working with one laboratory assistant and has been doing most of the interesting work himself. There is no natural way to teach others what he is learning, and since he is not much interested, he has not sought out opportunities for doing so. His manager knows that this is short-sighted and would cause difficulty if David should leave for any reason. Third, there have been some signs that David is getting restless. Even though vibration work is his specialty, he has now been doing it for quite a number of years. While it is possible to contend that every problem is different, the manager is well aware that there must inevitably be a certain sameness and repetition. Could David be fed up with his specialty? The manager decides that he must take action without delay on all these issues. Some discussion with David is clearly indicated.

FIRST DISCUSSION—DAVID'S FEELINGS
ABOUT HIS WORK

The manager watches for a good occasion. One day, a report comes in which he knows will interest David, and he goes out to his desk.

> "David, that was a remarkably fine piece of work you did on the gun mounting problem. The last report shows no field troubles yet with the new arrangement. You should be pleased."
>
> David: "Have we had a report since the *new* ones went into use?"
>
> Manager: "Yes, it came in this morning. Come on in and take a look."
>
> David comes into the office and studies the report with some care. He makes a note or two for his own reference and puts the report down. "Thanks. Always glad to have feedback on my recommendations."
>
> Manager: "It certainly helps, doesn't it? David, is this a good time to talk about your work?"
>
> "Sure."
>
> "You know, David, we ought to do something to bring along some young engineers in your field. You've been learning a lot, and somehow we ought to find a way to make it available to others. After all, David, you might decide some day you want to step out into other fields."
>
> "Well, that's not too likely. I'm still pretty interested in vibration. Oh, sometimes I get tired of all the travelling that's involved, but by and large, I like what I'm doing and intend to stick with it."

The manager learned one thing very easily. David is apparently not considering a change of specialty. The reason for his restlessness is not certain, but enlarging his vision of his work and interesting him in doing some new things is likely to have a positive effect. The manager would, of course, like to encourage him to take on the educational problem, but he knows that this is not likely to spark a great deal of enthusiasm on David's part. Perhaps a tradeoff would work. The manager decides to try it.

> "David, you've had a large number of emergency calls lately. Responding to them is, of course, vital to us, but I know they must interfere with longer range development work you're trying to do. Have you had to delay anything really important?"
>
> "Well, the big lag is in the . . ." and Dave describes with some enthusiasm a series of development tests he would like to run. "The real reason that work is off-schedule, though, isn't the trouble shooting I've been doing. We just haven't had the money or personnel for round-the-clock work."
>
> "How long would the test series take?"
>
> "I'd guess about six months, maybe eight."
>
> "And you feel the information would be really helpful?"

"I can assure you of that. Some of these emergencies wouldn't occur at all if we had these data."

"Well, we still don't have the money, David, or any extra people, but let me think it over. Maybe I'll have an inspiration."

The manager has already had half an inspiration, but he needs to work out the details. Why not use this work as a training vehicle? Managers would have to agree to release a few engineers on at least a part-time basis. The engineers would have to feel it worthwhile to do some routine work to gain a broader knowledge of the vibration field. David, probably in collaboration with someone else, would need to provide much more information than is usual in order to make it a rich learning experience. So the administrative problems are demanding and delicate, but if they could be worked out, it looks as if everybody would gain. David would get his test data, some of his wealth of experience would be transmitted to others, the laboratory would acquire information which would permit better mechanical design. The manager talks to some of his associates to get their reactions. It appears that if it is no more than half-time and lasts no longer than three months, they will be willing to make engineers available on a rotational plan.

SECOND DISCUSSION—THE TRADE-OFF

As soon as some of the details have been worked out, the manager approaches David again.

"David, I think I've found a way to help you get that experimental series done. It won't be exactly the way you want it, but at least it will get it done. You'll have to do something extra for us though."

"Like what?"

"Like helping with the vibration training for young engineers that I mentioned to you earlier."

"Listen, I hate to teach classes, and I don't think I'm any good at it either."

"I guess we agree on that," laughing. "No, we won't ask you to teach courses. Here's my idea."

The manager outlines his plan for borrowing engineers four hours a day to work on the vibration tests. "The other managers have agreed. The only condition is that you give the men enough background that they understand what they're doing, and that you keep them briefed on what is happening and conduct some discussions about the implications for design work in general."

David replies after some thought: "It *might* work, but don't expect me to give them enough information about the field to get them ready to understand what we're doing and why it's important. They have to have some basic information first."

"What would they need to know?" Then, as David begins to describe needed course work: "I'll tell you what—why don't you put together just a good general outline of the things you think are prerequisites. And don't forget the math they'll need, because some of them may be rusty. What we can do is pick six or eight young engineers and start by giving them—or seeing if the university will do it for us—a good basic course following your outline and any refresher math they need. That will probably take three or four months which will give you time to plan the experiments, get whatever equipment you need, and so on. We'll expect them to do the course work on their own time. When you're ready to run, we'll start the part-time assignment arrangement. What do you think?"

David seems a little hesitant, so the manager goes on with one more persuasive bit. "You know, if we get some of these beginners trained, we can send them out on the more routine trouble-shooting assignments and save you for the tougher ones."

"Well, that would be worthwhile," David says, "but they'll need more than this one laboratory experience to be ready to work on their own."

"I'm sure you're right. I am usually too optimistic about such things. What else would they need?"

"I think they'd have to work under supervision for their first few times. And that would give us a chance to see how well they do, too."

"Good. Would you be willing to take them along with you, first to observe and help and later to try out their own knowhow?"

"Yes. But don't count on everyone making the grade. This isn't an easy field. Some of them probably won't even like it."

"Look, even if we only get one or two who turn out to be good at it and interested, we'll still be farther ahead than we are now. Besides, what they've learned is bound to show up in their design work. And, of course, you'll get your test data and that's worthwhile. Will you give it a try?" David agrees.

Let's look for a minute at what the manager has done. First, he faced the problem as soon as he realized it existed. He did not put his head in the sand and hopes that David's interest would be reawakened by some lucky happenstance. He probed until he found something important that David wanted to do that would also be valuable to the organization. He found a way to do it, at the same time making inroads into another phase of the problem—transmitting David's information to others who needed it. He is thus taking out an "insurance policy" against the day when David might become dissatisfied and leave. He hopes that this will not happen, but he cannot afford the risk of that hope alone. By proposing an administrative solution that made it possible for David to do what he wanted and by involving David in the technical planning for both the tests and the training, he aroused the specialist's interest and got a commitment from him. Do not overestimate the solution, though. It is a temporary one. Any manager in such a situation will probably need to continue to find suitable trade-offs for as long as he wishes the specialist to stay on his job and as long, of course, as the specialist agrees that this is what he wants to do. In addition, the other fundamental aspect of the problem remains—how to recognize and reward such an individual appropriately.

THE DIFFICULTY IN DETERMINING REWARD

The major issue in determining reward is assessing what has been accomplished. When you are working with a specialist, regardless of the field, the likelihood is that you do not know as much about the technical quality of this work as the specialist. In fact, the more deeply specialized the person is and the more advanced the personal competence, the less likely you are to understand how "good" his or her output is. You can tell whether it fills business needs in a useful way, but you usually cannot appreciate how innovative the work was, how complex the problem was, how creative the solution was. And when longer-range or more fundamental research is involved, you may not even see clearly the implications for the organization nor the application to the practical accomplishments planned. Yet to reward a pedestrian piece of work and only nod at the unusual will do more harm than good. What should you do?

The first thing is to admit what you do not know so that you *can* look for solutions outside your personal judgment for evaluating specialized work. The specialist knows much that you do not know. As a manager, however, you also have areas of personal competence which the specialist does not share. It is, hopefully, the *joining* of these individual skills which leads to the accomplishment of organization goals. The manager in our illustrative example is faced with the need to evaluate work he does not fully understand. Let's see how he handles the situation.

HOW CAN DAVID'S WORK BE EVALUATED?

David's manager realizes that he must still solve the problem of rewarding David adequately. To do this, the manager needs sound evidence of his contribution. David also needs this so that his work will give him a sense of satisfaction.

The trouble-shooting work is the easiest to evaluate. Either the equipment works or it does not. Either the client is satisfied with the solution or he is not. The manager, therefore, begins with this factor by encouraging David to ask for reports on the function of equipment after his recommendations have been incorporated. He further suggests that he really should make a personal inspection after a reasonable period of operation. David agrees. He is really interested in knowing what happens. But he tends to get involved in new problems and forget the old ones. Together, they work out an arrangement whereby the laboratory assistant assigned to help him is responsible for maintaining a log of major emergency trouble-shooting work. No job will be considered finished until there has been an objective report

showing the desired improvement, a customer check to be sure of his satisfaction, and, on a sample basis, a personal follow-up inspection.

As far as the rest of the work goes, the manager knows that David sets
high standards. He would like to capitalize on this so that David's own
evaluation is as sound as possible, and so that he makes it available to his
manager. Since David has little patience for putting elaborate work plans on
paper, his manager decides to try to work out a series of discussions. He
wants to learn more about David's plans and at the same time help him think
through what he is trying to do, the various ways he might do it, and the final
choice of a course of action. The result should be that both will be more
aware of what has and has not been accomplished and why.

THIRD DISCUSSION—EXPLORING
THE EMPLOYEE'S PLANS

With this thought in mind, the manager suggests that he would very much
enjoy learning a little more about the technical aspects of David's proposed
experiments. David is a little surprised but agrees to talk with him.

> "David, I'm sure you realize that I have a relatively superficial knowledge of
> the vibration field, but I'd really like to know more about this series of tests you
> are planning. In simple terms, *what* are we trying to learn, *why* do we need to
> know it, what will we *do* with the information if we get it, what will happen if
> we *don't* obtain it completely and *how* are we going about doing the work? I
> assume there are several possible approaches, and that if the information is so
> important, others must have tried for it and failed. You must feel you have an
> idea which hasn't been tried before and, needless to say, I'd like to know what
> it is. That's quite a bit of territory to cover, but let's start with what you're
> trying to do and why it's important."

Notice that the manager needs no special technical information to set the
stage for this discussion. He is using sound interviewing techniques, asking
a broad enough question that David gets a good picture of the kind of
information he wants to hear.

David describes the information that he is trying to obtain and why he
thinks it is important. The manager probes to be sure that this is *necessary*
work:

> "How will this help us, David?"
> "How have we managed to get along without it all these years?" "*Have we
> made serious design mistakes?*"
> "Can you give me some examples?"
> "Is there any major program our agency is sponsoring in the next three to
> four years that would benefit significantly from this information?"
> "Tell me more about that."

The manager is making the assumption that if he probes methodically for
the advantages of and uses for the expected result, he will get understanda-

ble information and will, thus, be able to exercise sounder judgment about the worthwhileness of the project. He does not, of course, ask these questions all at once. They are samples of good probing questions to use in such a situation.

HOW WILL HE APPROACH THE PROBLEM?

He then probes thoroughly into how David plans to go about the tests. He explores *several* different approaches and asks David to compare his approach with that used by others. He has two objectives. He wants to be sure that David is current in his field, knows what has been done in the past and is not reinventing the wheel. He also wants to be sure that he has considered various approaches and has chosen the one that seems most advantageous.

> "Bring me up to date, David. Who else has worked on this problem and what did he find? Would you reach the same result if you were to take the same approach? Have his findings been used and verified? What will you do differently? Tell me more . . . Give me some examples . . ."
>
> "What other ways have you thought of approaching the matter? What about different amounts of time involved? Which will cost more? Which will take more people? How much risk is involved each way? What *don't* we know about in this approach? Which is likely to give the most results?"

Notice that the manager is getting David to weigh risk, resources, time, and likelihood of sound, useful results in each case.

> Then, "Should more than one approach be used? Should we safeguard our investment by setting up parallel programs? What would this cost? If we set up parallel programs, would we select two different approaches from the one we'd take if we choose just one?"

In this kind of a discussion, although the manager is unable to give technical "coaching" in the old-fashioned sense, he is able through sound questioning to help David explore many facets of the technical problem that he is working on and to crystallize his thinking about what it is he is trying to do. This, in effect, permits him to set meaningful standards which he will later use to measure his success. It also permits the manager to observe what happens and form his own judgment of its success.

OBTAIN JUDGMENTS
OF QUALIFIED EXPERTS

There are undoubtedly other technical specialists in the country who know this field and are qualified to make a technical evaluation of David's work. How can the manager get this evaluation in a way that will please David and be helpful to him and to the organization? This is probably not something to discuss with the specialist involved. This is a creative managerial task.

The manager thinks of as many things he might do as possible. One idea is to encourage David to write up his work for presentation at a technical meeting or publication in a technical journal. While David would probably be pleased *after* it was done, it is unlikely that he would consider it more than an unnecessary chore beforehand. The manager does not eliminate the idea, but he does decide to use it sparingly.

He thinks about hosting a discussion group, inviting vibration experts from all over the country. This might be a particularly good idea if the test series is successful. The younger engineers who assisted could help put much of the material on paper, and David could present his findings with discussion centered around implications for practical design and needed additional research and development in the field. It might even arouse the interest of one or two of the academic participants to pursue some of the issues on their own. The manager feels that this idea is worthwhile and logs it for later use when the work is farther along and looks promising.

What else? Vibration is not a field in a vacuum. Some of the most deserved recognition might come from associates working on other phases of projects but who need to consider potential vibration problems in their own work. Perhaps the manager could devise some vehicle for bringing David into closer contact with these people. Design Review Boards already exist for various phases of technical work. When major proposals are evaluated or when a contract has been awarded and the first paper designs and mockups are available, the Design Review Boards analyze them for possible design flaws and suggest better ways of incorporating past experience into the design. David certainly ought to be on some of these teams so that his vibration know-how is included in their recommendations. Such meetings are not frequent, but they are particularly influential in determining what the agency will and will not sponsor in the way of major technical programs. Participation in them would bring David into the mainstream of the agency's functions. The manager is pleased with this idea and takes steps to be sure that David is included the next time such a meeting is held.

Note that the manager, in making decisions which will involve David in meetings with distinguished colleagues, is careful *not* to schedule so many events of this kind that David is, in effect, prevented from devoting the major part of his time to creative work. A specialist is only likely to reach truly distinguished results if he is absorbed in his technical work and devotes the largest share of his time to it. Meetings, discussions, papers, and the like, no matter how pleasant or rewarding they may be, are distractors from an individual's main effort which brings him worthwhile results and marks him as a distinguished performer. Since this is probably the greatest reward he can receive, the manager needs to be careful not to destroy this possibility in his well-meant attempts to provide interim recognition. Note also that the manager must be extraordinarily careful to plan for rewards which the *employee* will view as rewards and to resist the temptation to set up situations that he would personally find rewarding.

WHAT ABOUT COMPENSATION?

The solutions suggested for evaluating and recognizing David's work avoided the problem of compensation. The facts are that our current compensation practices for rewarding the work of specialists lag behind our compensation practices for other kinds of work. Most organizations are sincere in their desire to pay specialists properly. But inability to measure their contributions, the frequent lapse of time between accomplishment and use of their work, and the lack of understanding of the case or difficulty of doing it have made it difficult to set a value on this kind of work. The worth of managerial positions is set largely by supply and demand and the going rate in the marketplace. A given specialist may not have a counterpart in other organizations—his or her work is so closely related to a unique combination of personality, training, and abilities. Even if the specialist has, the contribution may vary widely depending on the nature of the product or service of the institution and the perceptivity of its managers to possible applications and implications.

David's manager will undoubtedly do his best to match David's salary to that of other specialists of roughly similar competence. He will reconcile his salary with those of other vibration specialists. He will try to get the official grade of David's position raised to permit occasional merit increases. He will make sure that David understands how his salary is administered. Factually, he will probably not be happy with his performance in this area. This is a problem he will have until management tools, including compensation, are more incisive and sophisticated. Until such time, you will find that your compensation judgments will be improved by making certain that you understand the *purpose* of the employee's work to the organization; keeping abreast of what he is doing and why, so that you have a reasonable picture of his thought and action processes; getting his personal evaluation of his work's application to organization results; and devising ways of getting the judgments of others more technically qualified and doing this in such a way as to bring a sense of recognition for the employee. To do these things there must be a positive pattern of interaction between you and the specialist and an active involvement in what he is doing. You cannot back away from the specialist and his work because you feel that you do not understand either one. Withdrawal on your part actually limits the individual's contribution. You have information about the organization's goals, strategy, needs, and resources which provides the background or structure for his work. There is probably no instance where the joining of your individual knowledges and competences will mean more to organization results.

If you want to compensate a specialist adequately, therefore, do not abandon him on the assumption that he knows what he is doing. Work toward the effective pooling of what each of you knows. The outcome should be greater contribution on his part and greater recognition of what he has accomplished on yours. And this permits you to pay him appropriately. In our illustrative example, the manager's dialogues with David about the need for his test series show one way of bringing about the desirable interaction.

SUMMARY

To summarize, then, the major problems in dealing with an excellent specialist who is unlikely to become a manager are:

1. Sustaining interest and performance in the same field if greater depth is the individual's objective or in a different field if the current one is stale.
2. Contributing to the specialist's work even though you may not be technically qualified to do so.
3. Providing opportunities for influencing the plans of the organization by virtue of specialized knowledge.
4. Providing means for the specialist to evaluate his or her own work.
5. Providing recognition by those technically qualified to give it.
6. Paying the individual adequately—insofar as current tools permit.

You are most likely to be successful in solving these if you:

1. Through your continuing interaction with the individual, help to define personal targets better, and are systematic in probing the reasons for the work, the advantages and disadvantages of various ways of accomplishing it, the implications for full use, and exploitation of results. Out of this dialogue should also come better decisions on whether to attempt to leap-frog with higher risk, to inch along conservatively, or to take some middle position.
2. Look for reasonable trade-offs. That is, negotiate for an agreement to contribute certain things which the organization needs in return for pursuing some things which the specialist feels are desirable for the organization.
3. Devise ways for the employee to contribute to overall organization decisions whenever specialized knowledge is relevant. Do this even though it may involve going outside normal organization channels.

4. Encourage the use of objective data in evaluating his work and to seek the opinion of "customers" served either inside or outside the organization. In addition, help to set clear goals within the framework of organization needs so that accomplishments can be measured in these terms.

5. Devise infrequent but compelling reasons for interaction with distinguished colleagues in the chosen field and others with whom the work is related.

6. Make sure that the compensation policies and practices are understood and that you administer them consistently.

16

When a Manager
Reports to You

Accomplishing needed work by working through managers who report to you is a challenging situation. Not every manager is confronted with it since it implies a certain size organization and a higher level in the structure of the institution. When it exists, it creates a number of problems.

The first is communication. It is, of course, outmoded for managers to talk and work personally *only* with those who report directly to them. Nonetheless, much of the informal communication, as well as the interpretation of decisions and actions, are transmitted to the rest of the organization by this group. Their personal, powerful filters may consciously or unconsciously change the intent of the manager's message significantly.

A second problem is that the reporting managers undoubtedly have some personal ideas and methods which may conflict with yours. Many of these are, of course, excellent and helpful by themselves. Quick, constructive resolution of such differences, however, is needed so that individual workers at lower levels are not adversely affected. This means that the higher-level manager needs to develop personal negotiating and problem-solving skills to a high degree and needs to be receptive and open-minded about ideas which he or she does not originate.

Another special managing problem in this situation is that a manager to whom other managers report should, of course, devote major efforts toward improving their work performance. But their work is *managing* their respective departments or sections. Much of their interaction, therefore, should be about management. The goals toward which they should be primarily directed should be toward sounder managing practices. And the evaluation of their efforts and subsequent rewards should be based on how well they manage the work of their components.

This is a difficult concept to apply. There is a tendency toward one of the two extremes: to look only at component results and ignore the managing, or to look only at the managing *techniques* and ignore the results. We need to find a reasonable balance between the two. When we evaluate any process or technique, we first look to see if it has accomplished its purpose. So in managing we look first at its purpose—did this individual's managing accomplish key needed results? Next, we look at how effective these skills and practices were. Did the person get these results through innovative, economic methods—or were these wasted resources, human and otherwise, mismatched effort and priority, functions performed in a pedestrian way that ignored state-of-the-art information which might have helped accomplish a better job?

To make the vertical relationship between managers even more complicated, a manager lower in the organization usually makes a personal contribution. For example, he or she may carry out assigned projects, handle contacts with special customers, contribute to task force or study team efforts, and so on. In this work, the relationship to the upper level manager is similar to that of an individual worker. Keeping all these factors in mind, a manager intent on encouraging growth and motivation in another manager must focus attention on three basic elements—component results, managing skill, and personal work contribution.

THE CASE OF THE DISTRICT MANAGER

Since the situation described probably occurs more frequently in large industrial organizations than elsewhere, let us take our illustrative example from that source. Let's assume as a setting a 150-person component responsible for the installation and field servicing of heavy apparatus equipment. To simplify terminology, let us call the man who heads the component the top manager and the reporting managers district managers. These latter individuals are assigned responsibility on a geographic basis. They are physically located in their territories, and informal contacts with the top manager are, therefore, somewhat limited. The telephone is their major medium of communication; they meet at headquarters twice a year. The top manager usually visits each district three or four times a year unless special problems merit more personal attention. The district managers are all competent to do their jobs. Each, of course, has his special strengths and weaknesses, and the top manager has worked with them long enough that he recognizes what these are.

One manager, Hank Martin, is due in for a visit in a few days. The top manager wants to use the occasion to work with him on improving results in his district.

ADVANCE PREPARATION

The top manager knows that the way in which he approaches Hank will make quite a difference in his reception and so, he takes time to plan the discussion. First of all, he goes back over his records on Hank's territory. In general, they show that customers have been pleased with the work done for them. There are complimentary letters indicating that workmen do not leave a job until the equipment is functioning properly, and that they are careful to return to check out product performance during the first few weeks of operation. Field complaints are apparently handled promptly and given good attention. These things are all to the good.

On the negative side of the picture, however, is the fact that the cost of Hank's operation runs 2 to 3 percent higher than that of other district managers. Some of this is because he carries more employees on his payroll; some of it is because he simply takes more time with customers. His record of man hours per installation shows 10 to 15 percent more time than in other districts. In addition, he carries a larger inventory of component parts.

Since customers are pleased with the work he does for them, the top manager does not want to affect the quality of this service in any significant way. On the other hand, he wants Hank to be aware of the comparative data and try to bring his costs and inventory in line with other districts. It is a straightforward managing problem which needs attention, and the top manager would like Hank to solve it *without negative side effects*. He would also like to use the problem as a vehicle for helping Hank improve his managing skills.

If he worked nearby, it would be fairly simple to outline the situation and ask him to prepare for a discussion of ways and means of solving the problem. Since he is in another city, the top manager decides that it will work out better not to confront him with the unfavorable statistics over the phone. He feels that a more constructive reaction and greater dedication to accomplishing the objective can be obtained through a face-to-face discussion. This means a little initial delay, but the top manager believes that in the end the result will be better and will involve no longer total time.

PLANNED TACTICS

He considers his approach to Hank. He is a very good manager, and he especially wants to avoid modifying or undercutting any deserved compliments by telling him that he is "doing a great job, but . . ." After some thought, he decides to tell Hank only that he would like to review his operating plans for the next six months while he is at the home office for the meeting. This is done by phone and produces the expected response:

> "Okay, Larry, but you know it's almost impossible to plan our kind of work. We're literally at the beck and call of our customers, and the main thing we try to do is stay flexible and cover all the bases."
>
> "I'm aware of your consideration for your customers, Hank, and I certainly don't want to change that, but there *are* things we can plan in a field organization like yours if we give it a little thought. Frankly, your customer relationships are so good, and you are so on top of your service work, that I'd like to experiment a little with you if you don't object too strenuously."
>
> Hank groans. "All right. If you say so. What do you have in mind?"
>
> "Let's wait till you get here, Hank, because I think we have to feel our way a bit. If you will just think about your total operation and what you would like to be different—better I mean—that will give us a starting point."
>
> "Do you mean better shop facilities, more people, things like that?"
>
> "Well, that might be part of it. But what I have in mind is looking at the things you do, and, without sacrificing any essential customer service, what could we shoot for in the way of improved operations? Are there streamlining efforts we should be making? Cost reductions possible? Training we should be offering employees to upgrade their competence? More detailed information on failures relayed back to the factory or to engineering so that it can be factored into future design or assembly of equipment? You know the whole bit. You probably think about these things all the time. So don't do anything except *think* until we've had a chance to talk."

The top manager kept his opener very general because he does not want Hank to produce detailed plans before he has full information on the needed improvements. If this were to happen, Larry might be forced to turn down what Hank proposes, and he does not want to run this risk.

When Hank arrives for the meeting, Larry is careful to give him his share of public compliments for the work he has been doing and the fine customer relationships he has developed.

STEP 1—SETTING THE STAGE
FOR A CONSTRUCTIVE REACTION

When the time comes for the private talk, Larry begins:

> "I didn't mean to be mysterious, Hank, about this meeting. It's just that I wanted us to have a good discussion and get something started with you that could eventually be used with all the field operations. And I didn't want you to do a lot of work without really knowing what I have in mind. This isn't something we need to rush into. I'd like us to work it out rather carefully so that we know what we're doing and get some solid payoff from it."

These remarks take the urgency out of the situation. This usually helps minimize unfavorable reactions.

"All the service people in the districts do a lot of work on demand. The big installations can be planned for, of course, and the scheduled follow-up service calls. But complaint handling and trouble shooting can come up very suddenly and without much warning. I'd guess that it would be a great temptation to let the latter kind of work eat up most of the personnel time. On the other hand, *you* have a great many managerial tasks to get done. You have to fill vacant jobs, train new personnel, and be sure everyone is familiar with new equipment before they must work on it. You have all the usual appraisal and compensation functions, and at the same time you have to watch costs and stock and make sure the facilities and equipment you use are properly maintained. Then, over and above this, you have your personal customers and community activities. Because you're off by yourself you don't get many of the aids that would be available to you if you were based at one of our plants.

"Now my idea is this: I'd like to work with you to set some reasonable standards on the installation and service work. Nothing elaborate—just a few simple indicators we could look at to know whether that part of the job is being done well. In your case, we're sure it is—so this gives us a head start. If in the future anything falls below the standards we set, that would be a signal for you to develop remedial plans. Does this seem reasonable so far?"

Hank: "Sure. You mean things like customer reaction, completion within scheduled time, things like that?"

"Yes. Only we'd try to pin down what kind of customer reaction and how much time is needed for various kinds of installations. We'd try to be quite specific."

Hank: "I don't think that would be too hard to do. We've certainly had enough experience."

Notice that the top manager tackled standard-setting for important work of the component first. This is so that if the attempt to improve in certain other areas affects this work adversely, he and the district manager will be alerted to it and be able to take action to get it back to par. If this step were not taken, there might be a tendency to let regular work suffer while trying to gain improvement in new areas.

"After we have good standards in place for the main work of the organization, let's take a look at the managing part of the job—the work you do specifically. Let's try to evolve a few quite clear-cut results toward which you might work profitably."

Hank: "Okay. Do you want to begin this right now or what?"

"No. I think that would be the hard way. Why don't you see what you can dream up in the standards area first. Maybe when you've gotten one or two that you think are pretty good you could give me a ring and we could talk about them over the phone. Just be sure to include *customer reaction* and *cost* and *time*. There probably are other elements, but those occur to me right away."

Larry searches through a drawer. "Somewhere here I've got a list of questions which are supposed to help you develop useful standards. The point isn't to develop measures as an exercise—it's to give you enough information about work being done to indicate when corrective action is needed and when it's enough to just keep going. Ah, here it is." He hands the paper to Hank. "You can take this with you. I have a copy for myself. The examples aren't for our work. They were put together for a foreman's job and are intended to help you understand how to go about using the checklist."

Hank looks over the questions.

FIGURE 16-1   Standards Checklist (Examples given are for the work of an assembly foreman.)

---

1. What will be measured?

   Ex: Shipments against schedule; product performance against specs; manufacturing against estimate.

2. How will you measure it?

   Ex: Log of actual shipping dates; final inspection report; cost analysis report.

3. How frequently will you measure it?

   Ex: Monthly.

4. Will it give you objective, preferably numerical data about quality, quantity and time?

   Ex: Yes.

5. What number or range is considered about right?

   Ex: Shipping schedule met; performance within specified tolerances; cost with ±3 percent of estimate.

6. What number or range indicates that attention is needed?

   Ex: Delay in shipment in excess of 20 percent of total assembly time; performance outside specified tolerance; cost in excess of 3 percent over estimate.

7. Does the information obtained pinpoint what aspects of the work need attention?

   Ex: Yes.

Hank reads over the questions and laughs. "I guess it always seems easier to do this sort of thing for someone else's job than for your own. Somehow our work seems much more complicated than this foreman's."

"Well, don't try for perfection, Hank. The standards won't be fixed in concrete. We can always improve them as we go along. The main thing is to make a thoughtful start. When can I expect to hear from you?"

"Oh, a week to ten days at the outside."

"Fine."

Larry is pleased at Hank's reaction. He seems willing to try. He does not seem to feel that he is being punished or disciplined—a feeling Larry wanted to avoid. He may even feel a bit flattered that he is the first to try to do this. It looks like a good start.

THE FOLLOW-UP

The next problem is not to let this matter drag along endlessly. Larry wants Hank to give it a reasonable amount of attention and get the process functioning within a couple of months' time. Improvements can then be made as they work with the data.

A week goes by, and there is no word from Hank. He had said a week to ten days. Larry does not want that timing to slip, but he wants Hank to initiate the phone call. He has the occasion to write him a short note about a new installation coming up shortly and he adds a paragraph: "Incidentally, I'm most anxious to learn what you've been doing in the standards area. I'm looking forward to your call in the next few days." Three days later, Hank calls.

"This is much harder than I expected, Larry. Every time I put something down it seems to me it would take an awful lot of time and effort to keep track of the information. I assume that's not the idea; it ought to be relatively simple. Right? But anyway, here goes what I have so far. It seems to me that our first responsibility is that if something goes wrong with one of our products we have to fix it quickly and satisfy our customer. We want him to say: 'That's a good company to deal with. You can rely on them. I'll buy from them again.' Agreed, so far?"

"Yes, although we can't do this at *any* cost to us. It has to be done economically."

"Right. I ought to add that." There's a moment of silence while Hank presumably writes himself a note to this effect. "Well, what I wrote was: Responsibility—to service nonfunctioning equipment. Measures—(1) customer satisfaction shown by a poll immediately following service. (2) . . ."

Larry interupts: "I should wait until I hear it all, but I'm wondering what kind of poll you have in mind."

"I was thinking I'd sent out a simple little questionnaire and ask the customer to fill it out and return it to me."

"I wonder what a customer's reaction to that would be? It seems as if we're making extra work for him. Of course I may be prejudiced because I hate to fill out forms."

"Maybe you've got a point there. But how else can I find out if he was satisfied?"

"Rather than our speculating about it, Hank, is there a customer out there who is a good enough friend of yours that he'd be frank with you?"

"Oh, sure. Max Schilling would be willing to talk over almost anything. I've helped him out of a bad spot on a couple of occasions."

"All right. Why not find out how he'd feel about a questionnaire. Maybe you can think of some other possibilities before you talk to him so that you can get his opinion on several points at the same time. Well, I really shouldn't have interrupted. What else do you have?"

"Let's see. Where was I? Oh, yes. Second measure: Satisfactory equipment function as measured by performance against original specifications on completion of service work and at time of follow-up check one month later."

Larry: "That's good. It's objective and, of course, if the equipment is working as it should, the customer is quite likely to be satisfied."

"Right—unless his down time was so long that he lost profit. That's why I have a third measure on that point: (3) Customer down time as measured by elapsed time from breakdown or malfunction to full return to operation. The only problem is that I don't know how to put a simple numerical standard on that. It varies a lot, depending on the problem. If it's a motor repair job, it's a few hours probably, but if there's a system failure somewhere it might take a while to find out where the trouble is."

"Yes, I see your point. Could you collect data and gradually build a set of time standards for the more common problems at least?"

"Oh, we've already got the data. I could put someone on the job of getting it in shape so we can use it. It wouldn't be absolutely complete, but it would probably cover 75 to 80 percent of our trouble-shooting work."

"That'd be great, Hank, because that's one where we could probably get comparable data from other districts and make some inroads into cutting time wherever it seems out of line."

Hank: "Now about the cost of service you mentioned. I didn't have anything on that. Somehow it doesn't seem worthwhile keeping track of the cost of every service job. They range, you know, from a few minutes up to several days."

"I agree. But how about total man-hours on service work and total cost, including the payroll for that purpose and the cost of parts and equipment plus some overhead figure to cover clerical effort, stock room, inventory, etc.?"

Hank thinks for a minute. "Don't forget, Larry, we bill some of that."

"Right. I guess what I'm really getting at is whether, without a lot of your effort and some help from accounting, we could get a little profit and loss statement on the service part of your work."

"Now *that* sounds reasonable. I'll talk to our accounting man and see what he says. It may be that what we should look at is only the warranty period when we're stuck with most of the charges. But I'll look into it several different ways."

The discussion continues. It is a good start toward the development of a reasonable set of standards for the service work of that district.

Notice that there were no easy, ready answers. This had not been done before, and neither man knew what kind of standards or measures or information would prove useful to them. That is an important point, because most management lore implies that the higher-level manager ought to have the "answers." This is seldom true unless he is thoroughly experienced in doing the work and has already tried out various measures for it. Notice also that both parties contributed suggestions, but the district manager kept the responsibility for investigating, analyzing and finally recommending a set of standards. It is likely that he will never arrive at a complete, "final" set. Some chosen at first will prove too cumbersome and more work than they are worth. Others will prove ineffective in evaluating effort and correcting misdirected or inadequate performance. Over a period of time, however, a satisfactory list will gradually evolve. Then as each manager works with it and compares his data with other districts, improvement targets will be set in various areas: cut repair time on defective wiring by a certain percentage; reduce the cost of coil winding by a certain percentage; and so on. The standards are thus dynamic; they help control the work and point to needed improvements. They enable a manager to be very much on top of the basic recurring work of the component.

STEP 2—SETTING MANAGING GOALS

About a month's time has gone by. Larry and Hank have agreed on an initial set of standards, and Larry is now ready to work with Hank on setting a few goals for his *managing* work. Over the telephone, Larry says:

"Now that we have some reasonable standards for your service work, are you willing to take another step? I wonder if we could take a look at your personal work, Hank."

"Set standards for that?" Hank sounds a little incredulous.

"Well, maybe we can in some areas, but managing is mostly too intangible to measure." Larry is ready for this reaction. "I think the first thing to do would be for you to decide on two or three things you'd like to see accomplished as a result of your managing effort."

Hank says, "Mostly I want to make sure we get our work done."

"Yes, I appreciate that. But you must have some thoughts about certain work that could be done better or at less cost, or something like that. Tell you what, we've been getting much more information about our operations than we used to now that so much of our data is stored in the computer. Let me put a couple of reports in the mail to you. They may give you ideas, but be sure to add your own thoughts because these reports tend to be pretty much financially oriented."

The reports showing the cost and inventory figures that had alerted Larry to a problem in the first place are sent off. Within a day or two Hank calls.

"Larry, how come you didn't tell me our costs were higher than anybody else's?"

Larry smiles. This reaction is perfect. Instead of Hank's going on the defensive about his work, he is angry not to have been told sooner.

"I am telling you, Hank, by sending you the reports. But let me say right away that I frankly didn't realize the situation either until I saw the figures."

"Well, the first thing I'd like to suggest is that all of us in the districts get these reports, too, so that we know as soon as you do."

"I agree, and I'm sure that can be arranged. Now stop sputtering, and let's talk about goals for you for your managing work."

"We get one without even trying, don't we—to bring my costs down to, say, the average of the districts."

"It sounds reasonable, Hank, but we can't let your customer service suffer by doing it. So before you decide to work toward that goal, I think you ought to dig into the situation and find out *why* your costs are higher. There's always a chance they should be. Maybe your customers have more elaborate equipment or more custom stuff. Maybe your territory is more spread out than others or your labor costs run higher for some reason. I don't think this is the case, but I think *you* ought to get the facts before you try for a reduction."

This was a very important dialogue. The top manager did not jump at the first goal proposed by the district manager even though it was one he wanted. He made the effort to teach the district manager to negotiate with his boss on a rational basis, using facts rather than hunches, and to stand up for what he believes is right. This is an essential move if managers are to be encouraged to develop along lines of independent *and* sound decision making. It would have been easy to agree, but the opportunity for an important attitudinal lesson would have been lost.

Larry continues: "What about some other areas for your effort, like employee development?"

Hank is clearly surprised by the apparent shift in focus. "You mean courses and things like that?"

"Maybe courses, yes, but focused on your management goals. Is there any way that you could improve skills that would help cut costs and shorten service time and still make customers happy?"

Hank thinks for a minute or two. "I've been trying to develop specialists for certain kinds of work, and I do think our employees are good and really know their stuff. But maybe now we could start to aim for more flexibility so that employees would know each other's work. Then if one person were busy, another could substitute."

"That sounds like a particularly good idea, Hank, since perhaps in time it wouldn't take quite as many employees to carry the work load. Specialization is good, but it *is* expensive in a small operation. You'd need to have rather careful plans, though, to be sure we didn't hurt the customer during the learning period." Larry pauses. "It seems to me, Hank, that if you investigate the cost situation to see what you ought to do about that and work on this flexibility problem that's enough to tackle at one time. I'd rather see you get these two things pretty well planned out and underway before you start on anything else."

Hank agrees.

"When can you be ready to talk in specifics about both these projects?"

Hank: "It'll only take about a week or so to get the employee training worked out, but the cost figures will take some checking around. I'd rather do a little thinking before I set a date on that. Let me call you back in a couple of days."

Apparently the negotiating idea took hold. Hank has learned not to commit himself without some reasonable information. The top manager should be pleased. He wants the district manager's commitments to be worth something. Quite a lot has been accomplished so far. Standards have been set for the major work of the component, Hank has two worthwhile managerial goals, and the two managers have engaged in a planning negotiation which is teaching Hank personal skills that he either did not have or was not using before.

RECYCLING

It is three months later. Hank and Larry have agreed on the managing goals Hank will try to reach, and he has made specific plans to accomplish them. Hank is expected at headquarters on a routine visit, and this presents a good opportunity to review what has been done so far and to take a next step in forward-looking planning.

THE BRIEFING

When the two men meet, Hank reviews where the customer service work stands against the standards they had agreed on. It is clear that with one possible exception things are on target, and Hank has already developed action plans for improving that area.

Then Hank goes into some detail on each of the managing goals he set for himself. He begins with his "Add-A-Skill" Program as he calls it—his training program to make employees competent in all phases of the service work. He says:

> "Overall, Larry, this has been very successful. The engineers like it, and the technicians are pleased because they see a way for them to increase their value to us. They find it is much less boring, too. Of course, each man still has his number one specialty, and when we have a really tough problem, he's the man we call on."
>
> "Great. Glad to hear it. Just how have you been doing this?"
>
> "Well, first I had a general meeting and gave the men a picture of our operations and where we were strong and where I thought we could improve. I'm ashamed to say I hadn't done that in quite a while. Then I told them how I thought their being better rounded in what they could do would help them— with us and, frankly, with other companies too. I said we'd do it this way: we'd ask the man who is best acquainted with a certain kind of work to try to teach the others what he felt they need to know. They might have to help themselves, too, by doing some reading and boning up on their own. Later, as problems arose, the specialist could take someone out with him as helper. Now that adds to cost, but it's a sound investment, I believe. And, of course, we haven't added any help in order to do this. Eventually we send the 'helper' out on his own. It's really surprising how interested they are! Each person has an area of work picked out for himself as the first new one to learn. It'll probably take three to four years before everyone can do almost any job, so I've got a long-term program on my hands. I've been talking to some of the other district managers to find out what they do, and they've given me some ideas too."
>
> "Good. I'm pleased it's going so well. By all means check Charlie Burns on this if you haven't already done so. I think he had a program going a couple of years ago. He might have some good ideas."
>
> "He'll be here tomorrow. I'll try to see him then."

> "I gather that other than keeping it moving and encouraging employees, there isn't too much you need to do from now on."
>
> "Right."
>
> "What's the next step then toward reaching this target?"
>
> "I think it's setting up a good orientation program for new servicemen so that from here on we begin with built-in flexibility."
>
> "Sounds reasonable. How soon will you be ready to tackle that one?"
>
> "Probably in about a month. There isn't a great rush because I'm not expecting to hire any new employees until Bob transfers to the Western District. But I'll tell you something that probably *ought* to be started right away—a real solid study of the tools and instruments and work methods we're using to be sure they're as up to date and efficient as they can be. I've been finding in talking to the men that . . ."

Hank goes on with this thought. He seems really interested in putting new ideas into his program. When they get to the cost goal, it is clear that he is not only determined to get his costs down but has taken steps to do so. Apparently the system is working!

When the status of each goal has been reviewed and additional plans made for the future, Larry says:

> "Hank, I'm really pleased with the way this thing is going. I feel you've got a handle for improving operations in your district. Moreover, I feel we've both learned a lot from doing this. How about passing it along to the employees who report to you?"
>
> "How do you mean?"
>
> "Give them the same chance to plan their work. Of course, it will be a little different with them—they won't have managing work to be responsible for, just their personal work. And you already have a good start because you gave them a picture of the component's goals when you were setting up your "Add-A-Skill" program, and you say each man has targeted one new area of work to learn. So what you need are some standards for each man's work and some specific goals for work projects he may have to do or improvement targets where you and he feel the standard could be raised."

This suggestion reveals the reasons for many of the things the manager did previously. He took unusual care to go step by step through the process of standard setting, then goal setting, then sound work plans, then the careful review of progress and the recycling of plans for the future. At each step, he used tactics designed to keep the district manager's reaction favorable, to involve and interest him in problems discussed so that he would be constructive, not defensive, and committed to getting results. He did these things to teach by his personal example the skillful use of a managing tool. At this level in the organization, he probably could have gotten costs reduced by simply telling the district manager to do so. But his objective was broader than this—he also wanted to contribute to the younger manager's development as a manager.

SUMMARY

So now let's stand away from the detail and summarize the things to keep in mind in order to work effectively with a manager who reports to you:

1. The manager is responsible for the output of the organization. In order to control this work, it is helpful for him or her to set standards for measuring and evaluating recurring work and specific goals for the major projects and improvements which he or she intends to accomplish.

2. The major contribution of managers to the results of the organization is their system of managing, and you can focus their attention on this part of the job by working out with the person one or two key goals aimed at the solution of management problems and improvement of his or her managing skills.

3. Managers do some personal work—special assignments, customer contacts, etc.—which also contribute to results of the organization, and their goals should reflect this work.

4. You should review all *three* of these kinds of work (although not necessarily at the same time or in the same way) so that none is overlooked or under-emphasized. Note that the tendency is to forget the managing work.

5. You should involve the manager in the negotiation of all of his or her goals, in ways of accomplishing them, and in measures and standards. If the individual has an opportunity to influence his or her goals, he or she will feel a commitment to achieve them. This means that your personal negotiating skills must be good, and that you must find positive ways to encourage contribution.

6. Through your personal example and your interaction with the manager, you can "teach" improved management skills and help him or her to set high personal standards of skill in these areas.

17

What About You?

Yours may be an unusual situation—you may report to a paragon of managerial virtue. Your manager may have knowledge, skill, experience, and personal qualities which you would like to acquire. The person may be both introspective and communicative so that he or she knows, appreciates how things are done, and is able to explain them to you. This person may be demanding (of your best talent) and supportive (displays confidence in you). Your manager may be sincerely interested in your personal growth and helpful in exposing you to new concepts and experiences which promote your career plans.

The chances are that you are not so fortunate. The manager to whom you report is in all likelihood struggling to stay on top of the job. Many managers pull their share of boners, and, while their intentions may be good, they have neither the insight nor the wisdom to be of much help to you—that is, unless you help them help you. And that is the subject of this material: how you can capitalize on your work and help your manager help you grow in the direction of your career interests.

First of all, determine to give yourself as much time for this project as you would give any employee due an appraisal and career counselling session. And do not think of it as an "extra," something you really should not do on the job. This *is* work. This is an attempt to make yourself a better manager. This is an investment of time designed to help you obtain better results for the institution which you serve and to prepare yourself for more responsibility, if you decide that this is what you want.

KNOW YOURSELF

Let's begin at the beginning. First, you had better make a fairly objective appraisal of your abilities, interests, and personal values, or what you want to put first and actually do put first in your daily life. (These may be different.) You may have done this in college before you chose your major field and again before you undertook your research project in graduate school. But, assuming that you have been working for a few years now, your grasp of what it takes to be successful in certain kinds of jobs has grown quite a bit. It is worth remaking your evaluation. Anyway, you should not think of self-appraisal as a one-shot affair in which you arrive at all the answers. You change, circumstances change; new jobs, whole new technologies come into the picture. It would be foolish to settle for a relatively immature evaluation made ten years ago!

What is a good starting point? One good approach is to write down all the things that managers, work associates, and friends have said about you and your work. Put down both the favorable and unfavorable things. The negatives may enable you to exclude certain career targets. Assuming that you want to progress along the managerial route, focus especially on things that have been said about your *managing*. It is funny how we seem to overlook this rather critical point. And in considering your managing, what have people who have reported to you said about it? After all, they feel the brunt of it more than anyone else. Now, take a look at what you have written. You know yourself pretty well. What has been omitted? Why are there certain contradictions—have some things changed with time? Or do people who deal with you from different perspectives find you different? Add what you know about yourself, making sure that you have a good and fairly complete list of all the things you know that you do well both on and off the job. These are the data to be analyzed. These are the data from which you ought to be able to draw some conclusions about yourself. As an aid, pretend that it is an appraisal you have written for one of the employees. What would you say to *him or her?* What would you recommend that an employee undertake for personal growth? What sorts of possible future jobs should one think about as career targets?

SELF-PERCEPTION HAS ITS LIMITATIONS

You may not like the conclusions that you reach when you apply them to yourself. Most of us cannot be very objective when we do this, and we need someone to help us. So it may be a wise step to invest a little money as well as personal time in consulting a professional evaluator. In larger companies, in some government agencies, and in most educational institutions a counselor may be available. If not, a member of a reputable management consulting firm or a professor from a nearby college or university may be of assistance. Investigate their qualifications, though; check their educational background, previous contacts with the kind of institution in which you work, and make sure that he or she is experienced in working with adults. This is for *you*. You want one of the best counselors you can find.

When you have received an evaluation and any suggestions offered for your future, add these to what you had arrived at by yourself. How different are they? Does he or she interpret the same information differently? Have you learned something from the consultant about appraisal analysis that you can use to guide yourself in the future and also contribute to employees with whom you may be working on similar projects?

THINK ABOUT YOUR JOB—
AND THE NEXT ONE

Now get really practical. Take a hard look at your job. Is it drawing on your strengths—things you do well? Does it offer exposure to new knowledge and skill which leads you in the direction of your career interests? Normally, you will find that you have worked out an approach to your work which is built around things that you like to do and do pretty well. (If you honestly find nothing in the job which is compatible with your ability and interest, you had better analyze how and why you got into it and, more importantly, how you can gracefully get out of it. But yours is an exceptional case.)

It may, unfortunately, also be built around doing things that you have done many times in the past. For the sake of your personal growth, some new things must go into your work. You must experiment a little with new methods and new job content, if you want to *increase* the capability you have to offer an employer.

MANAGE YOUR TIME INTELLIGENTLY

The easiest way to do this is to make a little plan for your work—for *your* work, *not* the component's work. The plan should cover the things *you personally* do to help the organization get results, the contribution *you personally* make to the institution that you serve. As a beginning, make a list of the normal activity of your job—correspondence, meetings, reading for information and comment, tours of work areas within your jurisdiction, individual discussions held with employees, and so on. How much time do these things take? More importantly, how much time do they leave for important contributions to the current work of the organization and for looking ahead to future work and needed improvements? If you are typical, it is probably not enough. There is no rule of thumb for what is right, but most experienced managers agree that in proportion to the potential contribution they devote more effort to the minutiae of their jobs than to the important things. So make some decisions about the ratio of time that is right for you in the current situation and enlist the aid of a capable secretary to help you clear the time that you need for thinking and analysis, for important contacts and customers, for improving the capability of the organization to get results. Face the fact that devoting some time in that fashion may mean skimping on some of the daily routines. Can you find a more efficient way of handling them?

PUT SOMETHING NEW INTO YOUR WORK

Now, list the two or three most important things which you feel you should accomplish with or for the organization in the next year. They might include items like evolving a new concept of funding development work or expanding manufacturing facilities. Will these things involve your learning something new or learning how to do something that you have not done before? This is a critical point. If they do not, can you restructure them to make sure that they require substantial development on your part? Perhaps you could talk to a few successful managers whom you respect and find out various ways they achieve similar targets. Perhaps you might select a classic management book or two and a current book or a few recent articles which discuss similar material. Do they supply any new ideas for approaching this work?

For example, if you have tended to do all your work review on an individual basis, how about reading Argyris[1] and Blake[2] and then trying group planning as a possible effective change?

Or, if you have tended to take the former manager's recommendations pretty much at face value when filling an open position, why not read Fear[3] or Bassett[4] on evaluation interviewing and try some of their suggestions?

SELF-FEEDBACK WILL IMPROVE LEARNING

Putting something new into your own job is only the first step toward making your managerial work developmental for you. The second step is to get some feedback on how well you have succeeded in applying what you

[1]Chris Argyris, *Personality and Organization* (New York: Harper & Bros., 1957).

[2]Robert R. Blake and Jane S. Mouton, *The New Managerial Grid* (Houston: Gulf Publishing, 1978).

[3]Richard A. Fear, *The Evaluation Interview* (2d ed.; New York: McGraw-Hill, 1972).

[4]Glenn A. Bassett, *Practical Interviewing* (New York: American Management Association, 1965).

learned. Defining the results that you want to achieve in quite specific terms *in advance* and deliberately reflecting on how you are doing the work and whether you are on target will give you some needed feedback. For example, you may be using group planning and work review methods to acquaint employees with each other's work to prevent duplication and gaps and cut down on the amount of your personal coordinating time. After a trial period of three to six months, you should ask yourself if this different method is accomplishing these things. You can also ask employees how they feel about it. Do they find it helpful? Are there limitations? What supplements are needed to make it even more workable?

GET HELP FROM YOUR MANAGER

It would also be helpful if you could count on useful feedback from your manager. Obviously, he or she can provide feedback only if what you are doing is visible to him or her at least from the point of view of results. And even then you may need to help your manager help you.

Let's look for a moment at how you can tell what help he or she is likely to be able to give you. Start from the assumption that each manager to whom you report has something to offer you in the way of learning experience. Of course, after you have worked for your manager for four or five years, you may have learned most of it, but even then you can invite some additional inputs from him or her. Let's discuss ways to do this.

WHAT DOES YOUR MANAGER KNOW?

First, find out in some detail what your manager's training and experience have been and what valuable things have been learned from past managers. This means interviewing him or her—not all at once and not obviously—but certainly systematically and thoroughly. Unless you are widely separated geographically so that informal contacts are almost impossible, this is not too hard to do. Your manager probably will thoroughly enjoy talking about past accomplishments, and the obstacles which he or she overcame to make them. As you take on new assignments, do not be hesitant about asking: "Have you come up against anything like this before? Is there anything I should guard against or devices I should use? I want to be certain I'm not overlooking anything."

The manager who can help you most is not necessarily the one who is warm, pleasant, willing to listen, and considerate. Rather, it is the one who knows something you can use and is able to communicate it in relevant situations. A helpful manager is the one who expects you to accomplish very difficult things involving whole new approaches and gives you enough freedom to do them and a clean enough description of what is needed that you can tell when you have gotten there.

With these thoughts in mind, pick your manager's brain. If there is nothing more to be gained from doing this, then work with him or her as you take on each new commitment to learn as much as possible about what the result should be for the organization. For example, do not just agree to get out a monthly market report including orders pending, on hand, and in process. Instead, find out the purpose of the report, who will use it, and for what decisions. It may well be that when you know enough of these facts, you will want to include other data as well or change the timing of its publication or set up an automatic system using computer storage and print-out. Or, you may decide that the report is not enough—that you should develop a little plan for meeting the stated needs which will include periodic meetings, an informal contact system, *and* a report.

The idea is not, of course, to make you busier—although it may often have that effect—but, instead, to give your work richer meaning, maximum contribution to organization needs, and sufficient scope so that *you* improve your chances of developing your talents.

SET AN IMPROVEMENT GOAL FOR YOURSELF

Always have one improvement goal in your plans, no matter how busy you are. If you are able to enlist the help of your manager in determining what it should be, that is fine. But even if you are not, select one part of your work and determine to streamline it, reduce its drain on your time, get more results from it, eliminate it by substituting a better process or just dropping it because the payoff is not worth the effort. Do not overlook your managing work when you are selecting what the desired improvement should be. You might well upgrade the quality of the meetings that you call by outlining for those who attend the preparation that they should make. This might bring about more productive meetings, and it might also shorten the meeting time. Or you might enlist the help of your secretary to improve communication without the organization. Or you might want to increase the number and quality of work review contacts with individual workers in the organization, or their salary administration, or their whole reward system. The possibilities are endless, but always have one on which you are working and do not be vague and general about it. Set a good solid target for yourself and plan some specific actions and completion dates.

KEEP YOUR MANAGER INFORMED

Keep your manager informed of what you are doing, and especially of what has been accomplished. Stress has been placed throughout this book on how important it is for you to reinforce employee efforts that are in the right direction and reward them when they are successful. The same principle applies in dealing with your manager. If you get him or her to share personal experience and know-how, if you ask for more information about the "fit" of your work into the organization's needs, then reinforce this information-giving on your manager's part by showing him or her the role that it played in results which you achieved or how it influenced the program which you are undertaking or how much more worthwhile from the customer's point of view your enlarged program is. In addition to encouraging managers to give more information habitually, it will also give them something to talk about with pride to the manager's boss and associates, and this is desirable for both of you.

INCORPORATE YOUR CAREER
INTERESTS INTO THIS JOB

The discussion thus far has centered on increasing the growth pos-sibilities of your job and helping your manager contribute to your growth, Let's look at one additional area—adding some work which will help you toward your career goals. If you find your current position satisfying and are looking toward only a modest increase in responsibility during the remainder of your working career, your situation is no easier than that of the individual who seeks rapid upward mobility.

You cannot, of course, even think of *staying where you are* in the sense that you know enough and have had enough experience to permit you to handle this assignment until retirement. First of all, few assignments stand still. Organization structure changes to meet new business plans; external situations force expansion or contraction. So you cannot afford to risk making your present job your career.

Next, the whole concept of management is changing. Today's skills and skill level will not be good enough for tomorrow. New tools—some technological, some involving human skills—are constantly entering the pic-ture, and you must be prepared to use them early and well if you are to hold a position of leadership in the kind of work you are doing. You are, therefore, engaged in a personal battle against managerial obsolescence.

EVERY PROFESSIONAL WORKS
TOWARD A BETTER JOB

So in a sense, every professional worker is preparing for a new job all the time. You might as well be practical about it. This means finding ways to put elements of your somewhat new or radically new job into your present work so that you have a head start and can practice a little before your success or failure becomes critical. And, of course, it goes without saying that you must do this *without any sacrifice* of current needed results.

HOW TO GET READY FOR
THE FUTURE

It is not nearly as hard to do as it sounds. Go back to the plan that you made for your personal work. You are going to add to it. Now, on another sheet of paper write down what trends you see in the organization in which you are working. Is it becoming larger so that greater decentralization is likely, or is it contracting so that more centralization will probably occur? What might that mean for you—a larger staff with greater responsibility, a return to individual work, a requirement to get more results with even fewer resources?

Or, taking another look at predicting the future, are there rumors of reorganization, and what sorts of possibilities are being discussed? What would these mean for you in all probability; what problems, what opportunities? Or what is happening in the market place, and how will this affect the business plans of the firm, and what will it mean in terms of new manpower requirements? Or, what is happening in Congress, and what will this very likely mean about appropriations, and how will this affect the Agency? In other words, examine the current situation and the direction in which it is changing. You do not have to do this alone. Discuss it with your manager and with associates. Get the frankest, most objective picture you can, and make some interpretation of what it could mean to you. Focus on the *differences* from your current situation. Deliberately select one or two that seem major and figure out how you can begin to operate in this way *now* or what you need to learn in order to be effective in the new situation. Try to beat the trend!

Another way to prepare for your "next" job is to focus on your field and read the trade journals and magazines. Who seem to be the most progressive thinkers? Who are the people proposing what seem to be the "far out" ideas? Make their acquaintance if they are nearby, or start a little correspondence with them if they are too far away. Look for ways to try out a few of their ideas. Make up your mind that you will find a way to adapt at least one to your operation. Get help from employees if the ideas fit their functional interest.

INFLUENCE FUTURE TRENDS

All this assumes that when you examine the trends of the organization, you see opportunities for yourself that are compatible with your interests. If you do not, if you feel that the organization's future is not going to provide a satisfying career for you, determine to try to influence its direction in a way that is more compatible with your own talents. This is, of course, a serious responsibility. You cannot with integrity maneuver the organization into doing something that serves your interests but does not contribute to its total betterment. You are, therefore, faced with the difficult problem of finding a way to contribute to a better future for the organization and, starting from that point, evolve the opportunity for your more satisfying career. Realistically, the upward influence of most professionals only extends one or two organization levels above them. But this may be adequate for your purposes.

A CASE IN POINT

Let's take an example or two to illustrate the point. Suppose that you are responsible for shop functions including maintenance of the facility, equipment design, planning, parts manufacture, production control, assembly, inspection, and shipping. This involves a large organization, perhaps about a thousand employees. You become aware that the trend is away from large government production contracts and toward more development work involving relatively delicate, prototype manufacture and product testing. You realize that this will mean quite a different job for you (if the trend continues), even though on the surface your title and functions might sound the same.

You are interested in development manufacturing, and you see the advantage of having the top skilled mechanics and toolmakers that this kind of work requires. But you also feel that your particular strength lies in managing high volume work. You do not want to lose this skill and, in fact, you would like to improve it. You want to build your future career in this direction since you feel that for normal consumer and industrial business this is likely to have the greatest payoff for you.

What to do? Apart from quickly changing jobs (which most of us are unable and unwilling to do so readily), you must certainly begin to prepare for the differences inherent in development manufacturing. But, in addition, you can clearly seek ways in which you might diversify the shop to be more independent of government contracts. What would be both possible and profitable to do within the charter of the organization? Are subcontracts available from other parts of the firm or from other companies which would make good use of manpower, facilities, tools, and equipment, and bring profit to the company and permit you to keep your career on the course you desire?

It is worth some creative effort to examine the advantages and disadvantages of undertaking subcontract work. Once convinced that the advantages outweigh the disadvantages, you then face the task of putting together a businesslike proposal for the review of your manager and as many other levels of management as may be needed for approval. There is clearly risk involved. You may not succeed in selling your first suggestion. There may be some comfort in recognizing that repeated tries will at least develop your skills in this area! If you eventually succeed, it was worth the risk. And if you fail, the same career decision you faced earlier is still yours to make.

More often, the upward influence you wish to exert has a more philosophical base. You see a policy that you believe is not quite fair, and you pull together some recommendations for change. Perhaps you become aware of differences in interpretation of a communique from the Agency director, and you appeal for clarification by redrafting the communique. Or you feel that the Foundation is too stereotyped in its grants, and you suggest alternative guidelines. Or you feel that a business decision is being made without benefit of significant technical information, and you present these data to the people entrusted with the decision.

It is surely apparent that such activities would more likely to be acceptable and successful if they were carried out with the help, interest, and information of your manager. The point here is that you owe it to yourself to give thought to and take action on these fronts whether or not you have your manager's visible, positive support.

IF YOU KNOW WHAT YOUR NEXT JOB WILL BE

If you feel confident of your next job, it is relatively easy to conceive sound development plans. This might be the case if there is a natural upward progression step, or if you are on an executive training program and placement has already been determined, or if your manager has indicated a likely move. Sometimes, there is not a single next job but a family of probable ones. In such cases, it is primarily a matter of identifying some things in that job or job family which you are not currently doing but which might be advantageously incorporated into your present work.

For example, are there specific individuals with whom you might need to build strong working relationships? If so, begin now to consult such individuals where their thoughts and advice might be of help. Keep them abreast of your work where they should be current. Find ways of involving them in improvement studies where they might have a contribution to make. This is not to suggest that you work out contacts with them merely to advance your interests, but that you select work areas where it would be to your mutual advantage to be working together even now.

As another example, suppose you will need to defend your budget more effectively. Perhaps it will be a larger budget reviewed by higher-level individuals. Determine to do a more professional job this year on your current proposals. Do some reading, consult with financial or administrative people for their advice, and explore your manager's experiences. After you have presented your budget, make a point of seeing your manager or others who were present to ask for frank feedback on how the presentation might be improved, the defense made stronger, questions better anticipated, and so on.

The key, of course, is to recognize *critical* differences between a likely next job and your present one, and to put your effort and attention on these. Again, this should not be at the expense of present assignments, but rather to enlarge your contribution. There are two clear advantages in doing this— it prepares you for the more responsible position, and makes it more likely that you will be chosen for it because you are demonstrating improved capacity to handle some of its critical elements.

SUMMARY

Let us summarize, then, the key points about working on your own development:

1. Make an objective appraisal of your talents, abilities, and interests, with or without professional help and with or without the help of your manager, and set some general career targets for yourself.
2. Capitalize on your strengths in your current job.
3. Put some work into your present position which will benefit the organization *and* require you to add to your knowledge and skill. If it is directed toward increased capability for a likely next job, so much the better.
4. Help your manager to help you by asking about any relevant experience. Ask for his or her feedback on your work. Ask for more information about the purpose which your work serves in the organization. Keep your manager informed of your achievements, particularly when they reflect the application of information which you obtained from him or her.
5. Always include one work improvement goal in your plans.
6. Watch for trends in the function of the organization both to prepare yourself for them and to influence them.

RECOMMENDED PLAN

If you are a manager and feel confident that your future lies in managerial work, here are a few minimum development actions you might put into your plans:

A Skill Course in Interviewing.   This is the most fundamental of all managerial skills. Managers use interviewing to hire, to assign work, to discuss
appraisal, to obtain business information, to understand customers, and so
on.

Public Speaking and Conference Management.   A manager needs to communicate, to persuade, to defend, to make personal intentions clear. He or
she needs to be able to draw out individual opinions in a group situation and
to stimulate and resolve controversy on a constructive level.

Business Planning.   Whether or not managers are involved in a profit-
making business and regardless of their position in the organization structure, all managers must learn to think in terms of the purposes of the organization, the "customers" for its work, the strategy for aligning output and
customer, the information flow within the organization, the economic assignment of resources, and how to schedule and assess success. Reading,
courses, and deliberate reflection on how these subjects relate to the work
and to that of the next higher level in the organization will improve the
manager's skills in these important areas.

Personnel Evaluation.   Learning what to look for in people, how to judge
what they are able to do, and under what conditions they can do it is critical.
Managers must staff open positions, evaluate suppliers, customers, and their
own manager as well as those who report to them. Reading helps, but
tutoring by a professional is almost essential. If the personnel office cannot
supply help, seek a good management consultant, even if you must pay the
bill yourself.

Listening and Awareness of Others.   Being perceptive to what is in other
people's minds is hard to cultivate if it is not a natural talent. There are,
however, books and courses on listening[5] which may help. Sensitivity training or, more broadly, group dynamics sessions contribute to perceptiveness
as well as to improved interpersonal relationships.
   These are fundamental needs of all manager jobs. Beyond these, read
management books[6] and periodicals, and try to incorporate at least some of

[5]One helpful book is Ralph G. Nichols and Leonard A. Stevens, *Are You Listening?* (New
York: McGraw-Hill, 1957).
   [6]For example, see: W.F. Coventry and Irving Burstiner, *Management: A Basic Handbook*
(Englewood Cliffs, N.J.: Prentice-Hall, 1977); Ernest Dale, *Management: Theory and Practice*
(3rd ed.; New York: Mc-Graw-Hill, 1973); Edwin B. Flippo and Gary M. Munsinger, *Man-
agement* (4th ed.; Boston: Allyn & Bacon, 1978); Herbert G. Hicks and C. Ray Gullett, *The
Management of Organizations* (3rd ed.; New York: McGraw-Hill, 1976); D. E. McFarland,
Management Principles and Practices (4th ed.; New York Macmillan, 1974).

what you read into your managing. Be an experimental manager in the best scientific sense—build a reputation for trying new things, for developing people for better jobs, and for not only meeting but beating your commitments.

Index

A

Applying management theory, 14
   illustrations, 11–13
   impact of tradition on, 13
   manager's role in, 13–14
   need for individual adaptation, 12, 14
   preparing way for, 12
Argyris, Chris, 8–9, 10, 196
Attitude, change of, 143,161–65
   career planning, discussion on, 145–50
   climate for, 150–51, 164, 165
   role of encouragement in, 148
Attitude, manager's, 83–84
   on promotion, 157–58

B

Bassett, Glenn A., 37, 196
Beginner, 127–39
   evolving work measures with, 133–35
   giving first assignment to, 129–30
   guides for working with, 138–39
   importance of proper orientation of, 127–28
   planning work with, 130–33
   problem solving with, 138–39
   professional standards for, 133–35
Blake, Robert R., 10–11, 196
Briefing, 190–91
Burstiner, Irving, 204
Business planning, need for, 204

C

Career goals, addition of, 160–61
Career planning for yourself, 193–205
   feedback, 197
   improvement goal, 198
   influencing organization's future, 200–203
      illustrations, 201–3
   job analysis, 195–96
   predicting future, 200
   recommendations for, 203–5
   self-appraisal, 194–95
      use of specialists in, 194–95
Career planning with older employee, 145–52
   checking past record, 143–45
   encouraging the man, 148–49
   follow-up on, 150–51
   importance of building on strengths, 148
   obtaining his suggestions, 149
   setting it up properly, 145–46
Career planning with promotable employee, 156–66
   adding career goal, 160–61
   changing attitude, 161–64
      climate for, 164, 165
   investigation of interest, 156–58
   setting improvement goals, 158–60
Choice, employee, 94
Climate for changing attitude, 150–51, 164, 165
Commitment, generation of, 18, 22, 24, 33, 35, 39, 90–97, 102–11(*See also* Motivation)
   in beginner, illustrated, 127–39
   in managerial employees, illustrated, 180–92

Commitment, generation of *(cont.)*
  in nonpromotable specialist, illustrated, 167–79
  in older worker, illustrated, 140–52
  in promotable employee, illustrated, 153–66
Communication (*See* Information exchange)
Compensation, 20, 31, 42–43, 79, 87
  for a specialist, 167–68, 169, 173–78
Conflict, 10, 49, 109, 204 (*See also* Information exchange)
Coventry, W. F., 204

D

Dale, Ernest, 204
Debate, 52–53, 116
Development, employee (*See* Growth, employee)
Displaced employees (*See* Selection of employees, "un-staffing")
Drucker, Peter F., 5
Dunnington, Richard A., 14

E

Evaluation of employees, 27–28, 31, 34–44, 110, 153–54
  investigation of past record, 143–45, 155–56
  need for skill in, 204

F

Fear, Richard A., 37, 196
Feedback (*See* Information exchange)
Flippo, Edwin B., 204

G

Ginzberg, Eli, 3–4
Giving a first assignment, 129–30
Goals for management work, 188–89, 196–97, 198
  recycling, 190
Group interaction, 48–50
  effect of organization structure on, 70
  use for employee development, 162, 164
Group problem solving, 49–55 (*See also* Meetings, with employees)
  benefits of, 162
  use of debate in, 52–53
Growth, employee, 90, 104–8, 117–19
  adding new element to work, 147–48, 160–61
  climate during work review, 136–37

Growth, employee *(cont.)*
  for beginners, illustrated, 127–39
  for older employees, illustrated, 140–52
  for promotables, illustrated, 153–66
  for specialists, illustrated, 167–79
  group development, 108
  risk in, 160–61
Gullett, C. Ray, 204

H

Hall, Richard S., 66
Herzberg, Frederick, 8–9, 10
Hicks, Herbert G., 204

I

Improvement goal, 117–19
  for beginner, illustrated, 131–33
  for manager, illustrated, 119–20
  for promotable employee, illustrated, 158–60
  for self, 198
Inexperienced employee (*See* Beginner)
Information exchange, 30–31 (*See also* Conflict; Group interaction; Meetings, with employees; Negotiation, man-manager; Systems, information)
  deterioration of 120–21
  during career planning, 193–205
  during organization change, 77–78, 81–83
  during work reviews, 51–53, 103–4, 122
  effect of over-organization on, 69
  from senior to junior specialists, 170–72
  informal, role of, 140
  managerial role in, 46–47
  role in fighting obsolescence, 114–15
  unfavorable information during, 46, 136–38
Interpersonal relationships (*See* Professional workers, relationships among them; Relationships, man-manager)
Interpersonal relationships, theories of, 8–11
  9,1 relationship, 11
  9,9 relationship, 11
  partnership, 15–24
Interviewing, 37–39, 204
  for employee's past record, 143–45
  for manager's experience, 197–98
Investigating employee's record, 143–45, 155–56
Involvement of employee in work plans, 127–39, 188–89, 191–92
  in measurement of, 133–35, 184–88
  in problem-solving during, 137–39, 158–60, 174–75

J

Job analysis, in career planning, 195–96
Job description, 86–88 (*See also* Position design)
  in the partnership relationship, 87–88
  manager's, 87

K

Kellogg, Marion S., 42, 80, 103

L

Legal definition of partnership, 15–16, 21–22
Likert, Rensis, 10
Listening skill, need for, 204
Lopez, Felix M., 37

M

McFarland, D.E., 204
McGregor, Douglas, 9–10, 13–14
Management theory, application of, 11–14
Managerial employees, 180–92
  guides for working with, 192
  improving results of, illustrated, 181–92
  problems in working with, 180–81
  professional standards for, 183–88
  recycling plans for, 190
  setting goals for, 188–89
  setting standards for, 183–88
  teaching role of manager with, 191–92
Man-manager interaction (*See* Information exchange; Meetings, with employees)
Martix organization, 68
Measurement of results, 20, 87 (*See also* Performance evaluation; Results specification)
  as a basis for compensating specialists, 173–78
  for work improvement, 133–34, 138–39, 185
  illustrated, for beginner, 133–35
  to provide self-satisfaction, 130–34
Meetings, with employees, 29–32
  first, with individuals, 34–44
    adapting to individuals, 39–40
    agenda for, 36
    documentation of, 37
    notification of, 35, 40
  management of, need for, 204
  on organization change, 81–83
  recycling organization plans, 120–21
  skip-a-level, 101
  suggestions for improving, 121–22
  to negotiate work plan, 88–97

Meetings, with employees (*cont.*)
  with managers to plan work, 180–92
  with new employee to plan work, 127–39
  with older employee to motivate, 145–52
  with promotable to discuss career, 156–58
  with specialist to plan work, 167–79
Meetings, with manager, 26–27, 57, 62–64, 75
Motivation, 86–97, 98–111 (*See also* Commitment, generation of)
  effective supervision and, 10
  effect of partnership on, 21, 23
  impact of organization structure on, 8, 69
  impact of position design on, 69–71
  negative effect of casual management, 17
  role of recognition in, 109–11
  role of work in, 8–9, 40–41
Mouton, Jane S., 11, 196
Munsinger, Gary M., 204

N

Negotiation, man-manager, 88–89, 93–94, 99–100
  illustrated for manager with his manager, 188–89
  illustrated for new employee, 131–32
    establishment of standards, 133–35
  illustrated for promotable employee, 158–61
  illustration of trade-off with specialist, 170–72
New employee (*See* Beginner)
New manager, 25–33, 56–57
  agreement on responsibilities, 26–27
  aids to recognize employee ability, 153–54
  establishing partnership, 29–32
  first decisions, 32–33, 34, 57
  role of, 27–28, 40
Newness concept, 160–61, 165, 196
Nichols, Ralph G., 204
Nonprofit organizations, 3–4
  impact on managing of, 3–4
  increase in, 4

O

Obsolescence, prevention of, 112–23
  abandonment of low payoff work, 116
  employee mobility and, 115
  improvement goal, role of, 117–19
  in yourself, 113, 114, 119, 199
  of knowledge, 114–15, 116–17
  recycle work and, 120–22
Obtaining manager's help on career, 193–205
  learning what the manager knows, 197–98

Older employee, guides for working with, 152
(*See also* Career planning with older employee)
Organization, principles of, 66–69 (*See also* Position design)
  basis for grouping work, 67–68
  effect on managerial decision making, 68–69
  effect on work, 83–84
  matrix organization, 68
Organization review, 84–85
  checklist for, 84–85
Organization change, 76–85
  acceptance by employees, 76
  communication of, 77–78
  control of work during, 78
  information exchange, 77–78, 81–83
  involvement of employees in, 77
  personnel planner's role during, 78–79
  speed, need for, 75, 77, 83
  timing of, 77
Organizing specialized knowledge for result, 131, 135, 136–39
Orientation for beginner, 127–39
Outlook for Technological Change and Employment, Report for the National Commission on Technology, Automation and Economic Progress, 4–5, 6–7

P

Participation, employee (*See also* Negotiation, man-manager; Work plans, individual)
  in organization change, 77, 81–83
  in planning, 45–55, 63–64, 117–18
Partnership relationship, 15–24
  access to information in, 20–21
  common purpose in, 17–18, 22, 30, 73
  effect of over-organization on, 69
  effect on motivation, 21, 22–23
  employment negotiation in, 79–80
  establishment of, 29–31
  evaluation of, as model, 23–24
  individuality in, 18, 22
  investment in, 16–17, 19–20
  job description in, 86–88
  legal definition of, 15–16, 21–22
  personal responsibility in, 19–21
  reward in, 19–20, 23
  risks involved in, 21
  termination practices in, 23
  translation into industrial terms, 22–23
  work planning in, 96–97
Performance evaluation, 20, 22, 109–10 (*See also* Interviewing)
  danger of defensiveness, 145
  data collection for, 27–28, 31, 34–43
  of a specialized professional, 175–77
  self-appraisal, 23

Personnel planner, 78–79, 80, 82–83
Pfiffner, John M., 66
Planning, 45–64 (*See also* Work plans, individual; Work reviews)
  division of critical work, 71
  of business, need for, 204
  selling plans, 63–64
  work control during organization change, 77–78
Position design, 69–73 (*See also* Job description)
  administrative, 71
  basis for partnership agreement, 73
  long range, short range, 71
  relationships with other positions, 72
Praise, how to give, 156–57
Priorities, work, criteria for setting, 58–62, 118
  discussion with beginner, 130–33
Problem solving:
  with beginner, 137–38
  with promotable employee, 158–60
  with specialist, 174–75
Procedures, 72–73
Professional relationships (*See* Professional workers, relationships among them; Relationships, man-manager)
Professional workers, 4–7, 13 (*See also* Beginner; Managerial employees; Older employee, guides for working with; Promotable employee; Specialist, non-promotable)
  definition of, 15–16
  impact on managing of, 4–7
  impact on military leadership of, 6
  increase in, 4–5
  involvement of, in organization change, 77, 81–83
  involvement of, in planning, 45–55, 63–64, 117–18
  manager as a professional, 16, 25–26
  manager's past relationships with, 39, 41
  relationship among them, 15–24, 29
  reward of, 109–11, 123, 137
  stimulation of change by, 13
Progress reviews (*See* Work reviews)
Promotable employee, 153–66
  adding career goal for, 160–61
  career discussion with, 156–58
  changing attitude of, 161–64
  guides for working with, 165–66
  investigating past record of, 155–56
  manager's attitude toward, 158
  problem solving with, 159–60
  standards for, 158–60

R

Recognition, 109–11, 123, 137, 156–57 (*See also* Compensation)
  role in development of, 165

Recycling (*See* Work reviews)

Reitz, H. Joseph, 66

Relationships, man-manager, 127–205 (*See also* Interpersonal relationships, theories of)
with beginner professional, 127–39
with managerial employees, 180–92
with nonpromotable specialist, 167–79
with promotable employee, 153–66
with unmotivated older worker, 140–52

Resources, 46, 51, 54–55, 57, 58, 59–60, 61–62, 67, 79, 80, 89, 101, 122

Results specification, 17, 18, 20 (*See also* Evaluation of employees; Measurement of results)
for a department, 26–27, 62, 64
for a manager, 180–81, 189
for an individual, 92, 94–95, 110–11
for own work, 197

Review of work (*See* Work reviews)

Reward (*See* Compensation; Recognition)

Risk, in development, 160–61

S

Selection of employees, 19–20, 73–75, 79 (*See also* Interviewing)
partnership model, 73
role in fighting obsolescence, 114
"un-staffing," 74, 80–81

Self-appraisal, 194, 203
limitations of, 194–95

Self-development (*See* Career planning for yourself)

Self-feedback, 196–97

Sensitivity, need for, 204

Sherwood, Frank P., 66

Specialist, non-promotable, 167–79
exploring plans of, 174–75
guides for working with, 178–79
importance of concentrated work to, 176–77
managerial problems with, 178-79
man-manager relationships with, 167–79
problem solving with, 174–75
reward of, 173–78
use of trade-off with, 170–72

Staffing (*See* Selection of employees)

Standards, professional, 130–35, 174
checklist for development of, 185
for a beginner, 133–35
for a manager, 183–88
for a promotable employee, 158–60, 165–66

Stevens, Leonard A., 204

Systems, 72–73
information, 98–102

T

Tatum, Major Lawrence B., 6

Teaching role of manager, 82–83, 99–100, 103–4, 120
with beginner, 127–39
in first assignment, 129–130
in setting standards, 130–35
with managerial employee, 180–92
with older worker, unmotivated, 140–52
on-the-job, 150–51
with promotable employee, 163–65

Termination practices, in the partnership relationship, 23

Theory X, 9–10

Theory Y, 9–10

Time, managing own, 25–26, 32–33, 130–31, 195–96

Trade-off, 170–72

U

"Un-staffing," 74, 80–81

W

Williams, J. Clifton, 66

Work plans, individual, 87–97 (*See also* Growth, employee; Improvement goal)
errors in, 91–92
how to make, 89–90
objectives of, 88–90
of a beginner, 130–39
of a manager, 180–89, 196–99
of a promotable, 158–61
of a specialist, 174–75

Work reviews, 45–64, 103–4, 120–23 (*See also* Meetings, first, with individuals)
action plans, 53–54
assigning resources, 61–62
attendance at, 47–48
critical factors for success of, 53
frequency of, 150
managerial role in, 50–54, 93–97
meeting structure, 46, 50–54
setting priorities during, 55, 58–62
with managers, 190–92
with new professional, 136–39
with promotable employee, 158–61
with specialist, 174–75